GOD, THE GOOD, AND THE SPIRITUAL TURN IN EPISTEMOLOGY

In this book, Roberto Di Ceglie offers a historical, theological, and epistemological investigation exploring how commitments to God and/or the good generate the optimum condition to achieve knowledge. Di Ceglie criticizes the common belief that to attain knowledge, one must always be ready to replace one's convictions with beliefs that appear to be proven. He defends a more comprehensive view, historically exemplified by outstanding Christian thinkers, whereby believers are expected to commit themselves to God and to related beliefs no matter how convincing the evidence contradicting such beliefs appears to be. He also argues that both believers and unbelievers can commit themselves to God and the good, respectively, thereby creating a spiritual turn in epistemology that enables them to generate the best possible condition for conducting rational inquiries and discussion.

ROBERTO DI CEGLIE is Full Professor in the Department of Philosophy of the Pontifical Lateran University. The author of *Aquinas on Faith, Reason, and Charity* (Routledge, 2022), he has published in journals such as *Philosophy, International Journal for Philosophy of Religion, Sophia,* and *Philosophia.*

GOD, THE GOOD, AND THE SPIRITUAL TURN IN EPISTEMOLOGY

ROBERTO DI CEGLIE

Pontifical Lateran University

Shaftesbury Road, Cambridge CB2 8EA, United Kingdom

One Liberty Plaza, 20th Floor, New York, NY 10006, USA

477 Williamstown Road, Port Melbourne, VIC 3207, Australia

314–321, 3rd Floor, Plot 3, Splendor Forum, Jasola District Centre, New Delhi – 110025, India

103 Penang Road, #05–06/07, Visioncrest Commercial, Singapore 238467

Cambridge University Press is part of Cambridge University Press & Assessment, a department of the University of Cambridge.

We share the University's mission to contribute to society through the pursuit of education, learning and research at the highest international levels of excellence.

www.cambridge.org
Information on this title: www.cambridge.org/9781009203548

DOI: 10.1017/9781009203531

© Cambridge University Press & Assessment 2023

This publication is in copyright. Subject to statutory exception and to the provisions of relevant collective licensing agreements, no reproduction of any part may take place without the written permission of Cambridge University Press & Assessment.

First published 2023
First paperback edition 2026

A catalogue record for this publication is available from the British Library

ISBN 978-1-009-20355-5 Hardback
ISBN 978-1-009-20354-8 Paperback

Cambridge University Press & Assessment has no responsibility for the persistence or accuracy of URLs for external or third-party internet websites referred to in this publication and does not guarantee that any content on such websites is, or will remain, accurate or appropriate.

Contents

Acknowledgments	*page* vii
Abbreviations	ix
Introduction	1
PART I TOWARD THE OVERCOMING OF THE LOCKEAN VIEW OF FAITH AND REASON	9
1 Reformed Epistemologists and John Henry Newman as Critics of Locke's View of Faith and Reason	11
2 Thomas Reid: Philosophy, Science, and the Christian Revelation	28
PART II THE CHRISTIAN FAITH AS PART OF BOTH THE PROBLEM OF INCONCLUSIVENESS AND ITS SOLUTION	47
3 Thomas Aquinas: Primacy of Faith and Autonomy of Reason	49
4 Rethinking the Nature and Purpose of Debates: Mitchell, Practical Rationality, Religious Disagreement, A-Rational Commitments, and "Quasi-Fideism"	88
PART III THE SPIRITUAL TURN: WHY AND HOW TO TAKE IT	117
5 The Spiritual Turn: Process and Some Benefits. Divine Hiddenness, No-Fault Unbelief, and Religious Diversity	121

6 Comparison with Virtue Epistemology and Reinforcement: More Reasons for Believers and Unbelievers to Take the Spiritual Turn   168

Conclusion   211

Bibliography   216
Index of Names   230
Index of Subjects   233

Acknowledgments

For a couple of decades I reflected upon the idea that a spiritual turn in epistemology should be pursued. Only in the last years, however, had I the opportunity to realize this project. The person to whom I want to express special gratitude for having helped me along this path is David Fergusson. He is now Regius Professor of Divinity at the University of Cambridge. In the past few years he supervised my doctoral dissertation at the University of Edinburgh, where he generously assisted me in widening the theological breath of my views. People like him spontaneously attract other great minds, and so through him I had the opportunity to come into contact with scholars such as Mark Harris, Fergus Kerr, and Duncan Pritchard. To all of them I am profoundly in debt. In various ways, they have consistently lent support to my research.

Alvin Plantinga and Paul Moser, with whom I was in contact while in the United States, helped me develop my ideas as well. I have greatly benefited from their views regarding the limits of evidentialism and the proposal of a "Christ-shaped" philosophy, respectively.

A crucial role in contemporary academia is played by anonymous reviewers. Although at times this practice can be fruitless and frustrating, it is still a good way to see one's own work with outside eyes, so to speak. I would like to thank the anonymous referees for various journals, in which I published portions of this book (see below). I am especially grateful to the two anonymous reviewers for Cambridge University Press, who offered many and invaluable comments and suggestions, which I welcomed and developed in the final version of this book.

In this connection, I want to express many thanks to Beatrice Rehl, editor for Cambridge University Press. She has shown kind, constant, and vigilant attention throughout the process – from the submission of the manuscript to the choice of excellent referees and the final publication.

Last but not least, I am grateful to my family, especially my wife, Claudia, and my sister Margherita, for their endless support and encouragement.

Some sections of this book have been adapted from previously published essays. I give many thanks to the relevant editors and their offices who, in various forms, have granted permission for reproduction: "Faith and Reason: A Response to Duncan Pritchard," *Philosophy* 92 (2017), pp. 231–247; "No-Fault Unbelief," *Sophia* 60 (2021), pp. 91–101; "Thomas Reid: Philosophy, Science, and the Christian Revelation," *The Journal of Scottish Philosophy* 18 (2020), pp. 17–38; "Religions and Conflicts," *The Heythrop Journal* 61 (2020), pp. 620–632; "Divine Hiddenness and the Suffering Unbeliever Argument," *European Journal for Philosophy of Religion* 12 (2020), pp. 211–235; and "Intellectual Humility with Partial Application," *Philosophia* 2021, online first.

Abbreviations

DHA	divine hiddenness argument (see Chapter 5)
FU	fault unbelief (see Chapter 5)
IP	incompatibility problem (see Chapter 5)
ME	mere epistemology
NA	naturalistic assumption (see Part III)
NFU	no-fault unbelief (see Chapter 5)
SA	super-naturalistic assumption (see Part III)
ST	spiritual turn (see Part III)
SW	something wrong (see Chapter 5)

Introduction

Bertrand Russell once said that an exemplary philosophical investigation uncovers problems with matters that are apparently beyond controversy, and gives rise to intellectually fruitful debates.[1]

Among the beliefs whose acceptance seems beyond controversy in both philosophy and common opinion is that the search for truth is successful in proportion to the readiness of truth-searchers to put aside their own beliefs and accept whatever belief will appear to be proven.

Two quotations from classical thinkers exemplify this view. The first quote is from Plato's *Gorgias*, where Socrates emphasizes the primacy of evidence over his own beliefs:

> I am one of those who are very willing to be refuted if I say anything which is not true, and very willing to refute anyone else who says what is not true, and quite as ready to be refuted as to refute. For I hold that this is the greater gain of the two, just as the gain is greater of being cured of a very great evil than of curing another.[2]

Although Socrates does not mention the concept of evidence, this passage means that, if the available evidence suggests that one's beliefs are to be refuted, then the truth-searcher must change her mind, a change that Socrates sees as a sort of recovery from "a great evil" constituted by erroneous opinion.

The second quotation is from Locke's *Essay Concerning Human Understanding*. According to Locke, assent to propositions comes in degrees, and we should proportion our degree of assent to the available evidence. As he says, we should not entertain "any proposition with greater

---

[1] To use Russell's words, philosophy "keeps alive our sense of wonder by showing familiar things in an unfamiliar aspect" (Bertrand Russell, *The Problems of Philosophy*, 2nd ed. [Oxford: Oxford University Press, 1998], p. 88).

[2] Plato, *Gorgias*, 458 a3–b3. For more on this, see below, Chapter 4, note 6.

assurance than the proofs it is built upon will warrant."³ No commitment to one's beliefs should, therefore, prevent one from changing one's mind if the available evidence requires this.

I call this view *mere epistemology* (ME). I will later show my reasons for coining this expression. For now, let me describe it as follows: *One should always prefer beliefs supported by more evidence to beliefs supported by less evidence.* This view seems incorrigible, as shown by the fact that it is usually taken for granted by practitioners in every field and philosophers of various orientations, including epistemologists whose views are very different from the ones I have mentioned so far.⁴

ME is arguably aimed at achieving agreement among debaters. According to Thomas Aquinas, for example, evidence necessarily leads us to assent,⁵ from which follows that, once evidence in support of certain beliefs is provided, everybody should hold those beliefs. In this connection, Locke exemplarily devotes his *Essay* to showing that an agreement among debaters should follow if assent is proportioned to the available evidence. At the beginning of the work in question, Locke famously tells the reader that he formulated his new epistemological perspective as an attempt to help debaters "avoid the greatest part of the disputes and wrangling they have with others."⁶

This aim, however, has not been achieved. Locke's view has counterproductively fueled new controversies and disputes. This fact has led John Jenkins to affirm that "the very existence of the controversy attests the failure of Locke's epistemological project."⁷

This is a sign of a more general condition in which philosophers, as well as practitioners in other fields and even common people, find themselves.

---

³ John Locke, *An Essay Concerning Human Understanding* (London: Printed for Awhsham and John Churchil, 1700) (hereafter: *An Essay*), IV, xix, 1.
⁴ This seeming incorrigibility does not mean that ME is self-evident, perhaps in the way the principle of noncontradiction is. As Aristotle famously showed once and for all (see Aristotle, *Metaphysics*, 4, 4, 1006a35ff.), the self-evidence of the principle of noncontradiction can be confirmed by way of demonstration. ME, instead, simply falls into self-referential contradiction, as I will show later in this Introduction.
⁵ He says that "the assent of science is not subject to free will, because the scientist is obliged to assent by force of the demonstration" (Aquinas, *Summa theologiae*, tr. by the Fathers of the English Dominican Province, 2nd and revised ed. [London: Oates and Washbourne, 1920] [hereafter *Summa theologiae*], II-II, q. 2, a. 9, ad 2). In some cases, I will propose a different translation of the Latin text. (Aquinas's Latin texts are mostly taken from the Leonine and the Marietti editions.) "Evidence," for example, does not render "*evidentia*," as Aquinas takes it in regard to faith. It should be replaced by "full evidence" or "evidentness." For more on this, see below, Chapter 3, notes 45ff.
⁶ Locke, *An Essay*, Epistle to the Reader.
⁷ John Jenkins, "Faith and Revelation," in *Philosophy of Religion: A Guide to the Subject*, ed. by Brian Davies (Washington, DC: Georgetown University Press, 2007), p. 214.

In proportion to the interest they pay to the subject of their debates, debaters seem to be unwilling to accept the available evidence that disproves their original belief. More precisely, the more they care about certain views, the more they try to repropose such views by arguing against the evidence in question or starting to research anew from the beginning.

The attitude I have just described may be seen as positive support for research and its advancement, as recent debates on disagreement have opportunely noticed.[8] This means that the attitude in question, unlike what I have noted above, would be perfectly in line with ME. After all, there is more evidence than not that, at least in some circumstances, this is the best method to follow if one intends to take the research a step further.

This, however, does not have anything to do with the state of affairs I am describing here. I do not refer to those who, by way of hypothesis, try to further explore the outcome of their research by methodologically questioning the evidence they have at the moment. Once they find new evidence, they will accept it, however inconsistent with their original commitment. By contrast, I refer to those who, in proportion to their commitment to certain views, might indefinitely continue rejecting the available evidence that seems to disprove those views and continue reflecting on the subject to reaffirm them. This is simply unacceptable from the viewpoint of ME.

Debates on religious subjects are probably the most persuasive example of this attitude. Given the deep commitment to some fundamental beliefs that the faithful are expected to take on and the fundamental role that these subjects can play in the experience of both believers and unbelievers, it does not surprise that endless disagreement and consequent inconclusiveness copiously characterize debates when such subjects are at stake. Modern debates between believers and unbelievers seem to be almost always inconclusive, as both believers and unbelievers show usual recalcitrance to changing their original position.

Therefore, the inconclusiveness in question can be defined as the property of those debates whose protagonists are not ready to change their minds, *however convincing the evidence in support of such a change may be*. In other words, those who conduct inconclusive debates, *qua* inconclusive debaters, *prefer beliefs supported by less evidence to beliefs supported by more evidence*. This openly contradicts ME, yet debates conducted by supporters of ME frequently fall into inconclusiveness.

---

[8] See below, Chapter 4, Section 4.2.

In this book, I intend to explore why this is possible, and whether unexpected epistemological results might emerge from this exploration.

Before showing how I intend to develop this research, let me make two decisive points.

First, when I say that those who conduct inconclusive debates prefer beliefs supported by less evidence to beliefs supported by more evidence, I do not for a moment mean that they *always* conduct research in this way. I only mean that they do so *as protagonists of inconclusiveness*, that is, to the extent that they reject the available evidence because of their own commitments. But when do they act so?

As I said above, inconclusiveness is proportioned to the commitment of debaters to their original beliefs. Scientific and mathematical truths, for example, might be of no interest to debaters, in the sense that no one seems to care whether or not a molecule of water is composed of two hydrogen atoms and one oxygen atom. It follows that inconclusiveness cannot occur in scientific and mathematical debates unless debaters care about something related to the truths in question – debater's professional success, for example.

If my argument is correct, all debaters put ME into practice. However, they do so in inverse proportion to their commitment to certain beliefs. This has a substantial consequence. I mean that this fact allows debaters to avoid the self-referential contradiction into which ME would inevitably fall. If ME were always put into practice, it should apply to any belief, including itself, which is not plausible. In fact, there is no more evidence for ME than for its opposite. Saying that *one should* always *prefer beliefs supported by more evidence to beliefs supported by less evidence* is not supported by more evidence than the belief that *one should* not always *prefer beliefs supported by more evidence to beliefs supported by less evidence*.

Considering inconclusiveness, therefore, leads us to argue that ME should be included in a more comprehensive epistemological view. ME's fundamental tenet that *one should* always *prefer beliefs supported by more evidence to beliefs supported by less evidence* may turn into a more moderate view. Namely, *with some exceptions, one should prefer beliefs supported by more evidence to beliefs supported by less evidence.*

Second, one may object that there is no evidence that the inconclusiveness of debates is due to one's will to not change one's mind. After all, a disagreement might simply be caused by different competence levels among debaters, which might also be due to intellectual insanity and moral deficiency. It is known that debates on religion, which are probably the most inconclusive ones, have often been accompanied by mutual accusations of deficiency, both intellectual and moral, among believers and between believers and unbelievers.[9] This might explain why inconclusiveness, as I take it, has usually been overlooked by scholars. Different competencies among debaters, as well as forms of deficiency that afflict them, are unworthy of epistemological consideration.

In reply to this objection, it seems that the amount of inconclusiveness that characterizes debates, such as those on religious matters, is unlikely to be explained by recourse to different levels of competence. Persistent disagreement accompanies a long history of debates among apparently equally competent philosophers and theologians. Consequently, when equally competent scholars are involved, it is equally unlikely that accusations of intellectual insanity and/or moral deficiency can reasonably apply.

At any rate, my idea that inconclusiveness is due to a voluntary opposition to the possibility of changing one's mind is justified by substantial suggestions that emerge from religious debates, which are especially characterized by inconclusiveness. The suggestions at stake, which I find in Thomas Reid's and especially Thomas Aquinas's reflection, clearly show that inconclusiveness *is due to the will* of the faithful to stick to their religious commitments.

Let me make it explicit that by "religious," I mainly mean Christian, though I cannot exclude that aspects of other doctrines similar to the Christian one, especially Jewish and Islamic theism, may be included in this discussion. In other words, other religious beliefs might profitably expand and enrich this reflection. I focus on Christianity, however, for at least two reasons. First, because of the role that this religion has played in shaping Western culture. Second, because my reflection is stimulated by suggestions that emerge from the abovementioned Christian thinkers' thoughts.

Returning to how I intend to proceed with this research, let me point out that, in the case of debates regarding the Christian religion, an additional reason seems to lead scholars to overlook inconclusiveness. I say "additional" here because I have already listed the above reasons that apply to any debate – different competence levels among debaters, which may also be due to intellectual insanity and moral deficiency. I am referring to a restricted understanding of the Christian faith and its relationship to reason. This restricted understanding excludes what I argue is the specific way in which the Christian faith must be related to reason. Typical of this way is an attitude that causes inconclusiveness. The love

---

[9] See below, Chapter 5, Section 5.2.

for God, which should inspire (paradigmatic) believers in any activity, rational investigations and debates included, requires that they firmly commit themselves to God and the related beliefs – that God exists, loves us, sent Jesus Christ into the world for our salvation, and the like – no matter how convincing the evidence that contradicts such beliefs might appear to be. This does not mean that the believers in question cannot review any aspect of their faith if other views may suggest so. It only means that fundamental beliefs, such as those I mentioned above, cannot be given up.

The first three chapters of this book aim to reject the abovementioned restricted understanding of the relationship between the Christian faith and intellectual activity; then, they aim to support a more convincing, though unexpected, view of this subject. Chapter 3, devoted to Aquinas's thoughts on faith, reason, and charity, will allow me to advance several considerations that unequivocally support my thesis. In the following chapters, even more unexpected views will emerge.

First, the love and the commitments that I have mentioned above might be only one of the causes of the inconclusiveness here under consideration. Nonreligious commitments to the good and related beliefs might equally inspire debaters. From this, it follows that not only believers but also unbelievers – although this is not equally documented in the existing literature – can be responsible for inconclusiveness.

Second, stimulating perspectives that can reorient and make more effective any dialogues, on both religious and nonreligious topics, may emerge. On the one hand, believers are expected to increase their love for God and match it with love for the neighbor and the search for the good. On the other hand, the search for the good may inspire not only believers but also unbelievers. This may enable them to generate the best possible condition to successfully conduct rational inquiries and discussions. If they commit themselves to the good and consequently assume good habits, they can cause mutual understanding and friendship as well as increasing opportunities to achieve conclusiveness, at least in some cases. (I am only able to hypothesize such commitments. Unlike believers, unbelievers are – at least in principle – expected to commit themselves only to reason and arguments, which is equally expected to render them adopters of ME.)

I call the *spiritual turn in epistemology* this assumption of good habits (including its beneficial effects on the intellectual activity) as due to commitment to God and/or the good. Similarly to the *linguistic turn*, according to which the problems of philosophy are problems of language and of the relationship between language and the world,[10] the spiritual turn is based on the conviction that epistemological matters can fruitfully be treated by recourse to factors that are not strictly epistemic. The spiritual turn emphasizes the primary importance of human flourishing, taken as a commitment to God and the good. "Spiritual," therefore, is not opposed either to "nonreligious" or "physical." Rather, it designates the overall perfection of humanity.

This employment of the word "spirit" can be traced back to Georg F. W. Hegel. As is known, he was the first to use this word in philosophy to mean the totality of what exists, especially if taken *at its highest level of perfection*, which Hegel called "absolute spirit." This explains why, although it occurs when good habits are assumed, the turn here under consideration is "spiritual" and not merely "moral." Those who take the spiritual turn order everything, including the assumption of good habits, to the ultimate end, which is God and/or the good. They take a turn from ME, whose supporters first commit themselves to the mere search for truth – they maintain that every commitment must first be determined epistemically. This is why I call this view *ME*. ME, in fact, only considers merely epistemic factors such as evidence, whereas spiritual betterment and the assumption of good habits are taken into consideration to the extent that they are previously grounded in epistemic factors. One might object that searching for truth, wherever it can be found, is already a sign of spiritual profundity. I agree if this does not mean that we need first to attain the truth, from which every other good will follow. Unlike those who support this view, adopters of the spiritual turn first *commit themselves to God and the good*, based on the conviction that spiritual betterment brings the ability to perfect any human activity, including the intellectual one.

This conviction emerges from a theological reflection on the subject. I intend to develop our understanding of the epistemological consequences of the virtue of faith. This is in line with a traditional synergy between theology and philosophy, a synergy that started at least with Augustine's understanding of creatures, which he promoted and deepened on the

---

[10] As is known, this intuition was popularized by Richard Rorty in *The Linguistic Turn: Recent Essays in Philosophical Method*, ed. by Richard Rorty (Chicago, IL: University of Chicago Press, 1967). Let me also mention an edited book whose topic is whether good reasons for belief are *facts* and whose title resembles that of the present book: *The Factive Turn in Epistemology*, ed. by Veli Mitova (Cambridge: Cambridge University Press, 2018).

conviction that they show traces of the Trinity. This explains why this book focuses on epistemological matters and, nonetheless, was written starting from a theological point of view. Also, this explains why the cover is devoted to the evangelical story of Martha and Mary. The actions they take are both good, and nonetheless Mary's may successfully direct Martha's, whereas the reverse does not seem possible.

PART I

Toward the Overcoming of the Lockean View of Faith and Reason

The first three chapters of this book are devoted to supporting my view of the relationship that the Christian faith requires with intellectual activity. This relationship – so I intend to argue – leads believers to render debates on religion inconclusive. I will fully show this in Chapter 3, which explores Aquinas's theological approach to faith and reason. Only a theological perspective seems to offer an adequate understanding of the Christian faith and how it can be employed in rational debates.

However, this perspective has usually been overlooked in the course of the modern age, when debates on religion have been conducted from a merely philosophical viewpoint. I intend to argue that this viewpoint, which Locke exemplarily adopted, has inevitably restricted understanding of the Christian faith and its employment in the debates mentioned above.

Before moving on with Aquinas's approach to the relationship between faith and religion, which I believe guarantees a satisfactory understanding of it, I intend to focus on approaches that, compared to Aquinas's, seem only partly satisfactory. They have been taken by prominent modern and contemporary thinkers such as John Henry Newman and Alvin Plantinga (to whom I will devote Chapter 1) and Thomas Reid (to whom I will devote Chapter 2) to oppose the restricted view here under consideration.

In this connection, an objection needs to be responded to. This book's thesis is that a spiritual turn in epistemology is required, which implies a theological approach to faith and religion like the one I will argue can be found in Aquinas's thought. Why, therefore, devote a whole part (Chapters 1 and 2) of the three parts that constitute this book to the relatively satisfactory attempts in question? Doesn't this choice put exaggerated emphasis on them? My response is that the attempts made by thinkers such as Reid, Newman, and Plantinga provide an opportunity to show that, though rarely, modern restricted understandings of faith like Locke's have been determined and opposed. Furthermore, devoting a whole part of the book to the attempts mentioned above emphasizes the distinction with the subjects of the other parts. At the same time, if compared with those parts, the first is of limited length. The later parts of the book are more extensive as they comprise the constructive elements of the discussion.

CHAPTER I

Reformed Epistemologists and John Henry Newman as Critics of Locke's View of Faith and Reason

In this chapter, I first explore Locke's thought, which can be seen as an exemplar of the restricted view of faith and reason mentioned above. His thought is often seen as the one that has widely shaped how philosophers and even common people have become accustomed to considering the relationship between faith and reason in modern and contemporary times. I then devote Sections 1.2 and 1.3, respectively, to seeing how Reformed epistemologists and John Henry Newman have criticized Locke's perspective. I will argue that their original and intellectually penetrating criticisms are relatively satisfactory when considered from the viewpoint of the spiritual turn here under consideration.

1.1 Locke's Thought as an Exemplar of a Restricted Understanding of Faith and Reason

Locke's view of faith and reason has exerted an impressive influence on the philosophy of religion until recent times. As Jenkins has pointed out,

> it shaped the way non-philosophers spoke about, thought about and practised debate and enquiry regarding religious matters. There were important dissenters from Locke's approach in subsequent centuries, but it became embedded in training and practice so that both philosophers and non-philosophers came to have difficulty imagining an alternative.[1]

To do justice to this phenomenon, Jenkins adopts Charles Taylor's conviction that philosophy is "inherently historical."[2] Namely, our philosophical views are implicitly conditioned by historically dominant models.

---

[1] Jenkins, "Faith and Revelation," p. 213.
[2] See Charles Taylor, "Philosophy and Its History," in *Philosophy in History: Essays on the Historiography of Philosophy*, ed. by Richard Rorty, Jerome B. Schneewind, and Quentin Skinner (Cambridge: Cambridge University Press, 1984), p. 17, cited in Jenkins, "Faith and Revelation," p. 205.

Their influence is due "to what Taylor calls 'philosophical forgetting'; we have forgotten that the dominant model was one alternative among others."[3]

The model in question should not be attributed only to Locke. According to Nicholas Wolterstorff, "Locke was not a *solitary* genius." However, he "articulated better than anyone else"[4] that model, whose understanding can satisfactorily be achieved by focusing on his reflection.

Locke's reflection on religion was heavily influenced by the social and cultural problems of his time, especially the disagreements, conflicts, and wars that had accompanied the Reformation process. Wolterstorff rightly defines Locke as "an engaged philosopher,"[5] whose main interest was to solve the problems of his time. However, it was no longer possible to do so based on a unified tradition.[6] Locke, therefore, found a different way, which consisted of appealing to the deliverances of reason. He promoted a new method, which Jenkins calls the "epistemological project":

> It begins with the attempt to find universal norms and principles of correct human reasoning ... if we let these norms and principles guide our enquiries and debates we can make progress toward the rational resolution of some disagreements.... Subsequent thinkers would differ sharply with Locke on aspects of his epistemology or metaphysics, but the philosophical mainstream embraced the strategy of beginning by formulating the principles of a universalist epistemology, and then considering, in accord with these epistemological principles, arguments and evidence for and against the beliefs of faith.[7]

Therefore, the beliefs of faith can be accepted only to the extent that they can somehow be supported by reason. For Locke, the faithful should believe the divine revelation to the extent that they have arguments to demonstrate that it is really God who is the author of such a revelation:

> What I see I know to be so by the evidence of the thing itself: what I believe I take to be so upon the testimony of another: but this testimony I must know to be given, or else what ground have I of believing? I must see that it is God that reveals this to me, or else I see nothing. The question then here is, how do I know that God is the revealer of this to me; that this impression

---

[3] Jenkins, "Faith and Revelation," p. 207.
[4] Nicholas Wolterstorff, "Locke's Philosophy of Religion," in *The Cambridge Companion to Locke*, ed. by Vere Chappell (Cambridge: Cambridge University Press, 1994), p. 172.
[5] Ibid., p. 173.   [6] See ibid., p. 198.   [7] Jenkins, "Faith and Revelation," pp. 208f.

is made upon my mind by his Holy Spirit, and that therefore I ought to obey it?[8]

As is known, Locke reproaches those whom he calls "enthusiasts":

> If they believe it to be true, *because it is a revelation*, and have *no other reason* for its being a revelation, but because they are *fully persuaded without any other reason* that it is true, they believe it to be a revelation *only because they strongly believe* it to be a revelation, which is a very unsafe ground to proceed on.[9]

The safe ground to proceed on is instead *evidence* in support of belief: "The believing, or not believing that proposition, or book, to be of divine authority, can never be matter of faith, but matter of reason."[10] As is known, for Locke, assent to divine revelation comes in degrees, and we should proportion our degree of assent to the available evidence.[11]

Note that, among the Christian beliefs, God's existence is fundamental, without which no other belief can reasonably be held. (I use the expression "Christian beliefs" as a synonym for "truths of faith," as well as "revealed truths" and "the object of faith," namely, all of the statements that a believer assumes to be true since – so the believer thinks – they are revealed by God.) Furthermore, as Locke claims, that God exists is also the belief that is backed by such satisfactory evidence that we can claim that we have *knowledge* of God's existence.[12]

Consequently, Locke concludes that God's existence can firmly be held because it constitutes *knowledge*, more precisely *demonstrative* knowledge. Once this demonstration has been provided, other religious beliefs can be held with different degrees of firmness. Such beliefs constitute that which Locke names *judgment* (i.e., *probable* knowledge). Thus, once believers *know* that God exists, they will reasonably *believe*, at various levels of probability, religious statements such as "Jesus is the Son of God."

---

[8] *An Essay*, IV, xix, 10f. As Wolterstorff rightly notices, Locke offers a slightly different view in *The Reasonableness of Christianity*, which is not intended "to show that it is probable on satisfactory evidence that the New Testament records revelation from God, but to show that a great deal of the *content* of the revelation there recorded can be arrived at by reason – that is, can either be demonstrated or shown to be probably true" (Wolterstorff, "Locke's Philosophy of Religion," p. 192). In this case, therefore, reason plays an even more decisive role in the understanding of religious belief. Not surprisingly, the publication of the work in question raised controversies, including accusations according to which this book "would ultimately lead to atheism" (John C. Higgins-Biddle, "*The Reasonableness of Christianity* and Its Vindications," in *The Bloomsbury Companion to Locke*, ed. by S. J. Savonius-Wroth, Paul Schuurman, and Jonathan Walmsley [London: Bloomsbury, 2010], p. 270).

[9] *An Essay*, IV, xix, 11, my emphasis.   [10] Ibid., IV, xviii, 6.
[11] See ibid., IV, xix, 1. See also above, Introduction, note 3.   [12] See ibid., IV, x, 6.

Incidentally, let me mention that this view of faith does not apply to the experience of all believers. Locke distinguishes "original revelation" from "traditional revelation." The former occurs when an impression "is made immediately by God" on the mind of the prospective believer.[13] While paraphrasing the Pauline epistles, Locke explicitly mentions St. Paul as a recipient of this kind of revelation.[14] Instead, the latter occurs when someone believes on the ground that what she believes has been revealed by God. Obviously enough, Locke's view of faith applies only to the latter case. Consequently, as Wolterstorff points out, "it appears that Locke's definition of 'faith,' when combined with his account of original revelation, yields the result that the believer's *response* to original revelation is not a case of faith."[15] In fact, the distinction Locke proposes between the two kinds of revelation does not seem convincing. Thomas Aquinas's view of the object and signs of faith provides a more intellectually satisfactory view, according to which the distinction at stake disappears.[16]

At any rate, Locke saw his approach to religion as supportive of religious belief's credibility. Against the view that reason and faith are opposites, which he believed was common in his time,[17] he attempted to reconcile them with one another.

However, how Locke proposed this reconciliation was based on a restricted understanding of faith (i.e., the view of faith as just intellectual assent or propositional belief). I take here "faith" as a commitment to God, which includes trust in him (belief-in) and propositional belief (belief-that). I will extensively deal with this in Chapter 3, where I will focus on Aquinas's thesis, which traces back to Augustine, that faith is "believing in a God," "believing God," and "believing in God."[18] Newman's view, as I will show in the third section, is consistent with this tradition, as emerges when he says that "I mean by belief, not precisely faith, because faith, in its theological sense, includes a belief, not only in the thing believed, but also in the ground of believing; that is, not only

---

[13] See ibid., IV, xviii, 3.
[14] See Locke, *Works*, vii, 30–31, 34, 432, cit. in Nicholas Wolterstorff, *John Locke and the Ethics of Belief* (Cambridge: Cambridge University Press, 1996), p. 126, note 110.
[15] Wolterstorff, *John Locke and the Ethics of Belief*, p. 126, note 110.
[16] I will show this later. See below, Chapter 3, notes 53ff.
[17] Locke claims that "though it be in itself a very improper way of speaking, yet common use has so authorized it, that it would be folly either to oppose or hope to remedy it" (*An Essay*, IV, xvii, 24). Greg Forster appropriately finds this view "exaggerated," although he recognizes that "during the seventeenth-Century the influence of the Enlightenment, especially from the Continent in places like France, was issuing a major challenge to the view of faith and reason as natural allies" (Greg Forster, *Starting with Locke* [London: Continuum, 2011], pp. 63f.).
[18] See *Summa theologiae*, II-II, q. 2, a. 2. For more on this, see below, Chapter 3, note 75.

belief in certain doctrines, but belief in them expressly because God has revealed them."[19] Looking at faith as just propositional belief inevitably excludes what distinguishes religious experience from any other: the full reliance that believers – at the least the paradigmatic ones – are expected to place on the revealed doctrines. They should see such reliance as caused by their communion with God, which God himself grants to them. As a result, they should stick to their religious beliefs, no matter how convincing contrary evidence may seem to be.[20] By contrast, Locke's approach to religion can be seen as methodologically "naturalistic." By methodological naturalism, I mean the view according to which religious belief can only be taken as *the outcome* of a rational exploration of our experience. This view straightforwardly excludes any possibility that believing in God may somehow be due to a relationship with him, which God himself may grant to some of us. Locke's reflection implies the assumption that *every subject*, including religion, should be treated without taking into account that a supernatural being may exist and reveal to us an unexpected way to deal with our experience.[21] By contrast, whether they are right or wrong, religious believers are expected to ground their belief precisely in the conviction that God exists and may play a role in their believing. While referring to Locke's severe rejection of the enthusiast's position, Wolterstorff points out that "it's regrettable that, beyond this highly tendentious attack on the enthusiasts, Locke *never explores the possibility* that religious experience, of one sort or another, can provide evidence for theistic belief."[22] In other words, Locke chooses to exclude the possibility that, unlike any other belief, the religious one may be characterized by a high level of certainty that is divinely granted and is not due to rational justification.

---

[19] John Henry Newman, *An Essay in Aid of a Grammar of Assent*, edited with introduction and notes by Ian T. Ker (New York: Oxford University Press, 1985) (hereafter GA), V, Introduction. Among Reformed epistemologists, let me mention Dewey J. Hoitenga, according to whom "faith, although it includes belief, is more than just belief; it is belief that arises from trust" (Dewey J. Hoitenga, *Faith and Reason from Plato to Plantinga: An Introduction to Reformed Epistemology* [Albany: State University of New York Press, 1991], p. 35).

[20] However unsustainable this idea may appear to be at first sight, I will argue in its support while treating the way faith can be seen from Aquinas's viewpoint (see below, Chapter 3, Section 3.3).

[21] Naturalism can be taken in a more comprehensive way, as the view that no agent or force that stands outside the natural world exists. In this sense, Plantinga argues that naturalists don't accept the existence of God as well as that of "the Stoic's Mind, or Fichte's Absolute I, or Plato's Idea of the Good, or Aristotle's Unmoved Mover, or Hegel's Absolute." In other words, "naturalism is stronger than atheism, in the sense that it is possible to be an atheist but not a naturalist, but not possible to be a naturalist but not an atheist" (Alvin Plantinga, "Against Naturalism," in *Knowledge of God*, ed. by Alvin Plantinga and Michael Tooley [Malden, MA: Blackwell, 2008], p. 19).

[22] Wolterstorff, "Locke's Philosophy of Religion," p. 195, my emphasis.

Locke's choice may arguably be seen as caused by the abovementioned "attempt to find universal norms and principles of correct human reasoning," which he tried to apply to every subject to achieve agreement among interlocutors. However, this objective, which was the ultimate one of his epistemological project, was not achieved. Such a project has indeed given rise to further disagreement and disputes, which testify to its overall failure.[23]

My thesis is that the widespread disagreement in question is because, in proportion to their commitment to a certain view, debaters simply want to stick to that view, regardless of the available evidence that might convince them of the contrary. Religious doctrines explicitly include the abovementioned will to stick to one's beliefs. Therefore, at least religious debates manifestly call for an approach to epistemology that is an alternative to Locke's.

I will argue that an alternative approach can emerge from examining how religious experience requires believers to engage in debates. The approach in question is what I call a *spiritual turn* from ME, ME that Locke's project exemplarily shows.

Before moving on to this argument, however, I need to consider some reactions to Locke's thoughts, which are only partly satisfactory from the viewpoint of my argument.

1.2 Reformed Epistemologists as Critics of Locke's View of Faith and Reason

"Reformed epistemology" is a view developed by various thinkers, among which stand out William Alston, Wolterstorff, and Plantinga, in the last decades of the twentieth century.[24] Calvin College, situated in Grand Rapids, Michigan, is the academic institution where many of them have studied and taught, and it is to the thought of prominent Reformers like Calvin that their epistemology is associated. As I will show below, Calvin's thought has especially influenced Plantinga's research with the conviction that God implanted in all humans a *sensus divinitatis*, which, given

---

[23] See Jenkins, "Faith and Revelation," p. 214. See also above, Introduction, note 7.
[24] The first expression of this perspective is often considered *Faith and Rationality: Reason and Belief in God*, ed. by Alvin Plantinga and Nicholas Wolterstorff (Notre Dame, IN: University of Notre Dame Press, 1983). For a recent survey, see Anthony Bolos and Kyle Scott, "Reformed Epistemology," 2015, https://iep.utm.edu/ref-epis/, accessed September 24, 2020. Recent literature is explored by Andrew Moon, "Recent Work in Reformed Epistemology," *Philosophy Compass* 12 (2016), pp. 879–891.

appropriate circumstances, makes everyone able to believe religious statements *basically*, that is, in the absence of inference from other statements.[25] Reformed epistemologists, however, have also been influenced by epistemologists like Reid, and have especially reflected on Reid's argument that we are all born with belief dispositions, which form beliefs once triggered in a certain way. From this follows that, contrary to Locke's views, Reformed epistemologists have maintained that theistic belief, and other religious beliefs as well, can be reasonably held basically, and that to understand whether these beliefs are rational, we should focus on our dispositions, and not evidence in their support.

Plantinga is often seen as "the chief defender of Reformed epistemology."[26] Due to space constraints, I will focus on Reformed epistemologists' proposal, as shown by his reflection.

As I said above, this reflection can be seen as being inspired by Calvin's view that "there is within the human mind, and indeed by natural instinct, an awareness of divinity," which Calvin calls *sensus divinitatis*. It is "a tacit confession of a sense of deity inscribed in the hearts of all," which is testified by the fact that "from the beginning of the world there has been no region, no city, in short, no household, that could do without religion."[27] As Paul Helm has pointed out, adopting the *sensus divinitatis* means that "belief in God is natural in the sense of being part of man's original condition, part of what it means to be really or fully human."[28]

---

[25] As Moon points out ("Recent Work in Reformed Epistemology," p. 888, note 14) many scholars, from Derek Jeffries ("How Reformed Is Reformed Epistemology? Alvin Plantinga and Calvin's 'Sensus Divinitatis,'" *Religious Studies* 33 [1997], pp. 419–431) to Georg Plasger ("Does Calvin Teach a *Sensus Divinitatis*? Reflections on Alvin Plantinga's Interpretation of Calvin," in *Plantinga's Warranted Christian Belief*, ed. by Dieter Schonecker [Berlin: De Gruyter, 2015], pp. 169–190), have wondered whether Plantinga's view really coincides with Calvin's. Plantinga himself shows this doubt while wondering whether the model of religious belief he proposes is faithful to Calvin's view. However, he does not seem to pay exceeding attention to it, and says that "whatever Calvin thinks ... it's our model" (Alvin Plantinga, *Warranted Christian Belief* [New York: Oxford University Press, 2000], p. 173).

[26] Michael Bergmann, "Religious Belief, Epistemology of, Recent Developments," in *A Companion to Epistemology*, 2nd ed., ed. by Jonathan Dancy, Ernest Sosa, and Matthias Steup (Malden, MA: Wiley-Blackwell, 2010), p. 697.

[27] John Calvin, *Institutes of the Christian Religion* (Philadelphia: Westminster Press, 1960), Bk. 1, chapter 3, pp. 43f.

[28] Paul Helm, "John Calvin, the *Sensus Divinitatis*, and the Noetic Effects of Sin," *International Journal for Philosophy of Religion* 43 (1998), p. 88. The reference to the "original condition" may lead one to think that Calvin and Plantinga have in mind the unfallen condition of man. In reality, at least according to Plantinga's interpretation of the *Institutes*, "Calvin is pretty clearly teaching that all people, fallen as well as unfallen, have this knowledge" (Plantinga, *Warranted Christian Belief*, p. 173).

Plantinga argues that Calvin's view traces back to Aquinas. As he says, "we can usefully see Calvin's suggestion as a kind of meditation on and development of a theme suggested by Aquinas."[29] However convincing this harmony between them may be,[30] it is of interest to my argument that, by focusing on something that he believes is shared by prominent representatives of diverse branches of Christianity, Plantinga appears to think that a typically Christian approach to develop philosophical arguments on religion is possible and must be developed. This emerges from his famous article entitled "Advice to Christian Philosophers,"[31] where it is argued that Christian philosophers should choose their own subjects and treat them in a way that is different from the one adopted by philosophers who are not Christian.

It seems that it is on the basis of his religious experience that Plantinga rejects the typically Lockean view, according to which we should not entertain "any proposition with greater assurance than the proofs it is built upon will warrant."[32] It is his own experience as a Christian believer, combined with the abovementioned Calvinian conviction that the faithful believe because of a *sensus divinitatis*, that is, without any need of argument, that must have led him to propose an alternative to Locke's approach to religion. Plantinga finds this approach, which has been called "evidentialism" because of the crucial role it ascribes to evidence, incompatible with the experience of the vast majority of the faithful. These – so he observes – usually believe *basically*. Their belief does not need to be grounded in inference from other statements.

Incidentally, let me make two points. First, as Evan Fales has noticed, beliefs that emerge spontaneously in the absence of conscious inference from other beliefs may still be based on other beliefs.[33] This means that the distinction between basic and nonbasic does not seem to be very precise. In response, Plantinga shows that, for his purposes, having such a precise

---

[29] Plantinga, *Warranted Christian Belief*, p. 17.
[30] If, on the one hand, both Calvin and Aquinas claim that the existence of God can be affirmed without philosophical demonstrations, on the other hand, Aquinas's view is that all men by nature understand "in a general and confused way" (*Summa theologiae*, I, q. 2, a. 1, ad 1) that God exists. Needless to say, this view of God does not remind us of Plantinga's idea of the creator of all things who "is to be thanked and praised." Furthermore, when Thomas asks himself how to claim that an omnipotent, omniscient, and perfectly good creator of all things exists, he says that this claim can be advanced in only two ways, i.e., natural theology and faith. See *Summa theologiae*, I, q. 1, a. 1, and below, Chapter 6, note 76. See also Roberto Di Ceglie, "Alvin Plantinga and Thomas Aquinas on Theism and Christianity," *Philosophy and Theology* 27 (2015), pp. 235–252.
[31] Alvin Plantinga, "Advice to Christian Philosophers," *Faith and Philosophy* 1 (1984), pp. 253–271.
[32] *An Essay*, IV, xix, 1.
[33] See Evan Fales, "Proper Basicality," *Philosophy and Phenomenological Research* 68/2004, pp. 377ff.

distinction "doesn't really matter."[34] He has been interested in opposing evidentialist claims that religious beliefs can only be held on the basis of rigorous philosophical or scientific arguments.[35]

Second, Plantinga's view can be improved once combined with Aquinas's thought on faith. According to Aquinas, the faithful believe mainly because of God's grace and only secondarily because of arguments.[36] This means that they tend to *support* their religious belief through inference, which is not part of Plantinga's view. (From this, however, it does not follow that, for Aquinas, faith is *due* to such inference. As Aquinas says, before the same evidence, some believe whereas some do not,[37] and this is compatible with Plantinga's view.)

At any rate, what is of interest to my argument is that Plantinga seems to oppose the view that I call ME, at least in the sense that he rejects a substantial aspect of this view. The aspect in question consists in the fact that, for mere epistemologists, no commitment to God and religion is acceptable if not previously grounded in the available evidence.

Plantinga rejects this view precisely on the ground of religious experience. Due to this choice, he gives rise to an intellectual itinerary that might briefly be presented in three steps.

First, he argues that the epistemic standard applied to religious belief is more severe than the one applied to any other belief. Against this attitude, he employed an argument, which Terence Penelhum would later call the "parity argument."[38] In *God and Other Minds*,[39] Plantinga shows that, if believing in other minds is rational though unsupported by argument – we cannot observe the thoughts and feelings of other people[40] – then there is no reason to deny that believing in God is rational even if evidentially

---

[34] Alvin Plantinga, "On 'Proper Basicality,'" *Philosophy and Phenomenological Research* 75/2007, p. 614.

[35] I am in debt to Moon ("Recent Work in Reformed Epistemology," p. 885) for this reference to the debate between Fales and Plantinga. Moon refers also to more recent treatments of this subject, treatments among which it is worth the trouble to mention Michael Bergman, "Rational Religious Belief without Arguments," in *Philosophy of Religion: An Anthology*, ed. by Michael Rea and Louis Pojman (Stamford, CT: Cengage Learning, 2015), pp. 609–624.

[36] See *Summa theologiae*, II-II, q. 6, a. 1. For more on this, see below, Chapter 3, notes 68ff. and 80.

[37] See ibid., II-II, q. 6, a. 1.

[38] See Terence Penelhum, *God and Skepticism* (Dordrecht: D. Reidel, 1983), chapters 2, 5, and 6. After having been first used by Plantinga in *God and Other Minds* (1967, see next footnote), this argument has widely been used and also modified.

[39] Alvin Plantinga, *God and Other Minds: A Study of the Rational Justification of Belief in God* (Ithaca, NY: Cornell University Press, 1967).

[40] Thomas Reid had said something similar two centuries earlier: "The thoughts and passions of the mind are invisible" (*The Works of Thomas Reid*, ed. by William Hamilton [Edinburgh: MacLachlan and Stewart-Longman, Green, Longman, Roberts and Green, 1863], p. 450).

unsupported. Just as we sometimes "see" that someone is thinking, depressed, or in pain, so can a theist impressed by the harmony and beauty of the universe or the profundity of the Scriptures claim to "see" that God exists.

Second, Plantinga shows that there are problems with evidentialism and foundationalism once applied to religious belief. Let me focus on foundationalism, which in *Reason and Belief in God*, he rightly says is "the dominant way of thinking" in the epistemology of Western philosophical tradition.[41] According to foundationalism, knowledge consists of two types of statements: basic statements, which are immediately recognized as true, and other types of statements, which are inferred through reasoning from the basic statements. In Plantinga's discussion of foundationalism, "any statement must be proved through demonstration or, alternatively, must be accepted basically if it is self-evident, evident to the senses or incorrigible." The author of "Reason and Belief in God" concludes that the statement "any statement must be proved through demonstration or must be accepted basically if it is self-evident, evident to the senses or incorrigible" does not apply to itself, because it doesn't meet the criteria in question – that is, it has never been proved, nor is it self-evident, evident to the senses, or incorrigible. This shows that foundationalism, as Plantinga takes it, is self-referentially contradictory. It also shows that, since it has never been proved, its supporters must have held it basically, in a way that is clearly different from the ones I have mentioned above. The parity argument, therefore, can be employed again. If foundationalists act inconsistently with foundationalism, there is no reason to expect believers to act consistently with it. In other words, if there is no reason to maintain that a basic belief can only be self-evident, or evident to the senses or incorrigible, then it is possible to consider other perspectives.

Third, Plantinga considers other perspectives, which probably do justice to how Christians maintain their belief. He considers affirmations that Calvin and, as he believes, Aquinas have advanced jointly. He uses them as a model, which he calls the "A/C model," of both theistic and Christian belief. His goal is to show that, although held basically, such beliefs can reasonably be taken as "warranted" – where "warrant" is the quality "enough of which is what makes the difference between knowledge and

---

[41] Alvin Plantinga, "Reason and Belief in God," in Plantinga and Wolterstorff, eds., *Faith and Rationality*, p. 48. See also Nicholas Wolterstorff, *Reason within the Bounds of Religion*, 2nd ed. (Grand Rapids, MI: Eerdmans, 1984), p. 30.

mere true belief."[42] While taking part in the development of virtue epistemology,[43] Plantinga focuses on the intellectual faculties that yield theistic and Christian belief and considers the environment in which such faculties work. His objective is to show that, if the beliefs in question are true, the A/C model is very likely true. This means that Plantinga intends only to show how it *could* be that the belief in question is true or actual. The aim of his treatment of the A/C model is not to show "that it is *true* but, rather, that it is *epistemically possible*."[44] To show that the model in question is true would be – in Plantinga's own words – "to show that theism and Christianity are true; and I don't know how to do something one can sensibly call 'showing' that either of these *is* true."[45]

Such a conclusion can easily lead to criticism, which Richard Swinburne has summarized as follows: "There is ... a monumental issue which Plantinga does not discuss, and which a lot of people will consider needs discussing. This is whether Christian beliefs do have warrant (in Plantinga's sense). He has shown that they do, if they are true; so we might hope for discussion of whether they are true."[46]

At any rate, this brief outline of Reformed epistemology, as developed by Plantinga, serves an important purpose in criticizing the "methodologically naturalistic" approach to religion. Unlike Locke, Plantinga explores the possibility that religious experience, even if unsupported by arguments, can contribute to rational reflection. In this sense, he seems to oppose a fundamental aspect of what I call ME, that is, the conviction that commitments can be made only if they are previously supported by way of rational investigation.

If my argument is correct, Plantinga rejects ME, according to which one should always prefer beliefs supported by more evidence to beliefs supported by less evidence. He rejects philosophical arguments proposed by thinkers such as Locke, and continues believing, including when he is not yet in possession of adequate counterarguments. Of course, "not yet" means that, being a philosopher, Plantinga is expected to continue searching for such counterarguments.

---

[42] Plantinga, *Warranted Christian Belief*, p. xi.   [43] See below, Chapter 6, notes 12 and 13.
[44] Plantinga, *Warranted Christian Belief*, p. xii.   [45] Ibid., p. 170.
[46] Richard Swinburne, "Plantinga on Warrant," *Religious Studies* 37 (2001), p. 206. In reply, it can be said that "Plantinga's model achieves what he intends it to show, namely that provided Christian belief is true Christians are not irrational – or, more accurately, unwarranted – in holding the beliefs that they do hold" (Deane-Peter Baker, *Tayloring Reformed Epistemology: Charles Taylor, Alvin Plantinga and the De Iure Challenge to Christian Belief* [London: SCM Press, 2007], p. 95). A more recent debate on this subject is the one between Dieter Schonecker and Plantinga, a debate that is contained in Schonecker, ed., *Plantinga's Warranted Christian Belief*.

However, Plantinga does *not explicitly* claim that he continues committing himself to his religious belief, nor does he note that this commitment, even in the absence of argument, is required by religious doctrine. Accordingly, he does not explore the inconclusiveness here under consideration. Like anyone who engages in debates, be they conducted at an academic level or not, he takes into consideration contrary arguments and deals with how to maintain faith in the face of counterevidence.[47] However, he does not consider the possibility, which I will explore in this book, that, when related to religious debates, this inconclusiveness *is demanded by the specific way faith requires to be related to reason*. Consequently, Plantinga does not wonder whether or not, beyond mere inconclusiveness, other effects such as the spiritual turn here in question may follow from the Christian faith for both believers and unbelievers.

1.3 The Role of Newman's Notion of Inconclusiveness in His Criticism of Locke's View

Newman seems to have taken this debate on inconclusiveness a step further, which is why, though he lived a century before the Reformed epistemologists, I deal with his reflection after having focused on them.[48]

Born in London in 1801, he experienced a spiritual conversion during his adolescent years. This would determine his lifelong search for spiritual perfection. He quickly became an influential priest in the Church of England and the leader of the so-called Oxford Movement, started in 1833, intending to reform the Church of England by emphasizing the Catholic elements of the English religious tradition. He then left his Church and his teaching post at Oxford and converted to Catholicism in 1845. Facing no little opposition, misunderstanding, and resentment, he

---

[47] Not surprisingly, the fourth and last part of *Warranted Christian Belief* is devoted to defeaters for Christian and theistic belief, as Plantinga takes it. In his footsteps, see Erick Baldwin and Tyler McNabb, *Plantingian Religious Epistemology and World Religions* (Lanham, MD: Rowman and Littlefield, 2018), esp. chapter 11, "Objections to Plantingian Religious Epistemology."

[48] Closeness to my argument, therefore, is the criterion I have employed to decide the order in which to focus on these thinkers – they are presented in order of increasing closeness to my view. The same criterion will lead me to decide which affinities and differences between Newman and Reformed epistemology I will mention here. For a more general treatment of such affinities and differences, see Stephen R. Grimm, "Cardinal Newman, Reformed Epistemologist?," *American Catholic Philosophical Quarterly* 75 (2001), pp. 497–522. The author responds to those Catholic thinkers who had emphasized only the differences – he explicitly refers to *Rational Faith: Catholic Responses to Reformed Epistemology*, ed. by Linda Zagzebski (Notre Dame, IN: Notre Dame University Press, 1993). He also recognizes that similarities had already been detected by Basil Mitchell and Anthony Kenny (see p. 498, note 4).

continued working as an engaged theologian, whose importance in the life of England and devotion to the Church was recognized to the point that he was made a cardinal in 1879 and canonized in 2019.

This religious background might explain why Newman opposed Locke's view that assent to divine revelation must be proportioned to the available evidence.[49] Such a devout believer must have considered unacceptable ideas such as that "No religious tenet is important, unless reason shows it to be so" and "It is dishonest in a man to make an act of faith in what he has not had brought home to him by actual proof,"[50] ideas that are typical of ME. On the contrary, Newman's religious experience must have suggested, as John Lamont has pointed out, that "the belief in divine revelation that faith involves requires the strongest possible degree of assent,"[51] which is obviously more than the available evidence mostly allows.

In reply to Locke's view that assent must be proportioned to the available evidence, Newman devoted his *Grammar of Assent* to reflecting on "what it is to believe."[52] Reflecting on the nature of our intellectual activity led him to argue that assent can be certain in the absence of fully conclusive arguments. For Newman, "assent is in its nature absolute and unconditional."[53] This, however, does not mean that no preliminary reasons accompany assent. Newman only means that assent is independent of our acts of inference, as he points out in this passage:

> Indeed, I doubt whether assent is ever given without some preliminary, which stands for a reason; but it does not follow from this, that it may not be withheld in cases when there are good reasons for giving it to a proposition, or may not be withdrawn after it has been given, the reasons remaining, or may not remain when the reasons are forgotten, or must always vary in strength, as the reasons vary; and this substantiveness, as

---

[49] See *An Essay*, IV, xix, 1. See also above, Introduction, note 3. According to Gerald McCarthy, Newman was actually the "more articulate and forceful" among Locke's opponents. See Gerald McCarthy, "Newman, Foundationalism, and the Ethics of Belief," *Horizons* 8/1 (1981), p. 63.

[50] John Henry Newman, *Apologia pro vita sua: Being a History of His Religious Opinions*, edited, with an Introduction and Notes, by Martin J. Svaglic (London: Oxford University Press, 1967), p. 260.

[51] John R. T. Lamont, "Newman on Faith and Rationality," *International Journal for Philosophy of Religion* 40 (1996), p. 63.

[52] Newman, GA, V, Introduction. The fact that this work is devoted to exploring "what it is to believe ... what the mind does, what it contemplates, when it makes an act of faith" allows us to understand why Newman gave the work in question such an unusual title.

[53] Ibid., VI, p. 105.

I may call it, of the act of assent is the very point which I have wished to establish.[54]

For Newman, Locke's view is grounded in an attitude to start from philosophical reflection alone and not from the exploration of human experience. In other words, Locke "consults his own idea of how the mind ought to act, instead of interrogating human nature, as an existing thing, as it is found in the world."[55]

Newman does interrogate our experience and notices that our thought is often complicated by personal factors and hard to understand from the viewpoint of logics.[56] This is not surprising if we consider that we often have to do with *concrete facts* and *real things*, not *abstract notions*.[57]

Assent to real things is a *real assent*, which Newman typically calls "belief." This allows him to reject the accusation that religious belief is untenable because it has a-rational commitments at its core, and not evidence. For him, all beliefs, including those we usually see as properly held, presuppose a-rational commitments. To use Newman's words, "none of us can think or act without the acceptance of truths, not intuitive, not demonstrated, yet sovereign."[58] In this way, like Reformed epistemologists, Newman seems to develop a parity argument, as Duncan Pritchard has argued.[59]

While focusing on religious belief, Newman develops this reflection by saying that "to the devout and spiritual, the Divine Word speaks of things, not merely of notions."[60] Consequently, the faithful give a *real assent*, which I have already said is what Newman calls "belief," to an equally present reality, which is God. They do not simply give a notional assent that regards instead the mere *idea* of God.

---

[54] Ibid., VI, § 1, n. 3, pp. 113f. An aspect of this relationship between inference and assent is the fact that, as Newman notices, different people may hold different assent though the inference they possess is the same, which explains why philosophers have cultivated logics (see ibid., VIII, § 1).
[55] Ibid., VI, § 1. [56] See ibid.
[57] To be clearer, in some propositions, terms "stand for things external to us, unit and individual," whereas, in others, terms are "common nouns, as standing for what is abstract." This is the distinction that Newman formulated between, respectively, propositions that only admit of *real* apprehension and assent, on the one hand, and propositions that only admit of *notional* apprehension and assent (ibid., I, § 2).
[58] Ibid., VI, § 1.
[59] See especially his recent article entitled "Skepticism," in *A Companion to Atheism and Philosophy*, ed. by Graham Oppy (Hoboken, NJ: Wiley, 2019), pp. 277–290. I will also take into consideration other publications devoted by Pritchard to this subject in Chapter 4, Section 4.2. I refer the reader to that section for more on two related theses advanced by Pritchard: (1) Newman's parity argument is partly different from the one developed by Reformed epistemologists; (2) Newman's reflection exerted an influence on Wittgenstein's remarks contained in *On Certainty*.
[60] Newman, GA, IV, § 2, p. 57.

God, however, cannot be seen and perceived like other things in the world. An inference from the experience of such things to the transcendent God is, therefore, necessary. At the same time, this inference should not lead us to give a notional assent. Therefore, Newman argues that believers make an *informal* inference by way of a specific faculty, which he calls *illative sense*. The informal inference is the argument from concrete facts (e.g., miracles performed by Jesus and the apostles) to concrete facts (e.g., the divinity of Jesus). Unlike formal inference, the informal inference is not a causal conclusion from given premises. In other words, concrete facts, singularly taken, do not lead to any assent, whereas this is possible if the facts in question are taken collectively. In this connection, Newman speaks of "cumulation" and "converging" of such facts.[61]

A crucial role in this inferential process is played by the level of experience, culture, and maturity of the knowing subject. Note that, as I said above, the illative sense is the faculty that performs such an inference. Newman sees this sense as similar to the Aristotelian *phronesis* to the extent that it "is developed and matured by practice and experience."[62] In other words, this faculty varies among people. Its working depends on a complex of personal characteristics.[63]

A similarly relevant role is played by moral responsibility, whose importance for Newman's reflection we can easily understand while considering Newman's notion of conscience. For him, conscience is the fundamental premise of religious belief. It is the sense of moral obligation that spontaneously predisposes one to believe. In fact, it leads one to think of and revere God as the Supreme Governor, the Judge, which is "holy, just, powerful, all-seeing, retributive."[64] Nevertheless, Newman is aware that not everybody infers God's existence from the voice of conscience.[65] True, he is also aware of the force of conscience and its injunctions, as emerges when he asks himself: "Who can deny the existence of Conscience? Who does not feel the force of its injunctions?"[66] And nonetheless, he argues that conscience is fleeting and consequently insufficient to make one

---

[61] See ibid., VIII, § 2.
[62] Gérard Verbeke, "Aristotelian Roots of Newman's Illative Sense," in *Newman and Gladstone Centennial Essays*, ed. by James D. Bastable (Dublin: Veritas Publications, 1978), p. 179.
[63] See Newman, GA, IX, § 3.   [64] Ibid., V, § 1, p. 110.
[65] In this connection, Mark Wynn arguably notices that Newman "treats the data of conscience not so much as evidence for the existence of God ... but rather as presupposed in any religiously sensitive explication of what we mean by the term 'God'" (Mark Wynn, "The Relationship of Religion and Ethics: A Comparison of Newman and Contemporary Philosophy of Religion," *The Heythrop Journal* 46/4 [2005], p. 440).
[66] Newman, *The Idea of a University* (London: Basil Montagu Pickering, 1873), p. 514.

adhere to religious belief. When he focuses on the experience of "an ordinary child," he considers the one "who is safe from influences destructive of his religious instincts."[67] Moral responsibility, in conclusion, plays a fundamental role in the process that leads to religious assent. As V. F. Blehl says, the illative sense "requires a moral preparation for the perception of truth and for proper reasoning."[68]

All of the elements of Newman's thought that I have mentioned so far – the persuasion that assent is unconditional, the difference between real and notional assent, the informal inference, the illative sense, the role of conscience and moral responsibility – emphasize Newman's conviction that real assent is due to an amazingly high quantity of factors, only a few of which can be clearly determined. Even the "most elaborate exhibitions" of logic – so Newman says – "fail to represent adequately the sum-total of considerations by which an individual mind is determined in its judgment of things."[69] From this, it follows that the more distant the views adopted by debaters are, the more inconclusive their debates are destined to be. As Newman openly claims, "I do not talk to those who are too far from me on a number of questions."[70]

I should note that this approach to inconclusiveness is far different from what I focus on in this book. Newman endorses the idea that the inconclusiveness of debates is simply due to the exceedingly complicated nature of human knowledge. This leads to the conclusion that, had we the opportunity to reduce the complicatedness at stake, clarity and conclusiveness would inversely proportionally increase – which is confirmed by the fact that, for Newman, no inconclusiveness can be found in debates that are so simple and short that it is impossible to get confused.[71]

---

[67] Newman, GA, V, § 1. For more on conscience described as the "voice" of God, see Terrence Merrigan, "Revelation," in *The Cambridge Companion to John Henry Newman*, ed. by Ian Ker and Terrence Merrigan (Cambridge: Cambridge University Press, 2009), p. 51.

[68] V. F. Blehl, "The Role of Education in the Formation of Conscience and the Illative Sense," in *Internationale Cardinal Newman Studien*, ed. by H. Fries, W. Becker, and G. Biemer, vol. 11 (Nürnberg: Glock und Lutz, 1980), p. 146.

[69] Newman, GA, VIII, § 1, n. 2.   [70] Ibid., X, § 2, n. 1.

[71] "When an argument is in itself and by itself conclusive of a truth, it has by a law of our nature the same command over our assent, or rather the truth which it has reached has the same command, as our senses have. Certainly our intellectual nature is under laws, and the correlative of ascertained truth is unreserved assent. But I am not speaking of short and lucid demonstrations; but of long and intricate mathematical investigations; and in that case, though every step may be indisputable, it still requires a specially sustained attention and an effort of memory to have in the mind all at once all the steps of the proof, with their bearings on each other, and the antecedents which they severally involve; and these conditions of the inference may interfere with the promptness of our assent" (ibid., VI, § 1).

I instead hypothesize that believers are expected not to give up on their commitment to God even if the arguments that oppose their faith appear to them to be rationally sound and convincing. Therefore, the inconclusiveness at stake needs to be taken into consideration with reference to the specific way faith relates to reason – a way that Newman, like Plantinga and other Reformers, does not take into account. Unlike Locke, all these thinkers convincingly reject the idea that religious belief should be held by way of argument. However, they do not seem to focus on the proper tenacity of faith in the face of counterevidence, which I intend to argue depends on the specific relationship that faith requires with reason.

Plantinga and Newman engage in showing that religious belief is rationally plausible. They focus on the problem of evidentialism (i.e., they explore how Locke considers the relationship between assent and inference) and argue that, unlike Locke's view, their own is rationally acceptable. This strategy is perfectly understandable from the believer's viewpoint. However, if not accompanied by other approaches, it risks of boiling down faith to reason. My approach consists of considering what *distinguishes* faith from reason. Instead of focusing on the typically Lockean relationship between assent and inference, I explore its implicit presupposition – that is, Locke's taking for granted that faith has nothing specific compared with other kinds of experience. My purpose is to argue that the specificity in question allows faith to put reason in the best possible condition to function.

In the next chapter, I will focus on Thomas Reid's thoughts on religious belief. Unlike the thinkers considered so far, Reid refers to how faith requires to be related to reason. However, he does not develop a systematic reflection on the subject. Therefore, he cannot see what effects the relationship between faith and reason could have with respect to the theme here under consideration of the spiritual turn.

CHAPTER 2

Thomas Reid
Philosophy, Science, and the Christian Revelation

In this chapter I focus on Thomas Reid's reference to the specific way the Christian faith requires to be related to rational arguments. I start by showing that two aspects of his thought seem to be irreconcilable with one another. On the one hand, Reid constantly refers to the substantive benefits that mankind has received from the Christian revelation. On the other hand, the investigations – both philosophical and scientific – that Reid conducts are not supported by any appeal to religious beliefs. I argue that a closer inspection of these investigations shows, on the contrary, that the two aspects just mentioned are compatible with one another and that this compatibility is what Reid believes the Christian faith requires once related to reason.

2.1 On the Supposed Incompatibility, in Reid's Thought, between Divine Revelation's Influence on Reason and Autonomous Rational Investigations

For Reid, human beings are provided with knowing faculties – both sensory and intellectual – whose reliability has wrongly been put into doubt by the skeptic outcomes of the theory of ideas. Although Reid admires Hume's genius,[1] he famously rejects Humean skepticism, whose conclusions appear "so shocking to the common sense of mankind, and so contrary to the decisions of all our intellectual powers."[2] Against such skepticism, Reid praises not only the natural ability to make appropriate use of evidence,[3] which only some possess, but also the instinctive belief in the deliverances of our senses, with which all of human beings have been

---

[1] See Thomas Reid, "Letter to David Hume," in *The Correspondence of Thomas Reid*, ed. by Paul Wood (Edinburgh: Edinburgh University Press, 2002), hereafter *Correspondence*, p. 31.
[2] Thomas Reid, *Essays on the Intellectual Powers of Man* (1785), ed. by Derek R. Brookes (Edinburgh: Edinburgh University Press, 2002), hereafter EIP, II, xiv, p. 187.
[3] See ibid., II, xxi, p. 238.

provided.⁴ The author of everything must be thanked for this: "I consider this instinctive belief as one of the best gifts of Nature. I yield to the direction of my senses, not from instinct only, but from confidence and trust in a faithful and beneficent Monitor, grounded upon the experience of his paternal care and goodness."⁵ The reliability of our senses cannot reasonably be denied if we consider that "we come into the world without the exercise of reason; we are merely animal before we are rational creatures; and it is necessary for our preservation, that we should believe many things before we can reason."⁶

These few references to Reid's epistemology highlight the role played by the author of everything – whom Reid calls indifferently God, the Author of nature, and Nature; they also emphasize a line of reasoning that is developed autonomously from religious beliefs – the reliability of our instinctive beliefs emerges in fact as rationally undeniable.

It is unclear, however, how these two aspects of Reid's reflection relate to one another. Attempts to explain whether or not a logical priority is ascribed by Reid to his religious convictions over his philosophical and scientific reasoning have unsurprisingly given rise to mutually contrasting interpretations of his epistemology. On the one hand, there is the idea that Reid's reliabilism is justified by the belief that God would not let us be deceived by our natural faculties. He explicitly says that even "highly civilized" nations, "greatly enlightened in many arts and sciences," held "the grossest absurdities" with regard to various subjects. Human beings – so Reid claims – may be ignorant of even self-evident truths, and the "corruptions" that follow from such mistakes require "a light from heaven" so as to be corrected.⁷ On the other hand, there is the conviction that the reliabilism in question was developed without any appeal to religion. As a matter of fact, Reid never justifies rational beliefs by having recourse to religious ones and, not surprisingly, considers sciences such as mathematics exemplary because they make "no room for authority, nor for prejudice of any kind."⁸

---

⁴ See ibid., VI, iv, p. 464.
⁵ Thomas Reid, *An Inquiry into the Human Mind on the Principles of Common Sense* (1764), ed. by Derek R. Brookes (Edinburgh: Edinburgh University Press, 1997), hereafter IHM, VI, xx, p. 170.
⁶ EIP, II, xxi, pp. 238f.
⁷ Thomas Reid, *Essays on the Active Powers of Man* (1788), in *The Works of Thomas Reid*, ed. by William Hamilton, hereafter EAP, V, ii, p. 641.
⁸ Thomas Reid, *A Brief Account of Aristotle's Logic, with Remarks* (1774), hereafter *Brief Account*, in *Thomas Reid on Logic, Rhetoric, and the Fine Arts: Papers on the Culture of Mind*, ed. by Alexander Broadie (Edinburgh: Edinburgh University Press, 2004), p. 142.

For Norman Daniels, it is in a sort of providential order that Reid grounds the idea that, by natural constitution, we are not led to false beliefs: "Reid justifies natively given 'common sense' beliefs through a dogmatic appeal to God as a non-deceiver."[9] Derek Brookes has argued that such appeal to both God's existence and his providence has been made by Reid to justify natural laws and the reliability of our cognitive faculties.[10] In other words, that there are laws of nature and that we are not deceived by our cognitive faculties is ultimately due to the providential order established by God. Finally, for a scholar of Hume such as David F. Norton, Reid and other Scottish thinkers (especially George Turnbull, whose classes seem to have deeply shaped the adolescent Reid's thought) cultivated a "providential naturalism" or "curious supernatural naturalism."[11] According to Norton's reading of Reid's epistemology, our natural faculties "are God-given, are a part of the overall design of a providential nature, and can be trusted implicitly … What we naturally believe is in fact supernaturally guaranteed."[12]

Referring to Daniels's thesis mentioned above, Keith DeRose says instead that "Reid would be absolutely scandalized by the claim that he justifies common sense by an appeal to God as a non-deceiver."[13] This would in fact imply for Reid to make the same mistake of circularity he rightly accused Descartes of. In line with this view, Philip De Bary argues that Reid's response to skepticism "does not depend on his religious belief in any essential respect."[14] Reid, in other words, by no means needs a recourse to supernatural reality so as to rationally support the reliabilism he adopts. In the same vein, Lehrer and Warner[15] show that, from the fact that Reid believed that our natural faculties are a divine gift and are

---

[9] Norman Daniels, *Thomas Reid's "Inquiry": The Geometry of Visibles and the Case for Realism* (New York: B. Franklin, 1974), p. 120. Daniels modified such a view in the second edition of the work mentioned, as shown in Patrick Rysiew, "Reid and Epistemic Naturalism," *The Philosophical Quarterly* 52 (2002), p. 438.

[10] See his edition of Reid's *Inquiry* (University Park, PA: Pennsylvania State University Press, 1997), esp. pp. xivff.

[11] See David F. Norton, *David Hume: Common-Sense Moralist, Sceptical Metaphysician* (Princeton, NJ: Princeton University Press, 1982), esp. pp. 202ff. The term "providential naturalism" was coined by Norton in his PhD dissertation dated 1966.

[12] David F. Norton, "Hume's Scottish Critics," in *McGill Hume Studies*, ed. by David F. Norton, Nicholas Capaldi, and Wade Robison (San Diego, CA: Austin Hill Press, 1979), p. 318.

[13] Keith DeRose, "Reid's Anti-Sensationalism and His Realism," *The Philosophical Review* 98 (1989), p. 327.

[14] Philip De Bary, *Thomas Reid and Scepticism: His Reliabilist Response* (London: Routledge, 2002), p. 5.

[15] Keith Lehrer and Bradley Warner, "Reid, God and Epistemology," *American Catholic Philosophical Quarterly* 74 (2000), pp. 357ff.

trustworthy and not fallacious, it does not follow that he justified the trustworthiness and nonfallaciousness in question based on the assumption that God exists. These authors focus on what Lehrer in his 1989 book devoted to Thomas Reid[16] had called "the first first principle." This principle is one of the first principles of contingent truths, which Reid lists in *Essays on the Intellectual Powers of Man*. Lehrer also calls it a "metaprinciple," because it provides the general reliability of our intellectual powers: *the natural faculties, by which we distinguish truth from error, are not fallacious.*[17] Although this principle may seem to rely on the providential order mentioned above, it "does not require any other principle or assumption, not even that of the existence of God."[18] (In fact, any attempt to establish the trustworthiness of our faculties will presuppose such trustworthiness.) Lehrer's and Warner's conclusion is that the first first principle's truth is self-evident to both theists and atheists "as soon as they understand it: all reasoning, whether of science, religion or philosophy, rests upon the assumption of the cogency of the first first principle and all are powerless to refute it."[19]

Partly in line with the two views I have just mentioned, I am persuaded that in Reid's thought religion exerts an influence on intellectual investigation, but no religious statements are employed to justify rational beliefs. To appropriately argue this view, I will make reference to some arguments that can be found in Reid's works.

According to Reid, believers should not be tempted to overlook the strength and the autonomy of our intellectual faculties as "some good men" did "by zeal for religion." They were "led to depreciate the human understanding, and to put out the light of nature and reason, in order to exalt that of revelation."[20] Although Reid claims that there are things and phenomena "whose existence is certain though their cause be occult," this does not imply any form of religiously motivated agnosticism. On the contrary, "to acknowledge this, is only a candid confession of human ignorance, than which there is nothing more becoming a philosopher."[21] In regard to the widespread tendency to believe that qualities cannot exist without a related substance, for example, Reid confesses that he is not able to explain "how we know that they cannot exist without a subject, any more than ... how we know that they exist."[22]

---

[16] Keith Lehrer, *Thomas Reid* (London: Routledge, 1989).
[17] See EIP, VI, v, p. 480, my emphasis.
[18] Lehrer and Warner, "Reid, God and Epistemology," p. 361   [19] Ibid., p. 372.
[20] EAP, IV, xi, p. 636.   [21] EIP, II, viii, p. 120.   [22] Ibid., II, xix, p. 218.

Equally philosophically acceptable, and not in need of any appeal to God as a nondeceiver, is the criticism that Reid addresses against the ideal system, which in his eyes is simply not philosophically sustainable. While reflecting on those who ask us why we believe that the material objects we perceive really exist, and claim that we should reject this belief since we are not able to rationally argue in its support, Reid rhetorically asks: "Why, sir, should I believe the faculty of reason more than that of perception? They came both out of the same shop, and were made by the same artist."[23] (This passage might be read as an appeal to God, who is the creator of both the faculties at stake. What I intend to highlight, however, is the line of reasoning adopted by Reid: given the fact that both faculties have the same origin, which Reid's interlocutor apparently accepts, it would not make sense to accept one and reject the other.) Therefore, it is merely from a philosophical viewpoint that Reid offers arguments aimed at showing the limits that lie at the basis of the intellectual proposals advanced by great and influential thinkers such as Descartes and Hume.[24] Their system "admits only one of the principles of common sense as a first principle; and pretends, by strict argumentation, to deduce all the rest from it."[25] All of our natural faculties, and not only some of them, are instead trustworthy and nonfallacious.[26] That which the order of the world provides is entirely reliable, and must be used in accordance with its own nature. If so, our intellectual faculties do not fail, as it is confirmed by mathematics, which Reid praises as paradigmatic science especially because "in mathematics there is no room for authority, nor for prejudice of any kind, which may give a false bias to the judgment."[27]

After having shown Reid's support for the idea that philosophy and sciences should be developed without recourse to external authority, I intend now to deal with Reid's passages that may lend themselves to the belief that for him the process of knowledge relies on the presupposition of religious belief.

While focusing on the natural principles from which such a process develops, Reid claims they have been granted us by God:

---

[23] IHM, VI, xx, p. 169.
[24] Reid convincingly shows that there is significant inconsistency in the thought of both thinkers (see EIP, II, xx, pp. 229f. and IHM, V, vii, p. 71).
[25] IHM, VII, p. 210.
[26] For a convincing argument in support of this thesis, see DeRose, "Reid's Anti-Sensationalism and His Realism," p. 330.
[27] *Brief Account*, p. 142.

> The first of these principles is, a propensity to speak the truth.... Another original principle implanted in us by the Supreme Being, is a disposition to confide in the veracity of others, and to believe what they tell us. This is the counterpart to the former; and, as that may be called *the principle of veracity*, we shall, for want of a more proper name, call this *the principle of credulity*.[28]

Reid also concentrates on self-evident truths:

> Men may, to the end of life, be ignorant of self-evident truths. They may, to the end of life, entertain gross absurdities. Experience shews that this happens often in matters that are indifferent. Much more may it happen in matters where interest, passion, prejudice, and fashion, are so apt to pervert the judgement.[29]

Inappropriate moral orientation, passions, and prejudices negatively affect any activity, including the understanding of self-evident truths. By contrast, good habits, good examples, and precepts of virtue support such understanding. For Reid, they can openly be related to Christianity:

> The history of past ages shews that nations, highly civilized and greatly enlightened in many arts and sciences, may, for ages, not only hold the grossest absurdities with regard to the Deity and his worship, but with regard to the duty we owe to our fellow-men.... Such corruptions in religion and in morals had spread so wide among mankind, and were so confirmed by custom, as to require a light from heaven to correct them.[30]

2.2 Reid's Appeal to the Christian Revelation: Adherence to God and His Message

I intend now to argue that no contradiction between reason and revelation arises out of the view that I have described so far. I mean that it is precisely on the basis of his religious beliefs that Reid values the intellectual activity and its autonomy from external authority. He claims that "Reason as well as Revelation comes from God. Both are lights afforded us by the Father of Light."[31] Consequently, no contradiction can arise between such lights, to which it can apply what Reid says about reason and perception, namely,

---

[28] IHM, VI, xxiv, pp. 193f.   [29] EAP, V, ii, p. 641.   [30] Ibid.
[31] *Thomas Reid on Practical Ethics: Lectures and Papers on Natural Religion, Self-Government, Natural Jurisprudence and the Law of Nations*, ed. by Knud Haakonssen (Edinburgh: Edinburgh University Press, 2007), hereafter *Practical Ethics*, p. 9.

that "they came both out of the same shop, and were made by the same artist."³² As a consequence,

> we ought to make the best use of both [reason and revelation], and not to put out one that we may use the other ... As one Man may enlighten another in things that can be discovered by Reason, it is easy to conceive how a Revelation from Heaven may give men new Light in things which Reason can discover.... But this is no Reason why we should not make the best Use we can of our Reason.... Revelation is given to us as reasonable Creatures, not to hinder the Use of Reason, but to aid and encourage it.³³

For Reid, not only does divine revelation exert an influence on human reason; God's revelation also "encourages" our reason, of which we should make "the best Use we can." Elsewhere he emphasizes this persuasion by saying that "Revelation was not intended to supersede, but to aid the use of our natural faculties."³⁴ Furthermore, this use greatly helps to preserve a correct interpretation of divine revelation:

> Revelation was given (to) us not to hinder the exercise of our reasoning powers, but to aid and assist them. It is by reason that we must judge whether that revelation be really so; it is by reason that we must judge of the meaning of what is revealed; and it is by reason that we must guard against any impious, inconsistent, or absurd interpretations of that revelation.³⁵

It is now clear that in Reid's thought there is no room for Cartesian appeal to the providential order of the world and to God as a nondeceiver. Such an appeal would clearly "supersede the use of our natural faculties," which is something Reid openly rejects. At the same time, a recourse to God and his revelation is undeniable. Not only can revelation offer us "new Light in things which Reason can discover"; even the encouragement to its best use is supported and promoted by divine revelation.

Let me now proceed to offer some passages that clearly document Reid's optimism about the potentialities of reason. Reid's optimism emerges especially from some passages concerning the mistakes that have been made by the representatives of the ideal system. As I have already said, Reid considers their conclusions unacceptable. However, even if geniuses like Hume had made remarkable mistakes, we should not lose the trust in our intellectual abilities: "Is this to be despaired of, because Des Cartes and his followers have failed? By no means. This pusillanimity would be

---

[32] IHM, VI, xx, p. 169 (see also above, note 23). [33] *Practical Ethics*, p. 9.
[34] EAP, V, ii, p. 641.
[35] *Thomas Reid on Religion*, ed. by James Foster (Exeter: Imprint Academic, 2017); this quote is from the Natural Theology Lecture 73rd, p. 1.

injurious to ourselves and injurious to truth."³⁶ We should instead trust in our cognitive faculties and their philosophical deployment:

> If philosophy contradicts itself, befools her votaries, and deprives them of every object worthy to be pursued or enjoyed.... Is it not possible she may have been misrepresented? Have not men of genius in former ages often made their own dreams to pass for her oracles?... I have found her in all other matters an agreeable companion, a faithful counsellor, a friend to common sense, and to the happiness of mankind.³⁷

Reid's optimism about reason leads him to claim that we should value even the efforts made by those who have misrepresented philosophy and have made substantive mistakes:

> Instead of blaming the philosophers I have mentioned for the defects and blemishes of their system, we ought rather to honour their memories, as the first discoverers of a region in philosophy formerly unknown ... however lame and imperfect the system may be, they have opened the way to future discoveries ... have removed an infinite deal of dust and rubbish ... have put us in the right road.³⁸

This view, however, seems at first sight contradictory. It claims the coexistence of the influence of revelation on reason with the autonomy of reason from revelation. To assess the meaning and the reasonableness of this view, we need to have recourse to Reid's religious viewpoint. This may allow us to consider his appeal to the providential order of the world as based on a specifically theological conception of the Christian revelation and of the way it requires to be related to any human activity, including the rational one.

Unfortunately, no scholarly theological treatments of these topics can be found in Reid's works, mainly devoted to philosophy and sciences.³⁹ It is reasonable to believe, however, that, being not only a Christian but also a minister of his Church, the "Kirk," Reid was influenced by some theological views. As Alexander Broadie has pointed out, "the Kirk's belief system and its institutions informed his soul, and therefore informed his philosophy also."⁴⁰ Not surprisingly, Reid's reflection resonates with the typically Reformed stress placed not only on the limitations of philosophical

---

³⁶ IHM, I, viii, p. 23.   ³⁷ Ibid., I, viii, p. 24.   ³⁸ Ibid., I, iv, p. 18.
³⁹ While Reid had "a life-long interest in what we now call philosophy of religion issues," he "wasn't given to theological and ecclesiastical controversies" (Dale Tuggy, "Reid's Philosophy of Religion," in *The Cambridge Companion to Thomas Reid*, ed. by Terence Cuneo and René van Woudenberg [Cambridge: Cambridge University Press, 2004], p. 289).
⁴⁰ Alexander Broadie, "Reid in Context," in Cuneo and van Woudenberg, eds., *The Cambridge Companion to Thomas Reid*, p. 32.

knowledge but also on the gratitude and trust seen as appropriate characteristics of the human relationship with God.[41] Moreover, the belief that the divine revelation exerts an influence on human reason and that this may improve the employment of our intellectual abilities is a widespread one among various branches of Christianity, not only within the Reformed tradition; one may go so far as to claim that it characterizes the whole history of the relation between the Christian revelation and the development of Western civilization.

At any rate, Reid's conviction that the divine revelation can influence reason and at the same time promote its autonomy is precisely the one Thomas Aquinas extensively supports in his theological reflection, which is one of the most influential in the history of Christianity.[42] In the next chapter I will treat Aquinas's thoughts on this subject in detail. I will argue that Thomas Aquinas's theological reflection on faith and reason offers the opportunity to reconstruct a viable view of how Reid combines the influence of divine revelation with the autonomy of the rational activity. Like Reid, Aquinas was firmly persuaded not only that human reason, if appropriately used, cannot be wrong, but also that there cannot be contradiction between well-conducted rational investigations and religious beliefs. Unlike Reid, however, Aquinas was a theologian, and explicitly theorized about a view of how divine revelation can influence our knowing processes without replacing the autonomous employment of our rational faculties. According to Aquinas, the believers are expected to reject any rational argument that opposes their religious view – however convincing the argument in question may at first glance appear to be – and to confirm also from the merely rational point of view what they already accept as true by faith.[43]

---

[41] Wolterstorff argues that these three elements – humility, active gratitude and trust – characterize what he names "Reid's epistemological piety" (see Nicholas Wolterstorff, *Thomas Reid and the Story of Epistemology* [Cambridge: Cambridge University Press, 2001], chapter 10, esp. pp. 260f.; a longer version of this chapter is in *Thomas Reid: Context, Influence and Significance*, ed. by Joseph Houston [Edinburgh: Dunedin Academic Press, 2004], pp. 77–101). According to David Fergusson, in this view of Reid's epistemology Wolterstorff encapsulates a host of Reformed tenets, among which are "a stress on the limits of human knowledge" and "a sense of an overarching divine providence" (David Fergusson, "Reformed Theology in the British Isles," in *The Cambridge Companion to Reformed Theology*, ed. by Paul Nimmo and David Fergusson [Cambridge: Cambridge University Press, 2016], p. 256).

[42] This is often acknowledged in contemporary academic circles, as I show below, Chapter 3, note 1.

[43] Aquinas and Reid have already been compared to each other, although this has been done on another topic. In the book I have already cited in note 41, Wolterstorff focuses on affinities and differences between their understanding of the concept of wisdom (see Wolterstorff, *Thomas Reid and the Story of Epistemology*, pp. 250–255).

In this chapter, I limit myself to showing the effects that, in Reid's thought, adherence to God and his revelation seem to have on the intellectual activity. Because of such adherence, which is trust and faith in God, the faithful seem to firmly hold various beliefs, among which are the following: (1) Religious beliefs, at least the fundamental ones such as the existence of God and his revelation through Christ, are true; and (2) human reason, if appropriately employed, cannot contradict them. These convictions seem to take part in Reid's rational inquiries. On the one hand, Reid adheres to God and his revelation, from which follows that he holds (1) and (2). On the other hand, this does not limit the rational autonomy of his investigations. On the contrary, he believes that such investigations must be conducted autonomously from any authority, including the religious one. For Reid, "*in all matters belonging to our cognizance*, every man must be determined by his own final judgement, otherwise he does not act the part of a rational being. Authority may add weight to one scale; but the man holds the balance, and judges what weight he ought to allow to authority."[44]

Because of the adherence mentioned above, Reid employs (1) and (2) not only in the course of his epistemological investigations but also, and perhaps more significantly, in the context of his scientific research. While treating scientific topics, in fact, Reid clearly sticks to his religious views and rejects any scientific thesis that may be incompatible with them; he also seems to use reason to the best of his abilities, and effectively replies with the same methods employed by his opponents. In this way, he acts consistently with his rejection of Cartesian circularity. Unlike Descartes, he does not appeal to God as a nondeceiver. Instead, he limits himself to employing the abovementioned methods, which all scientists, not only those who believe in God, are expected to consider plausible. At the same time, given the adherence mentioned above, he endeavors to defeat any view that may appear to oppose his religious convictions; furthermore, he seems to be sure that the abovementioned methods will not lead us astray if they are consistent with the right employment of our cognitive faculties.

2.3 Reid as Critic of Religiously Unacceptable Scientific Views

In Reid's view, common sense, philosophy, and sciences are all intimately related to one another. For him, "philosophy has no other root but the principles of Common Sense,"[45] and Newton's *regulae philosophandi* "are

---

[44] EIP, V, viii, p. 528, my emphasis.   [45] IHM, I, iv, p. 19.

maxims of common sense, and are practised every day in common life."⁴⁶ In other words, "he who philosophizes by other rules, either concerning the material system or concerning the mind, mistakes his aim."⁴⁷ Consequently, the study of both matter and the mind is based on common sense, which Reid considers a trustworthy and nonfallacious means to the end of knowledge, gratuitously and providentially conceded by God to all human beings.

As a result, the optimism with which Reid looks at common sense as a reliable ground for knowledge can also apply to natural sciences. These disciplines occupy a significant portion of Reid's thought because, as has been said, the study of nature is for him an appropriate way "by which we come to apprehend the wisdom and design of the Almighty."⁴⁸ Not surprisingly, it has also been said that "among all the great eighteenth-century philosophers, Reid is arguably the most learned and expert concerning scientific issues."⁴⁹

In the study of nature, Reid is guided by the conviction that observation and experiment must be adopted,⁵⁰ while any inclination to build science on abstract convictions that lack reference to common experience must be avoided: "Conjectures and theories are the creatures of men, and will always be found very much unlike the creatures of God. If we would know the works of God, we must consult themselves with attention and humility, without daring to add anything of ours to what they declare."⁵¹

I intend now to focus on some disputes Reid had with philosophers and scientists who seemed to lack the abovementioned alliance and balance between, on the one hand, common sense – and its consistency with religion, which Reid considered indispensable – and, on the other hand, scientific disciplines. Among such philosophers and scientists, Reid numbered those who showed a tendency to reduce all beings to matter and consequently consider everything measurable (probably in an attempt "to replicate in moral philosophy the success of natural philosophy"⁵²).

---

⁴⁶ Ibid., I, i, p. 12.   ⁴⁷ Ibid.
⁴⁸ Robert Callergard, "Thomas Reid's Newtonian Theism: His Differences with the Classical Arguments of Richard Bentley and William Whiston," *Studies in History and Philosophy of Science* 41 (2010), p. 110.
⁴⁹ Cuneo and van Woudenberg, "Introduction," in Cuneo and van Woudenberg, eds., *The Cambridge Companion to Thomas Reid*, p. 3
⁵⁰ See IHM, I, i, p. 11.
⁵¹ Ibid., I, i, p. 12. For Reid, as has been said, "the 'votaries of the ideal system' display *hubris* not simply because they do not patiently observe nature ... but also because they prefer *their own* imaginings and thoughts ... to nature's laws" (Michael Pakaluk, "A Defence of Scottish Common Sense," *The Philosophical Quarterly* 52 [2002], p. 578).
⁵² Haankonssen, "Introduction," in *Practical Ethics*, p. xxxvi.

Though highly competent in many scientific fields, Reid resisted this widespread tendency, which was accompanied by a "totally misleading analogy between body and mind."[53]

I shall argue in two steps that Reid opposed such a misleading analogy as well as the confusion between mind and body with a stance that avoids the opposite extremes of materialism and idealism and consequently supports the traditional conception of human beings as both immaterial and material creatures of God.

2.3.1 Against Both Materialism and Idealism

In a short paper entitled *An Essay on Quantity*,[54] Reid argues against the possibility for the human mind to be measured. He criticizes the view promoted by Francis Hutcheson's *Inquiry into the Original of Our Ideas of Beauty and Virtue*, according to which the morality of our actions can be measured.

Like many of his contemporaries, Reid values mathematics and its incomparable perspicuity, accuracy, and certainty. From this, however, it does not follow that, for him, its method can apply to any possible subject. Reid disagrees with Hutcheson, according to whom things like tastes, smells, wisdom, virtue, and merit can be mathematically approached and measured. From the fact – which Reid acknowledges – that they are "capable of more or less,"[55] it does not follow that they can be subjected to *measurement*. The reason why is that

> whatever has quantity, or is measurable, must be made up of parts, which bear proportion to one another and to the whole; so that it may be increased by *addition* of like parts, and diminished by *subtraction*, may be *multiplied* and *divided*, and, in a word, may bear any proportion to another quantity of the same kind, that one line or number can bear to another.[56]

This empirical evidence is obviously incompatible with things like virtue and merit, and effectively supports Reid's conviction that operations of the mind cannot be measured. Reid therefore employs against the supporters of the universal application of mathematics the empirical method they themselves adopt.

---

[53] Ibid.
[54] This essay was Reid's first published paper: *An Essay on Quantity* (1748), in *The Works of Thomas Reid*, pp. 715–720, hereafter *On Quantity*.
[55] *On Quantity*, p. 715.   [56] Ibid.

A reflection against the inclination to consider all beings material is offered by Reid while discussing the view presented by Georges-Louis Leclerc, Comte de Buffon (1707–1788), in his *Histoire naturelle*. Natural history, comprising many subdisciplines such as the classification, anatomy, and physiology of plants and animals as well as the study of geology and human nature, was of interest to Reid for much of his life. A few years after the publication of Buffon's voluminous work had started (1748), Reid engaged in its reading and – as Paul Wood points out – "was soon caught up in a critical confrontation with Buffon's controversial ideas about classification, the history of the earth, the theory of generation and the nature of humankind."[57]

Of particular interest for our purposes is the fact that Reid rejected Buffon's idea that matter was self-organized.[58] Such a view should appear unacceptable to a thinker like Reid who engaged in "the physiology of plants, animals, and humankind, with the over aim of demonstrating that their vital functions were the result of the actions of immaterial causes."[59] Reid argued that efficient causes must be immaterial and equipped with active power. Consequently, he could not agree with Buffon's view, which Reid involved in the criticism that he addressed, with no little irony, against the overt materialism of Helvetius, namely, the "Extravagant Opinion ... that the chief Difference between Men and Brutes lies in this that Nature has given to Men finer Organs of Touch particularly in the hands and fingers ... it might be said that a man's Wit lies in his finger ends."[60]

Reid opposed not only materialism but also idealism, taken as the conviction that only ideas exist, and material objects do not. Reid perceived these opposite extremes as (ironically) related to one another. The theory of ideas conceived in fact the mental world on the basis of a strict analogy between mind and matter. This analogy consisted in looking at both mental and material world as composed of parts, which in the case of the former are the simple ideas of which complex ideas are in turn composed. Reid, however, noticed that there was no empirical evidence to support the analogy mentioned, as I have shown above while treating

---

[57] Paul Wood, "Introduction," in *Thomas Reid on the Animate Creation*, ed. by Paul Wood (Edinburgh: Edinburgh University Press, 1995), hereafter AC, p. 4.
[58] See AC, p. 87. [59] Wood, "Introduction," p. 4.
[60] Reid, MS 2131/4/i/29, 16, cited in Wood, "Introduction," p. 8.

Reid's conviction that no parts and consequently no *ratio* among them has ever been found in the realm of mental operations.[61]

2.3.2 In Support of the Traditional Coexistence of Matter and the Immaterial Mind

Reid's opposition to both materialism and idealism coheres with his idea that reality shows coexistence and some (although tenuous) commonality between matter and the immaterial mind. Evidence that for Reid matter and the human mind can sometimes be treated analogously is the conviction, which he shares with many of his contemporaries, that both matter and the mind belong to the natural world.[62]

In this view, both matter and the mind can be empirically investigated in an attempt to find natural laws and not causes, as Rebecca Copenhaver points out.[63] Natural laws are general laws under which we can subsume less general ones, which ultimately are observable facts. Consequently, we can find natural laws by induction, which Reid considers "the only way to attain any knowledge of Nature's work."[64] A cause is instead "that which has power to produce the effect": "by a cause I mean only an efficient cause which by its active power produces the effect."[65] Only substances with will, that is, agents provided with the active power to produce an effect, can be considered efficient causes: "a being which has no will can have no power ... Power in the proper sense is under the command of him who has the power."[66] As Copenhaver says, this leads Reid "to a radically non-necessitarian account of causation."[67] Only minds can – properly speaking – be called causes,[68] and "the voluntary actions of men can in no case

---

[61] Furthermore, Reid goes so far as to argue that, on closer inspection, there is no evidence in support of even the existence of ideas, as they are conceived by the theory in question. See above, note 22, and see also EIP, II, xiv, pp. 171ff.; John Greco, "Reid's Reply to the Skeptic," in Cuneo and van Woudenberg, eds., *The Cambridge Companion to Thomas Reid*, pp. 138ff.

[62] See AC, p. 185.

[63] See Rebecca Copenhaver, "Is Reid a Mysterian?," *Journal of the History of Philosophy* 44 (2006), pp. 449–466. It follows that Reid's view of the human mind is not "mysterian," namely, as if the mind were in principle inexplicable. Such a "mysterian" view can be found in Wolterstorff, *Thomas Reid and the Story of Epistemology*, p. 261.

[64] EIP, VI, viii, p. 535.

[65] Thomas Reid, "Of Power" (1792), ed. by John Haldane, *The Philosophical Quarterly* 51 (2001), pp. 6 and 9. Reid only accepts the notion of *active* power, while considers "a misapplication of the word" (EAP, I, iii, p. 519) the idea that there also are *passive* powers.

[66] Reid, "Of Power," pp. 10f. [67] Copenhaver, "Is Reid a Mysterian?," p. 454.

[68] Pakaluk concurs with Copenhaver. For him, "Reid regards only minds as having active power" (Pakaluk, "A Defence of Scottish Common Sense," p. 567).

be called natural phenomena, or be considered as regulated by the physical laws of Nature."[69]

The fact that the word "cause" is often applied to natural substances lacking will and freedom is a misunderstanding, due to the ambiguity that is typical of the employment of the word "cause":

> By the Cause of a Phenomenon nothing is meant but the law of Nature, of which that Phenomenon is an instance or a necessary consequence. The Cause of a body's falling to the ground is its gravity. But gravity is not an efficient Cause, but a general Law, that obtains in Nature, of which Law the fall of this body is a particular instance.[70]

Natural philosophy can only search for laws, which are nothing but the rules according to which the efficient causes operate: "natural Philosophy has no more to do."[71] Focusing on efficient causes is instead the task of natural theology or metaphysics, which are other branches of philosophy. Thus, from the viewpoint of natural philosophy and empirical sciences, both matter and the mind can be investigated only if the investigator searches for laws and not for causes. In this connection, Reid notices that, since practitioners of physical sciences have finally abandoned the search for causes, these sciences have significantly improved: they "are really sciences."[72] The same has occurred only partly with the science of mind, which is why this discipline "is but in a very low state."[73]

From what I have said so far it emerges that Reid makes convincing use of empirical evidence and is consequently able to show that matter is inert, namely, lacks the active power that characterizes the mind. Reid argues in defense of the traditionally religious persuasion that the core of reality, which is the cause of everything, is immaterial: "all causation in nature, then, is ultimately the result of the exercise of God's agent power or the power of agents subordinate to God."[74] Reid also supports one more traditional persuasion, namely, the idea that there is some commonality between matter and the mind. As I have shown, they can both be investigated by way of induction to the extent that such an investigation is aimed at finding natural laws.

Once having made clear that the active power and the cause that possesses it cannot be investigated and known from the viewpoint of

---

[69] AC, p. 185 [70] *Correspondence*, p. 142
[71] Ibid., p. 143. As Copenhaver says, "science cannot know the ultimate causes of things and must rest content with discovering laws of nature" (Copenhaver, "Is Reid a Mysterian?," p. 452).
[72] IHM, I, iii, p. 16. [73] Ibid.
[74] Cuneo and van Woudenberg, "Introduction," in Cuneo and van Woudenberg, eds., *The Cambridge Companion to Thomas Reid*, p. 11.

natural philosophy, it should be made clear whether or not this somehow limits Reid's research. Let us consider his treatment of muscular motion, which regards the relation between the nervous power and the will – and ultimately matter and the mind – and was widely investigated at Reid's time. While dealing with this subject matter, Reid may seem to indulge in a position of nescience, because for him "all we know is, that in the sound state of the Body the Exertion of the nervous Power immediately follows our Volition."[75] On the other hand, however, this sort of nescience does not limit – on the contrary, seems to improve – the exploration that Reid conducts of the subject in question:

> We have a natural Conviction of our being the Cause of our voluntary actions, and therefore accountable for them ... he that believes a certain Effect to be in his Power and exerts his Power to effect it, is undoubtedly in moral Estimation the Cause of that Effect and accountable for it, whether in Physical Consideration he be really the Efficient, or onely what the Cartesians call the occasional Cause.[76]

Although Reid agrees to the view that, from the standpoint of natural philosophy, it is not possible to deal with whether or not we are really the efficient cause of our voluntary actions, he cannot accept the conclusion some draw from this, which consists in *denying* our freedom and responsibility. If, therefore, the empirical method cannot be employed to show that we are free and responsible agents, Reid develops a straightforward argument that aims at defeating the inference from the limitations of natural philosophy to the negation of human freedom and responsibility. The argument advanced by Reid applies to the realm of ethics, and unfolds as follows: If we believe that we cause our actions, it is not possible for us not to consider ourselves responsible for them. As I said, this is a straightforward as well as effective argument, which allows Reid to support his conviction that we are free and responsible moral agents. Against occasionalism and mechanistic necessitarianism, which could both be taken as supporters of the idea that we are not responsible for our actions, Reid must have felt the urgency to support what he certainly considered extremely important in human life: that we can exercise freedom and responsibility in our relationship with God, ourselves, and others.[77]

---

[75] AC, pp. 119f.   [76] Ibid., p. 120.
[77] Some may object that Reid's insistence on libertarian free will is not based on religious convictions. However, some form of free will (and responsibility) is undoubtedly part of at least some branches of the Christian tradition, regardless of the exact way they relate it (free will) to God's favor. In this vein, Reid's debates against those who tended to *deny the existence of free will* (and responsibility) may plausibly be seen as due to his religious convictions.

According to Wood, "Reid's speculations on human physiology were thus conditioned by moral considerations," and Reid "emphasized our nescience concerning the physical connections between mind and body, in order to protect his beliefs in man's free will."[78] Elsewhere, while discussing Reid's treatment of Buffon's theories on natural history, Wood similarly claims that "his [Reid's] work on generation reveals that Reid was all too willing to withdraw into a posture of nescience about the processes involved in reproduction in order to protect his religious beliefs, and his anxieties about materialism led him to ignore questions which he should perhaps have addressed."[79]

All I have argued so far leads me to agree with Wood that moral and religious beliefs must have played a fundamental role in Reid's scientific investigations. At the same time, if the arguments that I have advanced in the course of this chapter are right, I have to disagree with Wood that Reid assumed a "posture of nescience" as a strategy aimed at protecting religious beliefs and avoiding further research. It is true that Reid seems to have conducted his research with the aim of rationally supporting his religious beliefs. From this, however, it does not follow that he limited the freedom to conduct research in any possible direction. He openly declared that no philosophical or scientific investigation, *if appropriately conducted*, would be proved harmful to religion,[80] and that his religious view could promote and encourage rational investigation without the fear of being contradicted. In line with this view, Reid seems to have carried out both his philosophical and scientific research. If the arguments I have developed here are correct, it must be said that Reid must by no means have considered his religious belief in need of being "protected" by recourse to a posture of nescience.

In conclusion, unlike Newman and the Reformed epistemologists, to whose reflection I devoted Chapter 1, Reid refers to the specific way the Christian faith relates to rational arguments. He clearly points to such a specificity when he affirms that, on the one hand, revelation exerts an influence on reason, whereas, on the other hand, reason cannot be replaced by revelation. The faithful are expected to rely on the persuasion that, if used appropriately and in accord with its own nature, reason cannot contradict religious belief. In line with this view, Reid seems to be reluctant to accept philosophical and especially scientific views – such as

---

[78] Wood, "Introduction," p. 30.   [79] Ibid., p. 19.
[80] "In Reid's eyes, the real danger to theism is from bad epistemology" (Tuggy, "Reid's Philosophy of Religion," p. 290).

materialism or the negation of human free will and responsibility – which must appear to him incompatible with his religious belief. At the same time, Reid rejects those views by employing against them the same philosophical and scientific strategies that are usually employed in their support. In this way, he seems to confirm the view that reason, if used appropriately, cannot but confirm religious beliefs.

However, Reid only mentions such a specific relation between faith and reason, a viable reconstruction of which clearly requires a theological exploration of the nature of faith. Reid never performed such a scholarly theological work. He was a Christian and a minister deeply involved in the life of his Church, and, for this reason, he might not surprisingly have been influenced by theological views, especially if authoritatively conveyed through the Christian tradition. That which in Reid's work may constitute an implicit application of solidly established theological views needs therefore to be made explicit by referring to Aquinas's theological works. These works reveal an impressive closeness to Reid's idea of how the Christian faith requires to be related to the intellectual activity.

PART II

The Christian Faith as Part of Both the Problem of Inconclusiveness and Its Solution

In this part, I first focus on Aquinas's theological view of faith and reason, a view to which Reid's philosophical and scientific investigations could only implicitly refer. Aquinas's view is that, since the Christian beliefs are taken by the faithful as true and revealed to them by God, the believers may rely more on faith than on reason. Accordingly, they may reject in theory all of those propositions that, even if seemingly convincing, contradict their faith. Obviously enough, this theological view of how the Christian faith needs relating to the intellectual investigation encourages the tenacity of religious believers in the face of counterevidence. This is why this theological view can be seen as part of the problem of inconclusiveness here under consideration.

I then argue that the abovementioned theological view is incompatible with ME, and I show why various attempts to minimize the gap between them should be rejected. At the same time, I argue that this theological view offers an opportunity to rethink ME and to turn it into a wider view, according to which it is the search for good, and not that for truth, that ultimately directs research and debates. The search for good entails the assumption of good habits in the intellectual investigation, from which follows that this investigation can be promoted and the inconclusiveness at stake may, at least in some cases, be overcome. If this argument is correct, the Christian faith is not only part of the problem of inconclusiveness; it may also be part of the solution. In other words, the reasonableness of this faith is affirmed, and, nonetheless, unlike the views that tend to minimize the gap with ME, this aim is attained by seriously facing the challenge represented by the gap in question.

CHAPTER 3

Thomas Aquinas
Primacy of Faith and Autonomy of Reason

In this chapter, I focus on Aquinas's conviction that contradiction between faith and reason is due to inappropriate employment of reason, since, unlike faith, reason may be mistaken. From this follows that, once confronted with this contradiction, the believer should engage in new investigations aimed at finding rational views that are compatible with religious faith.

Predictably enough, many objections can be raised to this view. I intend to demonstrate that they can plausibly be raised only from the viewpoint I have so far defined as "Lockean," namely, as if the relationship between faith and reason were looked at without taking into consideration what seems to be specific of faith, that is, the divine grace because of which the faithful (firmly) believe. I first examine and reject various Lockean interpretations of Aquinas. Then, I concentrate on the theological standpoint from which Aquinas looks at the matter. Finally, I consider the consequences of his view as to the inconclusiveness problem here under consideration.

3.1 "Lockean" Approaches to Aquinas's View of Faith and Reason

It is known that one of the most extensive and historically influential treatments of the relationship between faith and reason is the one provided by Aquinas.[1] It is equally known that Aquinas's texts can easily be

---

[1] His reflection can appropriately be seen as "the dominant Western tradition of thought on the subject," susceptible of being "accepted today by many both Catholic and Protestant Christians, as well as by the agnostic and atheist critics of Christianity" (John Hick, *Faith and Knowledge: A Modern Introduction to the Problem of Religious Knowledge*, 2nd ed. [Eugene, OR: Wipf & Stock, 2009], p. 12). More recently, Gregory Dawes claimed that "few Christians will have read Aquinas, but since his view is widely shared by theologians they may have absorbed it 'by osmosis'" (Gregory Dawes, "The Act of Faith: Aquinas and the Moderns," in *Oxford Studies in Philosophy of Religion*, ed. by Jonathan Kvanvig, vol. 6 [New York: Oxford University Press, 2015], p. 80). I have

misunderstood and are consequently susceptible to various and sometimes mutually contrasting interpretations. This is probably due to the fact that, as Rudi te Velde has noted, "only superficially is he [Aquinas] clear, but on analysis one discovers that he does not at all offer us a decently confined 'Anglo-Saxon' lucidity."[2] John Milbank, while referring to this consideration, claims that in Aquinas's works it is possible to find passages that seem to incontrovertibly support contrasting positions.[3] A well-known scholar of Aquinas such as Fergus Kerr has even devoted an entire book to "the very many ways of contemplating Aquinas," which are "rival, conflicting, even incommensurable" with each other.[4]

The variety I have just mentioned applies to readings of Aquinas's view of faith and reason also. Although scholars of Thomas usually agree with each other that the view in question seems to be an exemplary balance between Christian faith and natural reason, they equally disagree when it comes to the exact meaning of such a balance. Some maintain that Aquinas elaborated his rational views without being under the influence of faith, while others claim that the Christian faith constitutes an indispensable component of Aquinas's rational enterprise.

These conflicting interpretations were discussed on the occasion of the *querelle* on the concept of "Christian philosophy" that took place in France in the 1930s.[5] Among the readings of the relationship between faith and philosophical reflection in Aquinas's works there presented, I will mention the ones formulated and argued by Étienne Gilson, Pierre Mandonnet, and Jacques Maritain.

Before proceeding, however, I need to highlight three qualifications. First, the *querelle* regarded the concept of "Christian philosophy," which involved discussions on several pairs of concepts, such as faith and reason, faith and philosophy, and theology and philosophy, which do not perfectly coincide with one another. All of them, however, can easily be seen as based on the one in which I am interested here, that is, the relationship

---

devoted an entire book to treating Aquinas's view of faith and reason in the light that charity sheds on it. See Roberto Di Ceglie, *Aquinas on Faith, Reason, and Charity* (New York: Routledge, 2022).

[2] Rudi te Velde, *Participation and Substantiality in Thomas Aquinas* (London: E. J. Brill, 1995), pp. ix–xiv, cited in John Milbank and Catherine Pickstock, *Truth in Aquinas* (London: Routledge, 2001), p. 18.

[3] Milbank and Pickstock, *Truth in Aquinas*, p. 18.

[4] Fergus Kerr, "The Varieties of Interpreting Aquinas," in *Contemplating Aquinas: On the Varieties of Interpretation*, ed. by Fergus Kerr (London: SCM Press, 2003), p. 40.

[5] See *Reason Fulfilled by Revelation: The 1930s Christian Philosophy Debates in France*, ed. by Gregory B. Sadler (Washington, DC: Catholic University of America Press, 2011).

between faith and reason.[6] (Following Thomas, I broadly take here *reason* as a cognitive faculty that searches for evidence,[7] and *faith* as the virtue that leads one to firmly believe the divine revelation though it lacks full evidence.) Second, and more importantly, the fundamental problem with the concept of Christian philosophy coincides with the subject here under consideration. Christian philosophy is perceived to be a sort of oxymoron because it seems hard to see how philosophy can be helped and perfected by religious experiences (this is what the title of the book edited by Sadler, *Reason Fulfilled by Revelation*, effectively marks) without losing its ability to work on the basis of its own principles. The *querelle* therefore regarded precisely our subject, namely, how to explain the coexistence between the superiority of faith, which claims to perfect any activity, including the rational one, and the autonomy of reason. Third, the *querelle* may appear to be devoted not only to Aquinas but also to any believer who happens to deal with philosophical matters. In reality, the debates in question were mainly referred to Aquinas, whom all of the thinkers I will mention would certainly have described as follows: "one who had clarified the faith-reason relationship as perhaps no one else before his time."[8] Not surprisingly, the *querelle* started with speeches devoted to the more general idea of "Christian philosophy," but moved soon to more specific discussions of that idea in the context of Aquinas's thought. (Note that secular rationalists such as Léon Brunschvicg and Émile Brehier took part in the first phase of the *querelle*, which was later conducted mainly by Roman Catholics.) Furthermore, the thinkers whose views of faith and reason I am about to take into consideration mostly devoted their investigations to Thomas. What they affirmed regarding the relationship between faith and reason should therefore be taken as mainly offered in light of Aquinas's reflection.

It may be said that the *querelle* was caused by the spread of Gilson's idea of "Christian philosophy" in the early 1920s. In his investigations into the history of philosophy,[9] Gilson had focused on a number of Christian thinkers – especially Augustine, Bonaventure, and Aquinas. What he had concluded on the basis of such investigations was that the views of those

---

[6] "Faith" can exist without theology, whereas the contrary cannot be; the same can be said of "reason" if compared to "philosophy" as well as of "faith" and "reason" if compared to "theology."
[7] For what exactly "evidence" and "evidentness" mean in Aquinas's thought, see below, notes 45ff.
[8] John Wippel, "Thomas Aquinas and the Problem of Christian Philosophy," in *Metaphysical Themes in Thomas Aquinas*, ed. by John Wippel (Washington, DC: Catholic University of America Press, 1984), p. 1.
[9] See, for example, Étienne Gilson, *La philosophie de saint Bonaventure* (Paris: Vrin, 1924).

thinkers had promoted authentic philosophy. This conviction opposed a thesis that, especially in France, secular philosophers and historians of philosophy had largely endorsed. The thesis in question was that the abovementioned Christian thinkers had only developed a theology.[10] This was due to the conviction that one cannot develop any philosophy if one's research is somewhat associated to the Christian faith. Decades after the *querelle*, Gilson explained that not only philosophers who were not believers had endorsed this thesis. "A great many Catholic professors of philosophy"[11] had done the same thing. In the light of Descartes's view, so Gilson believed, they were convinced that "where theology begins, philosophy comes to an end. If we philosophize, we cannot be theologizing at the same time."[12] It is presumable that, so doing, they attempted to escape the accusation that their personal choice of faith had unduly influenced their philosophical investigation. At any rate, Gilson's view was an entirely different approach to the subject. According to him, an authentic philosophical reflection had emerged from theological affirmations throughout Christianity's history. Justin, Lactantius, Augustine, Anselm, Bonaventure, and Aquinas, to name a few, had promoted "a view of the world" that was "perfectly satisfying to the mind" and "incomparably more rational than the conclusions of reason."[13] In support of this view, Gilson offered the outcomes of his historical investigations. Based on the study of the thought of those thinkers, the French scholar argued that a Christian believer becomes a Christian philosopher "when amongst his [Christian] beliefs he finds some that are capable of becoming objects of science."[14] If this gives rise to an original philosophical perspective, this perspective is to be named "Christian philosophy." According to Gilson, this had happened since the beginning of the history of Christianity:

> A single God, creator of heaven and earth, Ruler of the world and its Providence, a God Who made man in His own image and revealed to him, along with his last end, the way to attain it – where, in the splendid achievements of Greek philosophy, could one find a view of the world as

---

[10] Let me refer especially to Emile Bréhier, a well-known historian of philosophy. He participated in the 1931 meeting, the meeting with which the *querelle* began, and strongly opposed Gilson's thesis that philosophy had achieved new heights because of a connection with the Christian faith.

[11] If we consider the various debates that Gilson developed on the subject in question, not only in the course of the *querelle*, we can say that, in this passage, Gilson referred to scholars such as Pierre Mandonnet (whom I will mention in a moment), Amato Masnovo, and Fernand van Steenberghen.

[12] Étienne Gilson, "What Is Christian Philosophy?," in *A Gilson Reader*, ed. by Anton Pegis (Garden City, NY: Doubleday, 1957), p. 184.

[13] Ibid., p. 178.

[14] Étienne Gilson, *The Spirit of Mediaeval Philosophy* (London: Sheed & Ward, 1936), p. 36.

clear and as perfectly satisfactory to the mind as the one revealed to men by Holy Scripture?[15]

Being an esteemed academician in the field, Gilson could authoritatively advance his thesis that there had been a Christian philosophy, that is, "every philosophy which, although keeping the two orders [reason and faith] formally distinct, nevertheless considers Christian revelation as an indispensable auxiliary to reason."[16] According to Gilson, this way of connecting philosophy and the Christian revelation had shaped the Middle Ages, and an original approach to philosophical problems had emerged.

Among the scholars who took part in the *querelle* and supported the view that no influence of faith is acceptable on philosophy there was Pierre Mandonnet, a Dominican friar who was a famous Thomist and an expert in medieval philosophy. According to him, what could be accepted was the idea that Christianity had somewhat promoted a general progress of humanity, not the idea that it had ignited specifically philosophical perspectives. In other words, the divine revelation should not be seen as a factor of philosophical advancement. This kind of advancement, in fact, "does not take place by Scripture but by reason."[17] Of course, philosophers who happen to be believers might be influenced by their faith while conducting their research. If this happens, then their research is to be considered *theology*, not philosophy. On the other hand, philosophers who are also Christians are expected to do research without any influence coming from their religious beliefs. In this case, the research that these philosophers as well as their colleagues who are unbelievers conduct is to be considered *philosophy*, not Christian philosophy.

Mandonnet did not reject the view that there were *Christian philosophers*, that is, philosophers who, like him, happened to be believers. (Note, however, that for him this coincidence was less frequent than Gilson thought. Mandonnet believed that only Aquinas, among the medieval thinkers Gilson had studied, should be seen as a philosopher.[18]) Mandonnet only rejected the view that the philosophical research they conducted could be thought of as a "Christian philosophy," as if a change in nature of philosophy should be taken into consideration when Christian

---

[15] Gilson, "What Is Christian Philosophy?," p. 178.
[16] Gilson, *The Spirit of Mediaeval Philosophy*, p. 37.
[17] *La philosophie chrétienne: Journée d'etudes de la Sociétè Thomiste* (Juvisy: Éditions du Cerf, 1933), pp. 67f., tr. by Sadler in *Reason Fulfilled by Revelation*, p. 81.
[18] See Pierre Mandonnet's review of Gilson's *Le philosophie de saint Bonaventure*, in *Bulletin Thomiste* 3 (1926), pp. 50–54.

believers philosophize. To put it otherwise, Mandonnet argued that there was a distinction between a *de facto* and a *de iure* union of the Christian revelation and philosophy, and that only the former could plausibly be accepted.

Gilson partly agreed with Mandonnet. The *de facto* union of faith and philosophical research does characterize those philosophers who are also believers. However, Gilson argued that, once the *de facto* union was accepted, the *de iure* one should also be accepted. According to him, "if there are relations of fact between faith and reason, between Revelation and philosophy in the concrete subject – if there are in fact relations, I say that it is impossible that there not be relations of right."[19]

However acceptable Gilson's view might be, what I am interested in showing is that a number of scholars rejected it, no matter whether they were unbelievers or believers. On the one hand, like Mandonnet, they found plausible Gilson's view that throughout history the Christian faith had somehow exerted an influence on philosophy – this is the *de facto* union. On the other hand, they did not consider this view compatible with Gilson's conviction that the Christian beliefs were "an indispensable auxiliary to reason" – this is the *de iure* union. Note that this criticism has been cultivated until recent times. One of his supporters, Ralph McInerny, said that Gilson "has persuaded everyone of the historical fact of the influence of the faith on philosophy." This, however, is a "far cry from holding that there is a continuing formal, objective dependence of philosophy on the faith."[20]

Maritain advanced a reflection that might be seen as an attempt to combine the abovementioned *de facto* and *de iure* unions. He agreed with Gilson that a Christian philosophy had really existed. On the other hand, since he thought that Gilson's merely historic-philosophical approach to the subject was insufficient, Maritain proposed to reinforce it by adopting a theoretical approach. After all, the fact that Gilson had concentrated on the subject from the viewpoint of the history of philosophy by no means was a sign that Gilson intended "to suppress the theoretical question." On the contrary, Gilson's view seemed "to leave it open."[21]

Maritain focused theoretically on the subject by considering "the classical distinction between the order of specification and the order of

---

[19] *La philosophie chrétienne*, pp. 63f., tr. in Ralph McInerny, *Praeambula fidei: Thomism and the God of the Philosophers* (Washington, DC: Catholic University of America Press, 2006), p. 94.
[20] McInerny, *Praeambula fidei*, p. 106.
[21] "La notion de philosophie chrétienne," special issue, *Bulletin de la Société française de Philosophie* 31/2 (1931), p. 59.

exercise."²² He proposed to see this distinction as a distinction "between the *nature* of philosophy, of what philosophy is in itself, and the *state* in which it is found factually, historically, in the human subject."²³ According to Maritain, when "considered in its pure *nature*, or essence," philosophy "depends only on the evidence and criteria of natural reason." However, if "taken concretely, in the sense of being a *habitus*," philosophy "is in a certain *state*." This state can be Christian or a-Christian and "has a decisive influence on the way it [philosophy] exists and develops."²⁴ (Note that Maritain advanced this argument only with regard to theoretical philosophy. When it comes to moral philosophy, he proposed another argument.²⁵ This argument was that not only the state but also the nature of philosophy should be considered under the influence of the Christian faith. A "moral philosophy adequately considered" – this is the expression that Maritain coined – "must be guided by the knowledge of our ultimate end, which, as Christians we cannot pretend not to know is supernatural."²⁶)

Although not exempt from criticism,²⁷ the distinction between nature and state appears, at least initially, to offer an acceptable balance between reason and faith. John Wippel has similarly distinguished between the *moment of discovery* and the *moment of proof*.²⁸ According to Wippel, the moment of discovery is to be distinguished from the moment of proof: "In the moment of proof his [the Christian's] procedure cannot be described as Christian philosophy." In contrast, "since in the moment of discovery it was his religious belief that first suggested this particular issue to him as a possible subject for philosophical investigation, one might refer to such a procedure as Christian philosophy in the order of discovery."²⁹ The moment of discovery, namely, the complex of traditions, cultures, opinions, and personal preferences of those who philosophize, is something

---

²² Jacques Maritain, *An Essay on Christian Philosophy* (New York: Philosophical Library, 1955), p. 11.
²³ "La notion de philosophie chrétienne," p. 59. See also Maritain, *An Essay on Christian Philosophy*, pp. 11f.
²⁴ Jacques Maritain, *Science and Wisdom* (London: Sheed and Ward, 1938), p. 79.
²⁵ According to Peter Redpath, these typically Maritainian distinctions have caused various problems, among which the controversial idea that philosophy should be taken *in itself*. See below, note 27.
²⁶ Maritain, *An Essay on Christian Philosophy*, pp. 38ff.
²⁷ Redpath points out that philosophy simply does not exist *in itself*, that is, apart from its state (Peter Redpath, "Romance of Wisdom: The Friendship between Jacques Maritain and Saint Thomas Aquinas," in *Understanding Maritain: Philosopher and Friend*, ed. by Deal W. Hudson and Matthew J. Mancini [Macon, GA: Mercer University Press, 1987], p. 110).
²⁸ See John Wippel, "The Possibility of a Christian Philosophy: A Thomistic Perspective," *Faith and Philosophy* 1 (1984), pp. 272–290.
²⁹ Ibid., p. 280.

other than philosophy, although beliefs can emerge – religious beliefs included – that might suggest new ways to philosophical inquiry. The moment of proof is the rigorous development of arguments, that is, the *nature* of philosophy, which all philosophers share, be they believers or nonbelievers.

A problem emerges that is crucial to these interpretations of Thomas's thought. Though different if not mutually conflicting, all of them end up overlooking the nature of faith and what is specific of it, namely, being caused by God and only partly responsive to rational criteria. The scholars in question treat the relationship between philosophy and the Christian experience as if it regarded, on the one hand, reason, and, on the other, faith as well as any other subjective or cultural condition. The *state* mentioned by Maritain as well as the *de facto* union mentioned by Gilson and Mandonnet and the moment of discovery depicted by Wippel may coincide with any possible experience and not only the Christian or the religious one. From this, however, a contradiction follows. These thinkers assume that prephilosophical experiences that are able to make philosophy move in the right direction may be of various kinds, and not only religious. However, the various cultural and subjective states in question are expected to be also criticized and even rejected by the philosophical reflection. In accordance with a classical view of philosophy, they should be rigorously examined so as to find which of them can be maintained and which of them needs instead to be discarded. But this, once referred to the Christian faith, may never be accepted by the thinkers here at stake. They are in fact all convinced that divine revelation is true and that it can only improve human enterprises, philosophy included.[30]

This problem is due to the fact that, unlike Aquinas, the thinkers mentioned so far do not focus on what specifically occurs once reason is related *to the Christian faith*, taken as *granted by God* and only partially responsive to rational criteria. They actually seem to start their reflection from the assumption that what may be proper to the faith in question, that is, its supernatural origin, cannot be taken into account in the context of their philosophical reflection. As a consequence, they do not seem to be in

---

[30] Of course, there are aspects of the experience lived by the believer that these thinkers as well as Aquinas may consider in need of being criticized and even rejected. In this case, it can be said that the believer mistakes her own conjectures for the Christian faith. According to Aquinas, "it is possible for a believer to have a false opinion through a *human conjecture* (*ex coniectura humana*), but it is quite impossible for a false opinion to be *the outcome of faith*" (Summa theologiae, II-II, q. 1, a. 3, ad 3, my emphasis).

a position to adequately evaluate the idea that faith may exert an influence on reason without compromising the autonomy of rational enterprise.

The abovementioned assumption that the theological origin of faith should be kept outside the philosophical investigation on faith and reason seems to perfectly coincide with Locke's approach to the subject. This approach lacks any consideration of what seems to be specific of faith, namely, characterized by a high level of certainty that is divinely granted and is not due to conclusive evidence. Such an approach to religious belief, based on which the firmness of belief comes in degrees and needs proportioning to the available evidence, has become the dominant model in the field until recent times. It can therefore have influenced many scholars of Thomas and their way of interpreting his view of faith and reason. For Jenkins, they have attributed to Aquinas the persuasion that

> the Christian believer is first convinced by metaphysical arguments of natural or philosophical theology that God exists. Subsequently he believes on the basis of testimony and other evidence that there were miracles and signs in biblical times and in the history of the Church. From these beliefs he is led to the conclusion that God has made revelations in history, and the essence of these revelations is contained in the Christian Creed as this is defined by the Church.[31]

However, no matter how widespread this view is, Aquinas cannot reasonably be considered a "proto-Lockean." While "Locke thought that in a normal case whether or not one assented to a proposition as divinely revealed is a matter of reason, ... Aquinas explicitly states that Christian faith requires something more than natural principles." Moreover – so Jenkins goes on – "Locke recognized that on his account the assent of faith is much less certain than that of knowledge." By contrast, in Thomas's view "the faithful hold the articles of faith with even greater certainty than the principle of non-contradiction."[32]

Unlike Locke, Aquinas considers the certainty of faith firmer than the one provided by reason. (There is also a viewpoint from which Aquinas says that it is the certainty of reason that prevails. However, he says that this viewpoint is of less importance when compared to the one from which he claims that faith is more certain than reason. I will elaborate on this later in this chapter.[33]) Thomas's perspective is a theological one. For him, faith

---

[31] Jenkins, "Faith and Revelation," pp. 215f.
[32] Ibid., pp. 216f. Jenkins is referring to Aquinas, *On Truth*, tr. by James V. McGlynn [Chicago, IL: Henry Regnery, 1953], q. 14, a. 1, ad 7. See below, note 115.
[33] See below, notes 72f.

is caused by God, from which follows that the firmness with which the (paradigmatic) believer is expected to believe does not need to be grounded on evidence. From this theological view of faith, Thomas draws conclusions on the relationship between faith and reason that are substantially different from not only the Lockean ones but also the readings of Aquinas's thought that I have mentioned above.

Before moving on to the next section, in which I will examine Aquinas's view of faith and reason as it emerges from his writings, I intend to further point out that the fact that Thomas's views are often seen as if they had rather been elaborated by Locke can also be confirmed by a recent debate on faith and reason. This debate deals with the relationship between faith and propositional belief and has received significant attention especially since John Schellenberg questioned the idea that faith involves propositional belief.[34]

That faith involves propositional belief is a traditional view. On the one hand, faith includes propositional beliefs such as that God exists; on the other hand, faith is more than propositional belief. According to Daniel McKaughan, given the conception of faith as involving propositional belief, "faith in God is justified only if the belief that God exists is justified."[35] This connection between belief in God and belief that God exists, which McKaughan rightly considers "a widely held principle,"[36] seems to resemble Locke's conviction according to which, in order to believe in God, God's existence must be supported by such satisfactory evidence that it should be said it is *known*.[37] According to McKaughan, given this "widely held principle," those who are instead persuaded that no sufficient evidence in support of the belief that God exists can be provided will consequently raise what the author in question names the "problem of faith and reason," namely, the conviction that believers believe inauthentically.

The typically Lockean idea that belief in God cannot be held if the belief that God exists is not rationally justified has often been ascribed to

---

[34] See John Schellenberg, *Prolegomena to a Philosophy of Religion* (Ithaca, NY: Cornell University Press, 2005), chapters 2, 5, and 6.
[35] Daniel McKaughan, "Authentic Faith and Acknowledged Risk: Dissolving the Problem of Faith and Reason," *Religious Studies* 49 (2013), p. 105.
[36] As a matter of fact, this principle, though with some variations, is held by many scholars. McKaughan mentions Plantinga, "Reason and Belief in God," p. 18; Anthony Kenny, *What Is Faith? Essays in the Philosophy of Religion* (Oxford: Oxford University Press, 1992); Richard Swinburne, "The Christian Wager," *Religious Studies* 4 (1969), pp. 217–228 (all cited in McKaughan, "Authentic Faith and Acknowledged Risk," p. 104).
[37] See *An Essay*, IV, x, 6.

Aquinas as well. Protestant thinkers in recent centuries have often argued that Thomas relied excessively on human reason. More precisely, as Arvin Vos has pointed out, they held "that Aquinas places too much confidence in natural theology and thereby compromises revealed theology."[38] For them, "Aquinas is an evidentialist ... he relies on proof of God's existence."[39] Plantinga reiterates this reading while claiming that Aquinas seems to say that "to believe in the mysteries of the faith is not to be foolish or to believe with undue levity, because we have *evidence for* the conclusion that God has proposed them for our belief."[40] Of course, since the thesis that God has proposed certain beliefs intuitively implies God's existence, Plantinga's claim is equivalent to saying that for Aquinas we believe in God since we have evidence for his existence. This is openly stated by Antony Kenny while concentrating on Aquinas's five ways. He claims that "if belief in the existence of God cannot be rationally justified, there can be no good reason for adopting any of the traditional monotheistic religions."[41]

Nevertheless, the idea that to believe in God one has to previously justify his existence would be unacceptable to Aquinas. (In reply to the Protestants' views mentioned above, among which Plantinga's may be numbered, Vos claims that "a thorough investigation of Aquinas's thought clearly shows that he actually contends that faith far surpasses reason both in the content it can grasp and in the certitude it can provide."[42]) Aquinas believes that arguing for God's existence is a useful support for the reasonableness of faith; at the same time, however, he also considers faith *theologically*, namely, as assent to revelation and trust in God, which are ultimately caused by God. In this connection, as has been pointed out, "the demonstration that God exists would not of itself be sufficient to

---

[38] Arvin Vos, *Aquinas, Calvin, and Contemporary Protestant Thought* (Washington, DC: Christian University Press; Grand Rapids, MI: Eerdmans, 1985), p. 125.
[39] Ibid.
[40] Plantinga, "Reason and Belief in God," p. 46. This, however, only regards the early Plantinga. In *Warranted Christian Belief*, Plantinga offers a different reading of Thomas's view of the theistic belief, as shown by the fact that he names "Aquinas/Calvin model" his own preferred account of theistic belief formation.
[41] Anthony Kenny, *The Five Ways* (London: Routledge & Kegan Paul, 1969), p. 4. Both Plantinga and Kenny, therefore, ascribe to Aquinas the view that belief in God needs a previous rational justification of the belief that God exists. Of course, they do so with different degrees of firmness, which can easily be explained given the fact that Plantinga only attempts to compare his own view to Aquinas's, of which Kenny is instead a distinguished interpreter. Furthermore, unlike Plantinga, Kenny shares in the alleged Thomistic view, which is here under consideration.
[42] Vos, *Aquinas, Calvin, and Contemporary Protestant Thought*, p. 162.

establish the truth of revelation for the religious believer. For this an act of faith would also be required."[43]

The readings according to which for Thomas *belief in* God cannot be held if the *belief that* God exists is not supported by evidence are therefore unconvincing. They apply to many circumstances (as Henry Price has rightly pointed out: "I cannot trust my doctor unless I at least believe that there is a person to whom the description 'being my doctor' applies"[44]), but not to the experience of the Christian faith. The readings in question simply overlook the fact that, for Aquinas, the act of believing in God is mainly due to divine grace.

The readings of Aquinas's view of faith and reason, which I have considered so far, seem to be affected by lack of consideration of the theological viewpoint, which Thomas typically assumes. This lack of consideration is pregnant with consequences to the "inconclusiveness matter" here under consideration. Overlooking the specificity of faith equals reducing debates on faith and reason to any possible debate. As a consequence, the inconclusiveness typical of discussions regarding faith and religion would remain unexplained. It is therefore advisable to proceed to explore the inconclusiveness that is typical of debates on faith's credibility by taking into account what is specific of faith. To offer a comprehensive account of faith and its specificity in Aquinas's thought is precisely that which I intend to do in the next section.

3.2 Aquinas's View of Faith and Reason: Evidentness, Human Will, and the Divine Grace

According to Thomas, faith is "an act of the intellect assenting to the Divine Truth at the command of the will moved by the grace of God."[45] Following the order in which Thomas treats the intellect, the will, and the

---

[43] John Wippel, *The Metaphysical Thought of Thomas Aquinas* (Washington, DC: Catholic University of America Press, 2000), p. 381. Elsewhere Wippel suggests that Aquinas "cannot mean that every Christian must first have demonstrated one or more of the preambles, such as the existence of God, before making an act of faith" ("Thomas Aquinas on Philosophy and the Preambles of Faith," in *The Science of Being as Being: Metaphysical Investigations*, ed. by Gregory T. Doolan [Washington, DC: Catholic University of America Press, 2012], p. 196).

[44] Henry Price, "Belief 'In' and Belief 'That,'" *Religious Studies* 1 (1965), p. 13.

[45] *Summa theologiae*, II-II, q. 2, a. 9. I will avoid citing the Latin text, unless I need to explain why I propose a translation that is different from the one I usually adopt. As I have already said (see above, Introduction, note 5), "evidence" is one of the words that, unlike the translation by the Dominican Fathers, I think should not be used to render Aquinas's text into English. For Aquinas, in fact, faith is not characterized by *evidentia*, because *evidentia* is the characteristic of what is *seen*, by either intuition or demonstration. Thus, I prefer "full evidence" or "evidentness" to "evidence."

grace of God, I intend first to concentrate on the relationship between the act of the intellect, evidence, and faith, and then to consider the singular shape this relationship takes because of the intervention of human will and divine grace.

The concepts of evidence and of faith are strictly related to each other, not only in Aquinas's thought but also in numerous other perspectives. If faith is often considered lacking in intellectual dignity and hard to harmonize with reason, this is due to the fact that, as Aquinas and many other thinkers claim, the truths of faith are not *evident*.

But which meaning does Thomas attribute to "evidence"? In line with a view shared by other medieval thinkers, which spans at least until the eighteenth century, he makes use of *evidentia* by way of analogy with the sense of vision to mean that which "marks the domain both of certainty and of *Scientia*."[46] Aquinas employs expressions such as "*visus,*" "*apparens,*" "*manifestus,*" "*per se notum,*" "*cognitus,*" and only infrequently does he make use of "*evidentia*" and its corresponding adjective "*evidens.*" However, Aquinas always intends to mean the characteristic of "those things ... which, of themselves, move the intellect or the senses to *knowledge* of them."[47]

Therefore, according to Thomas "*evidentia,*" which I will translate as "evidentness" to avoid confusion with "evidence," is typical of what we *know*, that is, what we apprehend

(1) directly, and not by way of testimony
(2) certainly, that is, accompanied by a sense of immoveableness,

and, in some cases,

(3) self-authenticatedly, that is, without any need for outside evidence.

Also, Thomas argues that we know by way of intuition and demonstration. According to him, the object of knowledge "is known either by itself (as in the case of first principles, which are held by the habit of understanding), or through something else already known (as in the case of conclusions which are held by the habit of science [*scientia*])."[48]

---

[46] Robert Pasnau, *After Certainty: A History of Our Epistemic Ideals and Illusions* (Oxford: Oxford University Press, 2017), p. 189. In Aquinas's works – so Pasnau argues – "'evidentness' is used to distinguish *scientia* of all kinds from mere opinion and faith" (p. 190).
[47] *Summa theologiae*, II-II, q. 1, a. 4, my emphasis. The Latin word Aquinas employs here is "*cognitio.*"
[48] Ibid., II-II, q. 1, a. 4.

Needless to say, Aquinas is focusing on the Aristotelian dianoetic virtues of understanding and *scientia*. As is known, he usually chooses Aristotle's views among the philosophical perspectives available at his time.[49]

On the basis of the Aristotelian epistemology, Thomas gives rise to his doctrine of faith. The starting point of his investigation is constituted by a consideration of faith from the viewpoint of its intellectual content and the arguments that can be found in its support. Aquinas adopts this epistemological approach while starting the section of *Summa theologiae* that he devotes to faith, which is usually called "treatise on faith" (II-II, qq. 1–16). In the first questions, Thomas treats, in order, the object of faith (q. 1), the act of faith (qq. 2–3), and faith taken as a theological virtue (q. 4).

Aquinas, therefore, starts his reflection by offering an epistemological view of the object of faith and the way the faithful assent to it; he then shows that a merely epistemological approach does not do justice to every aspect of the nature of faith. Unlike knowledge, in fact, faith does not have a fully evident object; that is, its object is not characterized by evidentness. This is why Aquinas says that this object is unable to cause our intellect to firmly assent, no matter whether this occurs intuitively or demonstratively. Consequently, although "faith implies assent of the intellect to that which is believed,"[50] the intellect can only assent "through an act of choice":

> the intellect assents ... not through being sufficiently moved to this assent by its proper object, but through an act of choice, whereby it turns voluntarily to one side rather than to the other: and if this be accompanied by doubt or fear of the opposite side, there will be opinion, while, if there are certainty and no fear of the other side, there will be faith.[51]

Aquinas is offering an accurate distinction between *knowledge* – which is achieved when the intellect *sees* the object of faith and consequently gives its assent – and *faith*, which occurs when the intellect *does not see* the object in question, which is why the assent can only be given because of the intervention of *the will*. Furthermore, this distinction is radicalized by Thomas's view that, although the intellectual content is unseen, faith is expected to be characterized by *certainty*. On the basis of this distinction, therefore, it can be concluded that, unlike knowledge, faith is unresponsive

---

[49] The Aristotelian account of cognition was, in Aquinas's time, questioned by those theologians who preferred the Augustinian account. For more on the difference between them, see Timothy Noone, "The Franciscans and Epistemology: Philosophy and Theology on the Issue of Universal Causality," in *Medieval Masters: Essays in Memory of Msgr. E. A. Synan*, ed. by Rollen E. Houser (Houston, TX: University of St. Thomas, 1999), p. 68.
[50] *Summa theologiae*, II-II, q. 1, a. 4.   [51] Ibid.

to rational criteria, since the believers give their firm assent (only) because they *will* to.[52]

It should be noted that in the passage that is here under consideration Aquinas is distinguishing faith not only from knowledge but also from opinion. Although he is focusing on the fact that faith consists in an act of choice, and this – so he says – is common to faith and opinion, Thomas seems to want to avoid, even for a moment, the impression that he is taking faith as a mere act of choice. Only something other than the mere will to believe can in fact explain why, though opinion and faith are both acts of choice, the latter, unlike the former, is certain. Something that is more than the mere will to believe, therefore, is to be found. As I am going to show below, Aquinas will argue that it consists in the intervention of God, whose grace allows believers to assent firmly to what is unseen.

Before taking into account theological considerations so as to determine why faith is certain though it lacks evidentness, I need to show that what distinguishes knowledge and opinion from faith is somehow nuanced by Thomas. If we take into account Aquinas's responses to the objections raised in the passage under consideration, it will immediately be clear that his treatment of the subject is more articulated than I have shown so far. Thomas seems even to deny the distinction just mentioned:

> Those things which come under faith can be considered in two ways. First, in particular; and thus they cannot be seen and believed at the same time, as shown above. Secondly, in general, that is, under the common aspect of credibility; and in this way they are seen by the believer. For he would not believe unless, on the evidence of signs, or of something similar, he saw that they ought to be believed.[53]

The second point Thomas makes seemingly denies the view that he offers in the *respondeo* I have cited above. He says that in some circumstances we *see* the object of faith; more precisely, we see a number of *signs* in support of this object ("object of faith," as I have said above, stands for those truths of faith to which the believer is expected to give her assent). To put it otherwise, Thomas only in part reproposes his view that one either knows or has faith, and that the truths of faith are not characterized by evidentness. He now says that his view does not regard the *signs* of faith. These

---

[52] This is effectively summed up by Hick, according to whom faith "consists in believing strongly various propositions, of a theological nature, which the believer does not and cannot *know* to be true … the lack of rational compulsion to assent is compensated by an act of will" (Hick, *Faith and Knowledge*, p. 11).
[53] *Summa theologiae*, II-II, q. 1, a. 4, ad 2.

signs, in fact, are characterized by evidentness ("they are seen by the believer"); though not conclusively, they point to the truth of the object of faith. As a result, given this argument that the signs of faith can be known, Aquinas seems to find a mediation between faith and knowledge.

Aquinas confirms this view while focusing on a famous episode of the Gospel according to John. It is the episode of St. Thomas the Apostle, which is often seen as an exemplary identification of knowledge with faith. It is usually believed that Thomas agreed to believe only because he could *see* the Lord. Jesus himself, according to the Gospel, told the Apostle: "Have you believed because you have seen me? Blessed are those who have not seen and yet have come to believe."[54] On this basis, an objection to Aquinas's persuasion that the object of faith is not fully evident can be advanced: "vision and faith regard the same object."[55] Thomas responds by quoting Gregory the Great, who distinguishes what the Apostle saw from what he believed: "He saw the man, and believing him to be God, he made profession of his faith."[56] In other words, Aquinas confirms his view by arguing that what the Apostle really saw was a man present in the flesh. The fact that that man was the Lord remains something that the Apostle only believed.

Aquinas's reading of such a famous story may be seen as somehow forced, especially if we consider that the episode at stake ends with the Lord reproaching the Apostle because the latter believed only to the extent that he saw. At first this seems to unequivocally confirm that the Apostle's believing coincides with his knowing. Jesus, however, does not say that Thomas saw and believed *the same thing*. No contradiction can therefore be seen with Aquinas's explanation. Moreover, a noticeable distinction between seeing a man and believing who he is should be considered. The former coincides with immediate knowledge, while the latter depends on a number of reasons, none of which – at least in the case in question – can really compel one to believe. This is a sharp distinction, which the way the episode in question is usually read tends to blur. The reasons in support of the belief that the man seen by the Apostle is Jesus are so numerous that one spontaneously becomes convinced that one simply knows the object in question. As a consequence, knowing and believing are seemingly coincident with one another. The number of arguments involved is impressively high, and it seems hard to deny that it is Jesus the man who miraculously shows himself to us after we have challenged him by claiming that, if he

---

[54] John 20:29. Hereafter, bible quotations are from NRSV translation unless otherwise specified.
[55] *Summa theologiae*, II-II, q. 1, a. 4, obj 1.   [56] Ibid., II-II, q. 1, a. 4, ad 1.

does not appear to us, we will not believe. Not surprisingly, the episode of St. Thomas the Apostle remains something unique for Christian believers, and as such it has famously been conveyed through millennia. At any rate, this episode seems to confirm the typically Thomistic distinction between object and signs. However numerous and seemingly convincing they may be, the signs are not compelling, nor are they able to bridge the gap between the assent (to the object of faith) and the reasons (signs of faith) for assenting, a gap that Aquinas says is typical of faith.

The relationship I have just mentioned between the assent to the object of faith and the arguments that lead one to assent allows me to explain Aquinas's conviction that faith neither is due to reason nor is irrational. In other words, faith is not due to rational arguments because no conclusive evidence can be offered in support of the act of faith. At the same time, faith does not totally miss arguments in its support. There are signs that point to the object of faith; however, they are only probable arguments, from which follows that, on their basis, the object at hand can be *believed* and not *known*.[57]

The faithful, therefore, do not see the object of faith; that is to say, they do not know that the object of faith is true. They only know that faith is internally consistent or, to employ Aquinas's words, "not impossible":

> The reasons employed by holy men to prove things that are of faith, are not demonstrations; they are either persuasive arguments showing that what is proposed to our faith is not impossible (*manifestantes non esse impossibile quod in fide proponitur*), or else they are proofs drawn from the principles of faith, i.e. from the authority of Holy Writ, as Dionysius declares. Whatever is based on these principles is as well proved in the eyes of the faithful, as a conclusion drawn from self-evident principles is in the eyes of all.[58]

An exception must be registered. Aquinas argues that we can *demonstrate* some of the Christian beliefs. He calls them "preambles of faith" (*praeambula fidei*) because they are logically presupposed by other truths of faith: "Things which can be proved by demonstration are reckoned among the articles of faith, not because they are believed simply by all, but because they are a necessary presupposition to matters of faith, so that those who do not know them by demonstration must know them first of all by

---

[57] The faithful "know them [the things that are of faith], not as by demonstration, but by the light of faith which makes them see that they ought to believe them" (ibid., II-II, q. 1, a. 5, ad 1).
[58] Ibid., II-II, q. 1, a. 5, ad 2.

faith."⁵⁹ These truths are "the existence and unity of God, and so forth."⁶⁰ The faithful usually believe them *by faith*, because only a few believers have the intellectual ability to achieve them *by demonstration*. Thus, one can have faith without being able to offer demonstration in support of the preambles of faith.⁶¹

At any rate, faith always implies a form of reasoning. This implication constitutes a significant part of the Christian tradition. It has been encapsulated in the well-known Augustinian conception of faith as "to think with assent." While reflecting on this, Aquinas is asked to respond to the following objection: "The Latin word 'cogitatio' ('thought') implies a research, for 'cogitare' seems to be equivalent to 'coagitare,' i.e. 'to discuss together.' Now Damascene says that faith is 'an assent without research.' Therefore thinking has no place in the act of faith."⁶² In reply, Thomas claims that John of Damascus is right to the extent that "research" stands for the demonstrative process whose outcome is conclusive evidence. There is, however, also a different meaning of "research," which is compatible with faith: "Faith has not that research of natural reason which demonstrated what is believed, but a research into those things whereby a man is induced to believe, for instance that such things have been uttered by God and confirmed by miracles."⁶³ Faith is, therefore, "thinking with assent"; namely, it combines the assent given to truths that lack evidentness with the investigation aimed at finding *probable* arguments in their support.

That said, Aquinas should conclude that the assent of faith is at best probable; he claims, instead, that faith enjoys certitude, that is, "firmness of the cognitive power in adhering to its own knowable object."⁶⁴ While comparing opinion (*opinio*), science (*scientia*), and faith, he says that faith should be placed between the other two, because it shares certainty with science and lack of evidentness with opinion.⁶⁵

---

⁵⁹ As I have already said (see above, note 45), there are problems with this translation. It employs "knowledge" in regard to both demonstration and faith, whereas the Latin text uses different words: "Ea quae demonstrative probari possunt inter credenda numerantur, non quia de ipsis sit simpliciter fides apud omnes, sed quia praeexiguntur ad ea quae sunt fidei, et oportet ea saltem per fidem praesupponi ab his qui horum demonstrationem non habent" (ibid., II-II, q. 1, a. 5, ad 3).
⁶⁰ Ibid., II-II, q. 1, a. 5, obj 3.   ⁶¹ See above, note 43.
⁶² *Summa theologiae*, II-II, q. 2, a. 1, obj 1.   ⁶³ Ibid., II-II, q. 2, a. 1, ad 1.
⁶⁴ Aquinas, *Commentary on the Sentences*, III, d. 26, q. 2, a. 4, tr. by Chris Decaen and Beth Mortensen, in *Opera Omnia: The Latin/English Edition of the Works of St. Thomas Aquinas* (Lander, WY: Aquinas Institute, 2012–)
⁶⁵ "Science is incompatible with opinion about the same object simply, for the reason that science demands that its object should be deemed impossible to be otherwise, whereas it is essential to

The idea that faith lacks evidentness and nonetheless enjoys the certitude that typically characterizes demonstrative knowledge is manifestly controversial. How is it possible for propositions deprived of evidentness to be maintained with certitude? According to Aquinas, this is possible in the case of the Christian faith, as he explains while commenting on the famous definition of faith contained in the *Epistle to the Hebrews*. As is known, the author of that Epistle says that faith, among other things, is "the evidence (*argumentum*) of things not seen." (Let me remind the reader that, unlike the English translation I usually adopt, I render Aquinas's "*evidentia*" as "evidentness" and not "evidence.") Someone predictably objects that attributing evidentness to "things not seen" constitutes a contradiction. In fact – so the objection goes – evidentness about certain things or propositions makes one *see* them. To put it otherwise, a proposition cannot remain nonevident (not characterized by evidentness) once evidentness in its support has been provided. In reply, Aquinas focuses on the meaning of the word "*argumentum*," which is employed by the author of the Epistle:

> "Evidence" is taken for the result of evidence. For evidence induces the intellect to adhere to a truth, wherefore the firm adhesion of the intellect to the non-apparent truth of faith is called "evidence" here. Hence another reading has "conviction," because to wit, the intellect of the believer is convinced by Divine authority, so as to assent to what it sees not.[66]

According to Thomas, therefore, the certainty that he attributes to faith in God is not due to evidentness. Unlike any other kind of assent, faith is not caused by human reason. As anticipated at the beginning of this section, the assent in question is due to the will of the faithful: "The intellect of the believer is determined to one object, not by the reason, but by the will, wherefore assent is taken here for an act of the intellect as determined to one object by the will."[67] Aquinas digs into the experience of the believers and offers an explanation of how they are expected to firmly assent to divine revelation. The fact that the faithful simply will to believe, if taken alone, makes the act of faith unreasonable. A different cause of faith must therefore be found, which is what Aquinas intends to do while devoting the sixth question of his treatise on faith to the causes of faith.

---

opinion, that its object should be deemed possible to be otherwise. Yet that which is the object of faith, on account of the certainty of faith, is also deemed impossible to be otherwise; and the reason why science and faith cannot be about the same object and in the same respect is because the object of science is something seen whereas the object of faith is the unseen, as stated above" (*Summa theologiae*, II-II, q. 1, a. 5, ad 4).

[66] Ibid., II-II, q. 4, a. 1.   [67] Ibid., II-II, q. 2, a. 1, ad 3.

According to Thomas, "two things are requisite for faith": first, the prospective believer happens to get in contact with divine revelation; second, she gives her assent to such revelation. The cause of both divine revelation and human assent must be God. In fact, since it appears to be superior to human comprehension, divine revelation cannot be either caused or understood by human beings. Only God is, therefore, the cause of both such revelation and human adhesion to it.

That said, how does God cause us to believe? More precisely, how does he lead us to adhere to his revelation? And what is the role played by the signs of faith, to which I have referred so far? Aquinas distinguishes between two factors that he believes are presupposed by the adhesion to the object of faith. One of them is "of external inducement, such as seeing a miracle, or being persuaded by someone to embrace the faith: neither of which is a sufficient cause, since of those who see the same miracle, or who hear the same sermon, some believe, and some do not."[68] Aquinas refers to miracles and arguments, which are only probable proofs for faith. It is not because of them that one believes in God's revelation, let alone in the firm way I mentioned above. The same can be said of the intention to believe. Aquinas refers to the Pelagians, who typically championed the idea that adhesion to God is only caused by our efforts. According to them, "the beginning of faith is from ourselves, inasmuch as, to wit, it is in our power to be ready to assent to things which are of faith ... the consummation of faith is from God, Who proposes to us the things we have to believe. But this is false."[69] Aquinas claims that not only signs or reasons but also our will are unable to make us (firmly) believe. The will, however, is unable to render us believers only in the sense the Pelagians took it. Unlike them, Aquinas takes the will as caused by divine grace. To those who object that, according to Augustine, "faith depends on the believer's will," Aquinas responds that "to believe does indeed depend on the will of the believer; but man's will needs to be prepared by God with grace, in order that he may be raised to things which are above his nature."[70]

---

[68] Ibid., II-II, q. 6, a. 1.   [69] Ibid.

[70] Ibid., II-II, q. 6, a. 1, ad 3. To those who may object that free will is incompatible with any external influence, it must be replied that for Aquinas, as Frederick Bauerschmidt points out, "God can move the will without compromising human freedom" (Frederick Bauerschmidt, *Thomas Aquinas: Faith, Reason, and Following Christ* [Oxford: Oxford University Press, 2013], p. 147). Bauerschmidt also refers to Aquinas's treatment of grace as both "operating," attributable to God, and "cooperating," attributable to the human being. This treatment is contained in *Summa theologiae*, I-II, q. 111, a. 2, ad 2, where Thomas says that "God does not justify us without ourselves, because whilst we are being justified we consent to God's justification by a movement of our free will. Nevertheless, this movement is not the cause of grace, but the effect."

The assent of faith must be caused by something that, unlike probable reasons or the mere will to believe, can effectively explain why Aquinas sees the Christian faith as certain:

> Since man, by assenting to matters of faith, is raised above his nature, this must needs accrue to him from some supernatural principles moving him inwardly; and this is God. Therefore faith, as regards the assent which is the chief act of faith, is from God moving man inwardly by grace.[71]

The certainty that Aquinas attributes to faith – at least to its paradigmatic instantiations – is even superior to that of demonstrative knowledge. Aquinas compares faith to intellectual virtues. Among them, art and prudence can easily be judged as less certain than faith, since they deal with contingent matters. (Faith is, therefore, "preferable in point of certitude, by reason of its matter, since it is about eternal things.") More interesting for our purposes is the comparison with the other three intellectual virtues, which share with faith the necessity of their object. Aquinas starts this comparison by elaborating on the concept of certainty:

> Certitude can be looked at in two ways. First, on the part of its cause, and thus a thing which has a more certain cause, is itself more certain. On this way faith is more certain than those three virtues, because it is founded on the Divine truth, whereas the aforesaid three virtues are based on human reason. Secondly, certitude may be considered on the part of the subject, and thus the more a man's intellect lays hold of a thing, the more certain it is. On this way, faith is less certain, because matters of faith are above the human intellect, whereas the objects of the aforesaid three virtues are not.[72]

Aquinas distinguishes two different points of view, that of the cause of certitude and that of the person who is certain. Note that this distinction is made by Aquinas since, from his theological point of view, he assumes that faith is caused by God. Were Aquinas an unbeliever, the distinction at hand would not make sense because the faithful would be seen as the cause of faith, and consequently there would not be any distinction between the

---

[71] *Summa theologiae*, II-II, q. 6, a. 1. Elsewhere Aquinas confirms this view while focusing on the role of the "visible miracles" performed by Jesus. According to him, "if Christ had not done visible miracles, still there remained other modes of attracting unto faith ... for men were held to believe the authority of the Law and the prophets. They were held also not to resist an interior calling" (*Quodlibetal Questions*, II, q. 4, a. 1, tr. by Urban Hannon, in *Opera Omnia*). Obviously, this emphasizes the primary importance of God's "moving man inwardly by grace (*interius movente per gratiam*)." It is only because of this intervention, which in the passage under consideration Thomas calls "interior calling (*interior vocatio*)," that the faithful believe the authority of the Law and the prophets.

[72] *Summa theologiae*, II-II, q. 4, a. 8.

cause of faith and the person who has faith. At any rate, once the distinction has been made, it can easily be said that, from the viewpoint of the cause, faith is more certain than any intellectual virtue. If the cause of faith is God and that of the intellectual virtues is human reason, then it is wholly reasonable to conclude that the cause of faith, unlike human reason, cannot be mistaken. The other point of view examined by Aquinas – that of the person who reasons or has faith – simply reverses the order I have just mentioned. In this case, intellectual virtues appear to be more certain than faith since they meet the believer's need for evidentness, which faith by definition cannot satisfy.

That said, Aquinas seems to ascribe equal dignity to the two kinds of certainty mentioned above. He identifies two points of view, from each of which any of those two kinds of certainty appears to be superior to the other. The two related points of view, however, do not have equal dignity. Since "a thing is judged simply with regard to its cause, but relatively, with respect to a disposition on the part of the subject, it follows that faith is more certain simply (*simpliciter*), while the others are more certain relatively, i.e. for us."[73] According to Aquinas, the viewpoint of the cause is more important because it allows for determining the nature of the object caused. In contrast, from the viewpoint of the person who believes or knows a certain object, it is only possible to determine what of that object can be seen from the specific viewpoint of that person. This argument is philosophically compelling. Aquinas brings it to the table so as to state that it is from the viewpoint that appears to be more decisive, that of the cause, that faith is more certain. Thus, his conclusion is that "faith is more certain simply." Nevertheless, this conclusion ultimately relies on his faith, because of which he believes that the certitude of faith is caused by God. In fact, once assumed that God causes this certitude, Aquinas can support his thesis that faith is more certain than any intellectual virtue.

When all is said and done, Aquinas's view of faith comes to light as built on three different factors. First, the believer assents to propositions (which she believes God has revealed); second, she gives her assent since she wants to; and third, she wants to believe since she is caused to do so by God, who acts into her interiority. While providing his definition of faith, Aquinas combines all of these three components, namely, the intellectual act, the will to believe, and the relationship with God, who ultimately causes the will of the believer. Faith is, therefore, "an act of the intellect

[73] Ibid.

assenting to the Divine Truth at the command of the will moved by the grace of God."[74]

A similar tripartition is the one that Aquinas draws on Augustine's work. According to this tripartition, faith is "believing in a God" (*credere Deum*), "believing God" (*credere Deo*), and "believing in God" (*credere in Deum*).[75] The first aspect of faith (*credere Deum*) emphasizes the fact that God is an object of intellectual activity. In other words, faith appears to be an act of the intellect with its noetic content. It is *fides quae*, which is different from *fides qua*, that is, the act of faith that is meant by the two other aspects of faith. The second aspect (*credere Deo*) emphasizes the fact that there is no faith without divine revelation. The third aspect (*credere in Deum*) emphasizes the fact that the object of faith is also its ultimate goal. It is the good itself that should be sought and not a mere truth or a person like any other. In other words, the first two aspects regard the content of faith (the material object: *credere Deum*) and how it is proposed to the believer (the formal object: *credere Deo*). The third aspect regards the proper task of the will that, because it aims at the highest good, causes the intellect to assent to the revealed truth.[76]

Aquinas argues that faith is formally an act of intellect. He also shows, as Peter Riga points out, "the large part which the will plays in the act of faith." As a result, Aquinas takes the act of faith as an act "intrinsically determined by affective elements."[77] More importantly, for him faith is not a merely human activity. Its object (*credere Deum*) is at the same time the *cause* of faith, in the sense that God causes the faithful to give their

---

[74] Ibid., II-II, q. 2, a. 9.
[75] "The object of faith can be considered in three ways. For, since 'to believe' is an act of the intellect, is so far as the will moves it to assent, as stated above, the object of faith can be considered either on the part of the intellect, or on the part of the will that moves the intellect. If it be considered on the part of the intellect, then two things can be observed in the object of faith.... One of these is the material object of faith, and in this way an act of faith is 'to believe in a God'; because, as stated above nothing is proposed to our belief, except in as much as it is referred to God. The other is the formal aspect of the object, for it is the medium on account of which we assent to such and such a point of faith; and thus an act of faith is 'to believe God,' since, as stated above the formal object of faith is the First Truth, to Which man gives his adhesion, so as to assent to its sake to whatever he believes. If the object of faith be considered in so far as the intellect is moved by the will, an act of faith is 'to believe in God.' For the First Truth is referred to the will, through having the aspect of an end" (ibid., II-II, q. 2, a. 2).
[76] Hick argues that, on the "Thomist-Catholic" view, faith is intellectualist, fideistic, and voluntaristic: "It is intellectualist, in that it regards faith as a propositional attitude; fideistic, in that it regards faith and knowledge as mutually exclusive; and voluntaristic, in that it sees faith as the product of a conscious act of will" (Hick, *Faith and Knowledge*, p. 23). Based on what I have said so far, however, for Aquinas faith and knowledge are only in part "mutually exclusive," which is why his view does not seem to be "fideistic."
[77] Peter Riga, "The Act of Faith in Augustine and Aquinas," *The Thomist* 35 (1971), p. 168.

assent. He does so *exterius* since "those things which are of faith ... do not come to man's knowledge (*cadunt in contemplatione hominis*), unless God reveals them [*credere Deo*]."[78] God's being the source of faith can also be connected to *credere in Deum*. By definition, God is the good, since he is the principle and end of all things. Thus, the faithful tend to God and love him because of the work he does in their interiority (*interius*) to move them to assent. Aquinas is aware that the faithful believe for a number of reasons, as his view of signs clearly shows. Nevertheless, he insists that the cause of the believer's *firm* assent to divine revelation is "the inward instinct of the divine invitation."[79] In other words, God is "the chief and proper cause of faith."[80]

Once faith has been examined by considering all of the aspects mentioned above, it is possible to see its relationship with the other theological virtues of hope and charity. In regard to the relationship with hope, let me recall that the faithful tend to God, the union with whom they see as their highest possible good. This good, however, cannot be completely achieved by them in this life. It is "eternal life, which consists in the enjoyment of God himself,"[81] and the achievement of such a good implies eternal happiness, which is precisely "the proper and principal object of hope."[82] Regarding the relationship between faith and charity, let me focus on the idea that the faithful tend to God in that God grants human beings the opportunity to partake of him by arousing their desire to love him increasingly and to believe his revelation.[83] According to Aquinas, charity, which God grants to believers, is the heart of the Christian faith.[84] It is

---

[78] *Summa theologiae*, II-II, q. 6, a. 1. The expression "*cadunt in contemplatione hominis*" should rather be rendered with "become aware." According to Aquinas, with the exception of the preambles of faith, we cannot achieve "knowledge" of the revealed truths.

[79] Ibid., II-II, q. 2, a. 9, ad 3.

[80] Aquinas states that "science begets and nourishes faith, by way of external persuasion afforded by science; but the chief and proper cause of faith (*principalis et propria causa fidei*) is that which moves man inwardly to assent" (*Summa theologiae*, II-II, q. 6, a. 1, ad 1).

[81] Ibid., II-II, q. 17, a. 2.   [82] Ibid.

[83] William Mann insists on the fact that faith is not simply cognitive or propositional in nature, and emphasizes a similarity between Aquinas and Luther: "For both accounts [Aquinas's and Luther's], then, genuine faith entails love of God and neighbour" (William Mann, "Theological Virtues," in *Routledge Encyclopedia of Philosophy*, ed. by Edward Craig [London: Routledge, 1998], vol. 9, p. 329).

[84] Dawes emphasizes that, for Aquinas, "it is charity, a love for God as first truth, which leads us infallibly towards what ought to be believed" (Dawes, "The Act of Faith: Aquinas and the Moderns," p. 71).

charity that makes faith perfect: "Charity is called the form of faith in so far as the act of faith is perfected and formed by charity."[85]

Aquinas also offers a definition of faith while commenting on the *Epistle to the Hebrews*, which I mentioned above. According to that *Epistle*, as I have said, faith is "the substance of things hoped for" and "the evidence (*argumentum*) of things not seen." Even if these words "are not arranged in the form of a definition," Aquinas looks at them as including all of the components of faith.

To show that the seeming definition at hand does not lack any aspect of faith, Aquinas proceeds to explain how the two parts it consists of should be interpreted. This explanation is necessary because the concepts of both substance and evidentness, which are used in the first and second part, respectively, seem at least at first sight to be mistakenly and even contradictorily employed. While saying that faith is "the substance of things hoped for," the sacred author seems to misunderstand the meaning of "substance," which is something other than a virtue or act. While saying that faith is "evidence of things not seen," the author in question seems to go so far as to contradict himself, because – as I have already said above – evidentness aims at making the things to which it applies seen and not unseen.

In defense of the sacred text, Aquinas finds a solution to both issues. Regarding the employment of the concept of substance, he says that it can stand for "the first beginning of a thing, especially when the whole subsequent thing is virtually contained in the first beginning." He provides an example from epistemology and says that "we might say that the first self-evident principles are the substance of science, because, to wit, these principles are in us the first beginnings of science, the whole of which is itself contained in them virtually." It is therefore possible to offer the following conclusion: "Faith is said to be the 'substance of things to be hoped for,' for the reason that in us the first beginning of things to be hoped for is brought about by the assent of faith, which contains virtually all things to be hoped for."[86] Regarding the employment of the concept of evidentness, I have depicted above how Aquinas responds to the objection according to which such employment was inappropriate.[87]

---

[85] *Summa theologiae*, II-II, q. 4, a. 3. While commenting on Aquinas's view of faith, Mark Wynn says that "the assent of faith is both 'cognitive' (insofar as it involves beliefs) and action-orienting (since it serves a practical goal, and requires an associated mode of life here and now)" (Mark Wynn, "Religious Faith," in *The Routledge Handbook of Contemporary Philosophy of Religion*, ed. by Graham Oppy [London: Routledge, 2015], p. 2).
[86] *Summa theologiae*, II-II, q. 4, a. 1.   [87] See above, note 66.

Having concluded this debate, Thomas replaces the seeming definition at hand with one that he claims can properly be said to be a definition: "Habit of the mind, whereby eternal life is begun in us, making the intellect assent to what is non-apparent."[88] In this way, Thomas seems to insist on maintaining that faith is a virtue (not surprisingly, this occurs at the beginning of question 4, which Aquinas devotes to faith as a virtue). Faith is a good habit, which leads us to give our assent to the revealed truths and to somehow begin enjoying the eternal life. By faith, the believers desire to do good and become better, which is precisely what a virtue is able to produce.[89] Aquinas's definition focuses, therefore, on the role not only of the intellect but also of the will; not only on the initiative of the believer but also on the gratuitous intervention of God that allows the faithful to firmly trust in him.

This does not coincide with the readings of Aquinas's doctrine of faith that insist on its intellectual feature. According to Swinburne, for example, Aquinas looks at faith as mainly "belief-that," while it is another view of faith, which Swinburne calls "Lutheran," that "involves *both* theoretical beliefs-that (Thomist faith) *and* a trust in the Living God. The person of faith, on this view, does not merely believe that there is a God (and believe certain propositions about him), he trusts Him and commits himself to Him."[90] However, if my argument is correct, Aquinas's view involves all of the elements in question.[91]

Crucial to Thomas's reflection is his considering faith an intellectual act as well as a theological virtue. On the one hand, he assesses with philosophical rigor the relationship between faith and evidentness, and takes faith as a propositional attitude. On the other hand, from this it does not follow that he is impeded from arguing with theological reasons for the peculiarity of the intellectual act of faith, a peculiarity that is due to grace. For Thomas, the believers place a firm trust in God, which God himself grants to them, and can consequently steadfastly stick to their belief, however convincing contrary arguments may appear to them to be. If

---

[88] *Summa theologiae*, II-II, q. 4, a. 1.
[89] Aquinas totally agrees with Aristotle, for whom "virtue is that which makes its possessor good, and his work good likewise" (*Summa theologiae*, I-II, q. 55, a. 3 s.c.). In the same question, Aquinas also points out a more clearly theological character of virtue, and makes reference to Augustine, according to whom "virtue is a good quality of the mind, by which we live righteously, of which no one can make bad use, which God works in us, without us" (ibid., I-II, q. 55, a. 4, obj 1, and s.c.).
[90] Richard Swinburne, *Faith and Reason*, 2nd ed. (Oxford: Oxford University Press, 2005), p. 140.
[91] For a reading of Thomas and Luther that supports this interpretation, see above, note 83.

my argument is correct, Aquinas's insistence on the intellectual aspect of faith should not be taken as somehow opposed to the view of faith as a personal relationship, characterized by love and trust, between God and the faithful. As is known, this opposition has instead been often proposed in the course of the last century. Hick has insightfully put forward a "desire to escape from the older image of faith as merely the acceptance of theological propositions, and to draw into the doctrine of faith the 'I-Thou' encounter between God and man which has been so much stressed in modern Protestant theology."[92] Hick looks at the abovementioned desire directed "toward a less rigidly intellectualist view" as something that "sounds very different from the traditional view of faith as a believing of theological propositions on the authority of God who has revealed them."[93] At any rate, if, as he says, "God ... is the divine Thou, who deals with us as a Person with persons, as a Father with children," this does not seem to sound significantly different from Aquinas's view, which emphasizes the idea that the love for God perfects faith. The real difference is that, unlike Hick, Aquinas emphasizes the connection between the love relationship with God and the intellectual aspect of faith. Since God gives rise to an intimate relationship with them and intervenes in their interiority, human beings come to believe in him *firmly*.

This gives rise to the inconclusiveness here under consideration. If the faithful believe firmly in God, they must not have reasons for changing their mind, however convincing contrary arguments may seem to them to be. Once the believer is persuaded because of the influence God exerts on her that revealed beliefs cannot be mistaken, it follows that she will remain steadfast in her religious conviction.

In the next section, I intend to show that this stance is manifestly confirmed by Aquinas's reflection on how to employ rational arguments in support of faith. In this way, I will also reply to the objection that my argument seems to point in the direction of a kind of religious relativism. If the Christian believer is expected to persist in her faith in the face of counterevidence because of her commitment to the idea that faith is divinely caused, then the same could be said of other theistic traditions. As I said, however, once reflected on the persistence in question as related to the promotion of the rational investigation, I will be able to show why my argument does not lead to any religious relativism.

---

[92] Hick, *Faith and Knowledge*, p. 23.   [93] Ibid.

3.3 The Inconclusiveness of Debates between Believers and Nonbelievers as a Consequence of the Peculiar Nature of Faith

While starting his *Summa contra Gentiles*, Aquinas takes St. Hilary's words as orientation for his reflection: "I am aware that I owe this to God as the chief duty of my life, that my every word and sense may speak of him."[94] For Thomas, this is a *duty*, as it is confirmed by the words he uses – "*officium*" and "*debere*." Such a duty arises from his *desire* to completely devote himself to reflecting on God and his works.

Aquinas employs St. Hilary's words at the beginning of a work that is purposely devoted to how to conduct disputes with those who do not believe in Christ. The words in question effectively show Thomas's disposition toward debates on religious matters: taking such debates as an opportunity to spread the faith in Christ and make interlocutors convert to Christianity.

From this, however, it by no means follows that Aquinas believes that nothing can be learned from those who do not share his faith. It is well known that he extensively takes advantage of pagan philosophers' teachings; accordingly, he states that "no doctrine is so false as not to have some truth mingled with error."[95] Furthermore, Thomas is aware that not every aspect of the object of faith, *as perceived by believers*, is necessarily true. The fact that the faithful firmly hold the Christian belief does not exclude that they may mistake their own conjectures for the Christian faith.[96]

Faith, therefore, if taken as the assent to revelation, assent that is granted by God, is simply infallible because God cannot be mistaken. Believers are therefore expected to totally rely on the revealed truths. As a result, any debate conducted with those who do not believe should be aimed at converting them to the Christian faith.

This is seen by Aquinas as highly meritorious. Rational investigations – so he argues – do not deserve merit if the investigators are ready to accept any possible news, including the replacement of the religious truth. Rational inquiries are instead meritorious to the extent that they are conducted by believers who, having already accepted the Christian beliefs, intend to confirm their truth also by way of rational investigation. This is what Aquinas argues while comparing two kinds of arguments in support

---

[94] Aquinas, *Summa contra Gentiles*, tr. by Anton Pegis, James F. Anderson, Vernon J. Bourke, and Charles J. O'Neil (New York: Hanover House, 1955–1957), vol. I, chapter 2.
[95] *Summa theologiae*, I-II, q. 102, a. 5, ad 4.
[96] See ibid., II-II, q. 1, a. 3, ad 3. See also above, note 30.

of faith, those that one develops before adhering to faith and those that one employs after having already adhered to it.[97] Those who intend to adhere to faith only once they have found sound arguments in its support do not have merit;[98] by contrast, those who conduct rational investigations to confirm the truth of the Christian faith have merit.

This is based on the conviction that faith in God is meritorious:

> Our actions are meritorious in so far as they proceed from the free will moved with grace by God. Therefore every human act proceeding from the free will, if it be referred to God, can be meritorious. Now the act of believing is an act of the intellect assenting to the Divine truth at the command of the will moved by the grace of God, so that it is subject to the free will in relation to God; and consequently the act of faith can be meritorious.[99]

Nothing seems to be more exemplarily meritorious than believing in God, since the Christian faith is by definition a free act moved by God, who is nothing but the good itself.[100]

The thesis that faith is meritorious is so crucial to Aquinas's thought that defending it leads the medieval thinker to argue for the merit of knowledge (*scientia*) and opinion (*opinio*). This occurs because there are those who question the merit of faith by saying that, since religious belief "is a mean between opinion and scientific knowledge or the consideration of things scientifically known," and "the considerations of science are not meritorious, nor on the other hand is opinion,"[101] then faith is not meritorious. This objection is based on the idea, which Aquinas accepts and supports on several occasions,[102] that faith shares something with science and something else with opinion, namely, certainty in the former case and lack of evidentness in the latter. Consequently, if neither science nor opinion has merit, so the objection runs, how can faith, which is determined by features of either of them, be seen as meritorious? Aquinas

---

[97] "Human reason in support of what we believe, may stand in a twofold relation to the will of the believer. First, as preceding the act of the will; as, for instance, when a man either has not the will, or not a prompt will, to believe, unless he be moved by human reasons: and in this way human reason diminishes the merit of faith.... Secondly, human reasons may be consequent to the will of the believer. For when a man's will is ready to believe, he loves the truth he believes, he thinks out and takes to heart whatever reasons he can find in support thereof; and in this way human reason does not exclude the merit of faith but is a sign of greater merit" (*Summa theologiae*, II-II, q. 2, a. 10).

[98] This is exemplified by the evangelical episode of St. Thomas Apostle, on which see above, notes 54ff.

[99] *Summa theologiae*, II-II, q. 2, a. 9.

[100] On the (at least seemingly) paradoxical relationship between God's influence and human freedom, see above, note 70.

[101] *Summa theologiae*, II-II, q. 2, a. 9, obj 2.   [102] See above, note 65.

shares this view. However, he notes that the objector misunderstands the meaning of "science," which the objector reduces to the "scientific assent" without thinking about the role that in science is played by the "consideration of things scientifically known." According to Aquinas, science includes, on the one hand, the scientist's assent to a scientific fact and, on the other hand, her consideration of that fact:

> Now the assent of science is not subject to free will, because the scientist is obliged to assent by force of the demonstration, wherefore scientific assent is not meritorious. But the actual consideration of what a man knows scientifically is subject to his free will, for it is in his power to consider or not to consider. Hence scientific consideration may be meritorious if it be referred to the end of charity, i.e. to the honor of God or the good of our neighbor.[103]

If assent is not a matter of free will (before the "force of demonstration," one cannot withhold assent), the same cannot be held with respect to *consideration*: this *is* a matter of free will, because one *can decide* whether or not to reflect on something that is already known.[104] As a consequence, merit can be gained if the reflection at hand is "referred to the end of charity, i.e. to the honor of God or the good of our neighbor."

Aquinas says something analogous in regard to opinion.[105] Consequently, both science and opinion can be meritorious from the viewpoint of the consideration of what is already scientifically known or opined, respectively. In both cases, one has merit if, because of charity, that is, "the honor of God and the good of our neighbor," one goes on to reflect on what one already knows or opines.

According to Aquinas, therefore, not only in the case of faith but also in that of science and opinion, merit depends on charity, that is, the love for God that God himself grants to us. Consequently, when one searches arguments in support of faith, one acts meritoriously. For Thomas, the readiness to believe, which is due to charity,[106] enables the faithful to use

---

[103] *Summa theologiae*, II-II, q. 2, a. 9, ad 2.

[104] On Aquinas's view, "it is possible for an agent to have sufficient motivation for believing a proposition, and nonetheless to be able at least to withhold assent from it, or even to dissent from it (that is, to be free with respect to coming to believe it)" (Claudia Murphy, "Aquinas on Voluntary Beliefs," *American Catholic Philosophical Quarterly* 74 [2000], p. 586).

[105] Of course, in this case (the case of opinion) "there is no firm assent, since it is weak and infirm, as the Philosopher observes (*Poster*. I, 33), so that it does not seem to proceed from a perfect act of the will: and for this reason, as regards the assent, it does not appear to be very meritorious, though it can be as regards the actual consideration" (*Summa theologiae*, II-II, q. 2, a. 9, ad 2).

[106] "The measure of charity . . . makes the will ready to believe them [the revealed truths]" (ibid., II-II, q. 2, a. 10, ad 2).

reason to the best of their abilities: "When a man's will is ready to believe, he loves the truth he believes, he thinks out and takes to heart whatever reasons he can find in support thereof."[107]

For Aquinas, the opportunity to successfully employ reason in support of faith seems to be proportional to the readiness to believe. From his words, it seems to emerge that not all believers have the same faith, and the more they love God the more they seem to be ready to believe in him and argue in support of faith. If this is correct, it should be concluded that one who has a paradigmatic faith engages in debates with those who do not believe to show the reasonableness of one's religious experience.

In effect, Aquinas openly claims that the Christian faith can be lived and experienced at different levels of intensity. Of course, the fact that the faithful experience faith at different levels of both certainty and charity is also a common opinion among believers. As Saint Paul says, "the righteousness of God is revealed through faith for faith" (Rom 1:17). Aquinas deals with this topic and offers a picture that is consistent with his concept of faith. He wonders "whether faith can be greater in one man than in another." It is worth the trouble to report the whole *respondeo*:

> The quantity of a habit may be considered from two points of view: first, on the part of the object; secondly, on the part of its participation by the subject. Now the object of faith may be considered in two ways: first, in respect of its formal aspect; secondly, in respect of the material object which is proposed to be believed. Now the formal object of faith is one and simple, namely the First Truth, as stated above. Hence in this respect there is no diversity of faith among believers, but it is specifically one in all, as stated above. But the things which are proposed as the matter of our belief are many and can be received more or less explicitly; and in this respect one man can believe explicitly more things than another, so that faith can be greater in one man on account of its being more explicit. If, on the other hand, we consider faith from the point of view of its participation by the subject, this happens in two ways, since the act of faith proceeds both from the intellect and from the will, as stated above. Consequently a man's faith may be described as being greater, in one way, on the part of his intellect, on account of its greater certitude and firmness, and, in another way, on the part of his will, on account of his greater promptitude, devotion, or confidence.[108]

In this passage, Aquinas summarizes in an impressively effective way his view of the different levels of faith. He employs the tripartition of faith

---

[107] Ibid., II-II, q. 2, a. 10.   [108] Ibid., II-II, q. 5, a. 4.

I mentioned above.[109] According to that partition, faith means "believing in a God," "believing God," and "believing in God."

From the viewpoint of "believing God," there is no diversity of faith among Christians. In fact, they all assent to that which God has revealed, without which there is just nothing to believe.

Something similar may be said of "believing in a God," because all Christians are required to believe the same revealed truths. However, a believer can believe explicitly more things than someone else. To explain this stance, Aquinas refers to both the intellect ("on account of its greater certitude and firmness") and the will ("on account of his [of the believer's] greater promptitude, devotion, or confidence"). The point Thomas makes is that the faithful believe with more or less certitude, firmness, promptitude, devotion, or confidence. At the heart of this diversity, there is charity, from which the readiness to believe follows. This can easily be seen in Aquinas's reply to the first objection contained in the article at hand. Let us consider the objection:

> It would seem that faith cannot be greater in one man than in another. For the quantity of a habit is taken from its object. Now whoever has faith believes everything that is of faith, since by failing in one point, a man loses his faith altogether.... Therefore it seems that faith cannot be greater in one than in another.[110]

In his reply, Aquinas emphasizes the role played by the readiness to believe:

> A man who obstinately disbelieves a thing that is of faith, has not the habit of faith, and yet he who does not explicitly believe all, while he is prepared to believe all, has that habit.[111]

Note that the objection deals with the material object of faith ("believing in a God"). On this basis, those who fail to believe even only one truth cannot be considered believers. Aquinas shifts the attention from the material object of faith to the virtue of faith, namely, the readiness to believe, which he also names "the participation of faith by the subject." Those who "obstinately" do not believe a thing alone are not worthy of the habit of faith, while those who are "prepared to believe all," have such habit. While responding to another objection, Aquinas adds that "some submit to it [the first truth] with greater certitude and devotion than others; and in this way faith is greater in one than in another."[112]

---

[109] See above, note 75. [110] *Summa theologiae*, II-II, q. 5, a. 4, obj 1.
[111] Ibid., II-II, q. 5, a. 4, ad 1. [112] Ibid., II-II, q. 5, a. 4, ad 2.

Thomas, therefore, emphasizes the role played by the readiness to believe. This readiness is caused by the love for God,[113] which is divinely granted to believers in various degrees. Consequently, it is especially from the viewpoint of "believing in God," that is, the determination of the will to the good, that there is diversity among believers.

Let us now turn back to the subject here under consideration, that is, the inconclusiveness of debates due to believers' wish to stick to their faith, regardless of contrary arguments. I can now argue that those who possess a paradigmatic level of faith are ready to reject any kind of argument that opposes their religious belief. This is exactly what Aquinas openly says in a famous passage devoted to faith and reason. He says that, if natural reason attains conclusions that contradict the truths of faith, the arguments developed are certainly wrong:

> If ... anything is found in the teachings of the philosophers contrary to faith, this error does not properly belong to philosophy, but is due to an abuse of philosophy owing to the insufficiency of reason. Therefore also it is possible from the principles of philosophy to refute an error of this kind, either by showing it to be altogether impossible, or not to be necessary.[114]

On the one hand, Aquinas maintains that any argument contrasting with the truth of Christian revelation, even if it appears to be rationally convincing, must be rejected as wrong.[115] On the other hand, this conviction ends up highlighting the importance of the role that reason is expected to play, since Aquinas's thesis is that once certain arguments have been rejected – because of their being in contradiction with faith – reason must start anew from the beginning, "from its own principles." In so arguing, Aquinas promotes the idea that, on the one hand, *scientia* needs to be grounded in arguments, and, on the other hand, that the search for arguments is to be promoted by the readiness to believe.

In this way, not only does Aquinas highlight his conviction that, unlike rational conclusions, faith is always true;[116] he also emphasizes the intellectual value of "the love for the truth believed," that is, the love for God that leads believers to reflect on him and his works in order to attain as many arguments as possible. From this follows that, for Aquinas, once

---

[113] See ibid., II-II, q. 2, a. 10, ad 2.
[114] Aquinas, *Super Boetium de Trinitate*, q. 2, a. 3, tr. by Rose E. Brennan (New York: Herder and Herder, 1946).
[115] According to Aquinas, "faith is more certain than any understanding [of principles] and scientific knowledge (*omni intellectu et scientia*)" (*On Truth*, q. 14, a. 1, ad 7).
[116] Again, let me mark Aquinas's awareness that not every stance, which seems to come from God, is authentically revealed by him. See *Summa theologiae*, II-II, q. 1, a. 3, ad 3. See also above, note 30.

caused to investigate by faith, reason functions in the best possible way. If the believer has confidence that reason cannot contradict faith, then they should be ready to follow reason wherever it leads.

Two questions arise. First, is it really possible for faith to exert an influence on reason when it comes to revealed truths that can also be demonstrated (the preambles)? In this case, reason alone is expected to demonstrate their truth. Does Aquinas really claim that faith intervenes in this case? If so, and this is the second question, how exactly can faith exert an influence on reason without depriving the latter of its autonomous way of proceeding?

In reply to the first question, let me point out that for Aquinas faith does play a role in the rational investigation regarding subjects that can be known. In such a case, the faith conceived as a certain amount of nonevident truths disappears, whereas the form of faith – that is, charity – keeps operating. It is precisely the case of the *praeambula fidei*:

> Demonstrative reasons in support of the preambles of faith, but not of the articles of faith, diminish the measure of faith (*ratio fidei*), *since they make the thing believed to be seen*, yet they *do not diminish the measure of charity* (*ratio caritatis*), which makes the *will ready to believe them, even if they were unseen*.[117]

On the one hand, evidentness has been provided, which is why what Aquinas calls "*ratio fidei*" – that is, its nonevidentness – turns out to be diminished or eliminated, depending on the amount of the available arguments. On the other hand, the faithful continue loving God and committing themselves to the revealed truths, which means that "*ratio caritatis*" – that is, the love for God that is divinely bestowed on the faithful – does not disappear. Thus, if belief regards the love in question and is not taken as just propositional belief, it can be said that the faithful know and believe at the same time. In contrast, if belief is taken as mere propositional belief, which is not the case in the passage that I have just taken into consideration, then we can confirm Aquinas's view that there is incompatibility between knowledge and belief when it comes to the same object and the same time.[118] In other words, knowledge, taken as the adherence to certain statements *due to evidentness*, cannot replace belief taken as the adherence to God's revelation *due to charity and divine grace*. According to Aquinas, in fact, natural processes cannot replace divine

---

[117] Ibid., II-II, q. 2, a. 10, ad 2, my emphasis.
[118] See ibid., II-II, q. 1, a. 4, ad 2. See above, note 53.

grace: "Grace is more perfect than nature, and, therefore, does not fail in those things wherein man can be perfected by nature."[119] Consequently, even if the object of faith has become fully evident, one continues to have faith, provided that faith is taken as adhesion to God and his revelation caused by charity.[120]

In reply to the second question, let me show how exactly Aquinas believes and argues that faith keeps exerting an influence on reason without depriving the latter of its autonomy. Let us recall his view regarding the question of whether faith can be held with more certainty than that which characterizes intellect, science, and wisdom taken as intellectual virtues.[121] From the viewpoint of *the cause* – so Thomas says – there is more certainty on the side of faith, because the cause of faith is God. From the viewpoint of *the subject*, that is, the person who searches for evidentness, there is more certainty on the side of reason. In fact, evidentness can only be searched for by human reason, whereas the object of faith is not fully evident. It follows that from the viewpoint of the subject of faith, natural reason functions without being under the influence of faith.

In support of this relationship between faith, reason, and charity we find the passage, mentioned above, in which Aquinas reflects on what to do in case reason and its arguments deny the revealed truths. According to him, the believer should immediately reject such arguments simply because they oppose the truths in question. She should then start reasoning anew from the beginning, based on reason and "its own principles." In this way, Aquinas confirms the view that only by way of reason can we look for evidence and arguments. Furthermore, by saying that reason should recommence its work, he shows that, however mistaken reason might have been, the believer is expected to maximally trust in its potentialities.[122] This follows from Aquinas's firm conviction that faith coincides with the truth and that reason should be consistent with faith because it is not possible to demonstrate what is false: "Since faith rests upon infallible

---

[119] Ibid., II-II, q. 9, a. 1.
[120] A conviction that is widespread among Christians, as rightly pointed out by Penelhum, can therefore be rejected: "It is common for Protestant, as well Catholic, thinkers to say that there cannot be conclusive reasons for the commitment that faith involves, since if there were such reasons, there would be no freedom in the commitment and hence no merit in making it" (Terence Penelhum, "The Analysis of Faith in St. Thomas Aquinas," *Religious Studies* 3 [1977], p. 140). On the contrary, "perhaps what makes faith voluntary is not that its grounds are inconclusive, but that even if they are conclusive, men are free to deceive themselves and refuse to admit that they are" (ibid., p. 153).
[121] See *Summa theologiae*, II-II, q. 4, a. 8. See above, note 72.
[122] For a similar account of reason provided by Reid, see above, Chapter 2, notes 36ff.

truth, and since the contrary of a truth can never be demonstrated, it is clear that the arguments brought against faith cannot be demonstrations, but are difficulties that can be answered."[123] Notice that the trust Aquinas places in reason does not seem to be strictly due to reason. Rather, it seems based on two principles, neither of which is affirmed by way of argument. In fact, the former (faith rests on infallible truth) is clearly due to faith; the latter (it is impossible to demonstrate what negates the truth) is proposed by Aquinas neither as a first principle nor as a demonstration (after all, such a demonstration would fall into circularity). In conclusion, love for God and firmness of adherence to his revelation[124] grant the believer *orientation* of her speculative investigation. She takes this activity to further confirm the truth of revelation and to respond to objections and criticisms. Also, divine revelation, which she believes and loves, becomes for her *criterion* of her rational activity. According to Aquinas, in fact, she is supposed to accept or reject the conclusions of reason on the basis of their agreement or disagreement with revelation, respectively.

The fact that, even if influenced by faith, reason can work in full accordance with its own principles seems to be shown by Aquinas while comparing the difference between a rational investigation that starts from purely rational principles and that which instead "starts from God":

> God is indeed that by which all things are known, not in the sense that they are not known unless he is known (as obtains among self-evident principles), but because all our knowledge is caused in us *through his influence*.[125]

These words respond satisfactorily to the second question here under consideration. On the one hand, it is claimed that rational investigation is ultimately based on self-evident principles. Consequently, since revelation does not enjoy full evidence, its truths do not play any role in this. On the other hand, it is claimed that we can know (we can achieve evidentness regarding) everything because of God's influence. This influence, in fact, puts the believer in a condition to love God, trust him, and take his revelation as true. As a result, that which I have said above is confirmed: the believer takes the revealed truths as *orientation* and *criterion* for her

---

[123] *Summa theologiae*, I, q. 1, a. 8.
[124] The certainty of faith consists of *adherence* – "to adhere" (*inhaereo*) – to the revealed truths. Faith can be seen as surer than any rational certainty: "Understanding and knowledge are more perfect than faith with regard to clearness, not with regard to more certain adhesion (*quantum ad certiorem inhaesionem*)" (*Summa theologiae*, II-II, q. 4, a. 8, ad 3, my translation). See also *On Truth*, q. 14, a. 1, ad 7, where Aquinas says that the certainty of faith is "firmness of adherence (*firmitas adhesionis*)."
[125] *Summa contra Gentiles*, I, 11, my emphasis.

rational investigations. Let me now add that, once the believer has employed those truths as a *criterion* and has consequently rejected any arguments that contradict divine revelation, she should adopt faith as *orientation* again, and resume reasoning with the aim of demonstrating that such arguments deserve rejection also from the viewpoint of reason.

Let me point out that it is only because of the divine influence that one may plausibly will to hold on to one's beliefs against apparently convincing evidence. Apart from that influence, in fact, believing under the command of the will would be mere *wishful thinking*, which is simply unacceptable.[126] Once reference to that influence is added, instead, things change. As a scholar of Aquinas such as Herbert McCabe appropriately argues, we should "disentangle two senses of 'wishful thinking': a bad sense, in which I think religious belief isn't necessarily wishful thinking, and a good, or at least harmless sense, in which I think it is."[127] Consider the possibility that God exists and intervenes in support of our intellectual enterprise, especially if this enterprise is aimed at knowing as much as possible about him and everything is related to him. If so, it is fully plausible to think that because of love for God, which is divinely bestowed on them, believers stick to their belief, however convincing contrary evidence may seem to be. It is their *readiness to believe*, which is caused by charity, that leads them to behave in this way, no matter how incompatible this may be with ordinary epistemological views. This is confirmed by the fact that, as I have already pointed out in the course of this chapter, although Aquinas adopted Aristotle's epistemological doctrine, he also modified that doctrine to try to explain how believers could be certain in the absence of full evidence. He was aware that, given Aristotle's views, what he – Aquinas – was proposing about faith should appear implausible. Believing firmly what is not fully evident is simply unacceptable on the basis of those views. And nonetheless, he was also aware that divine intervention can plausibly change things, as confirmed by the fact that the modification he introduced to Aristotle's perspective clearly regards his view of religious belief, and not belief in general.[128]

---

[126] Against the so-called doxastic voluntarism, according to which one has voluntary control on one's beliefs, Swinburne says that one cannot change one's belief at an instant. As he says, "one's beliefs about whether the evidence favours a proposition determine one's beliefs about that proposition" (Swinburne, *Faith and Reason*, p. 135).

[127] Herbert McCabe, *Faith within Reason*, ed. by Brian Davies (London: Continuum, 2007), p. 2.

[128] Stump seems to confirm this when she says that "nothing in Aquinas' account of the relations between the intellect and the will contravenes the common view that we do not have direct voluntary control over our beliefs ... But in cases where the object of the intellect is *not* sufficient to move the intellect by itself, then Aquinas thinks that it is possible for the will to have an effect

Let me note that, in contemporary terms, this view can arguably be seen as "externalist" to the extent that a belief-forming process, which is supremely trustworthy, is clearly involved, and the faithful are expected to firmly believe without being in possession of accessible reasons.[129] However, when it comes to *debates* about the revealed truths, Aquinas's perspective should be seen as "internalist," since factors that are internal to the subject obviously play a crucial role. This also regards debates that focus on the belief-forming process here under consideration. I mean that when Aquinas discusses the entitlement of the believer to take her Christian beliefs as divinely enabled, he assumes an internalist position. If my argument is correct, then *qua* believer, Aquinas is externalist, whereas *qua* scholar who reflects on his belief, he is internalist. (This does not exclude that, while debating to rationally support his belief, he also continues believing, as I have said so far. From this viewpoint, which is the viewpoint of the believer, he continues acting as an externalist.)[130]

In conclusion, Thomas Aquinas's reflection on the nature of faith and its relation to reason does offer a viable view of how believers combine the influence of divine revelation with the autonomy of reason's employment. In other words, Aquinas's view may explain how believers are not expected to change their mind, however convincing contrary arguments may appear to them to be, and at the same time are expected to appropriately and competently engage in rational debate. They are encouraged to do so

---

on intellectual assent to propositions. In this way, a person's will can influence his beliefs" (Eleonore Stump, *Aquinas* [London: Routledge, 2003], p. 362).

[129] I will focus on externalism, including the way it emerged in the course of the last decades, in Chapter 6, Section 6.1. See also Stump's reading of Aquinas as a champion of "a species of externalism, with reliabilist elements" (see below, Chapter 6, notes 75f.).

[130] A different perspective has recently been proposed. According to Gregory Stacey, internalism can be attributed to Aquinas *qua* believer. He refers to "phenomenal conservatism," according to which, in the absence of reasons for doubting what appears to us, we should assume that what appears to us is as it appears. This view is seen as internalist because the assumption in question is justified, although the justification occurs *noninferentially*. Stacey says that, according to Aquinas, God's intervention in our interiority (the interior calling) "generates basic belief that the gospel is credible," and this belief is "*prima facie* justified in an 'internalist sense'" (Gregory Stacey, "Towards a Catholic Epistemology," PhD dissertation, University of Oxford, 2019, p. 200). My view is that Stacey is right in seeing the revealed truths as (noninferentially) justified when no contrary evidence emerges. I also believe, however, that contrary evidence may sooner or later emerge. In that case, we know that, according to Aquinas, at least those who are paradigmatic believers should persist in their faith, and at the same time should start reasoning anew from the beginning (see Aquinas, *Super Boetium de Trinitate*, q. 2, a. 3; see above, note 114). This means that Aquinas expects the believer to be internalist while debating in support of her faith. Instead, while firmly adhering to God and his revelation, the believer is expected to act as an externalist. She wants to continue believing because of a belief-forming process constituted by God's intervention, and not because no objection to her belief has shown up.

because not only are they expected to maximally trust in God and rely on the truth of what he has revealed. They are also expected to rely on natural reason, which, according to Aquinas, once under the influence of such a religious faith, can best function in accordance with its own rules. This supports believers' tenacity of faith in the face of counterevidence, which gives rise to the inconclusiveness here under consideration.

Someone may object that the tenacity in question not only gives rise to inconclusiveness; it also paves the way to religious relativism. In other words, my argument can, at first sight at least, be used to support the view that followers of different theistic traditions are expected to persist in their own faith even if convincing counterevidence may show up. If all of them are committed to the view that their faith is divinely caused – so the objection goes – none of the traditions in question can claim to be the true one.

In reply, let me draw a distinction between the viewpoint of the tenacious believers and that of those who reflect on the rational plausibility of religious traditions. No relativism can affect the former viewpoint. Being persistent in one's faith in the face of counterevidence because of love for God is an attitude that, in itself, does not have anything to do with the understanding of different religions and the comparison among them. Not surprisingly, I did not focus on the subject of this book to support *the truth* of Christianity, but only to show, among other things, that ME is not applicable always, especially when it comes to Christianity. The problem of relativism may affect instead the other viewpoint, that of those who compare religions with each other. They do not focus on the tenacity or the love for God that may inspire the debaters, since only evidence and arguments are of interest to them. This, however, is beyond the scope of my research. Nonetheless, let me point out that what I have argued so far (and which I will further develop in the next chapters) shows that those who tenaciously intend to persist in their faith, once engaged in debates, are put in a condition to employ reason to the best of their abilities, which should increase their chance to overcome relativism.

CHAPTER 4

Rethinking the Nature and Purpose of Debates
Mitchell, Practical Rationality, Religious Disagreement, A-Rational Commitments, and "Quasi-Fideism"

In the previous chapter, I argued that, according to Aquinas, Christian believers are supposed to stick to their belief against contrary evidence, however compelling this evidence may seem to them to be. In this chapter, I first show that this is incompatible with ME, according to which one should always prefer beliefs supported by more evidence to beliefs supported by less evidence. I then consider and refute some perspectives that more or less implicitly minimize this incompatibility. Finally, I argue that the Christian faith offers an opportunity to rethink the nature and purpose of debates, a rethinking that allows for a wider epistemological view than ME. In this new light, intellectual investigations and debates should ultimately be directed by the search for good.

4.1 ME and the Christian Faith

In Chapter 3, I focused on how Aquinas believes that the Christian faith should relate to rational investigations and debates. In short, faith mainly consists of a relationship with God, which is divinely granted to believers. Because of this privileged relationship, the faithful – at least the paradigmatic ones, who firmly believe in God and trust him – are expected to hold on to their religious beliefs when confronted with arguments that, in regard to such beliefs, may arouse serious doubts. Furthermore, since they are expected to believe that no sound and truthful arguments against divine revelation can be found, the faithful are supposed to trust human reason and use it to the best of their abilities.

I decided to focus on Aquinas's thought since it can convincingly be labeled "a touchstone for Christian reflection on faith."[1] This probably led me to spill more ink than necessary on typically Thomistic arguments. It

---

[1] William Jay Wood, "Faith's Intellectual Rewards," in *Religious Faith and Intellectual Virtue*, ed. by Laura F. Callahan and Timothy O'Connor (Oxford: Oxford University Press, 2014), p. 37.

nonetheless enabled me to offer a view of some aspects of the relationship between intellectual activities and the Christian faith, aspects that are widely accepted by Christians. Among them, the firmness with which the believers should adhere to the divine revelation, the conviction that such firmness is a divine gift and must consequently be seen as superior to the one that our cognitive faculties can provide, and the idea that the autonomous and unprejudiced employment of those faculties should be encouraged and not limited, as may seem to be the case at first sight.

In Chapter 2, I showed that these aspects of the relationship that the Christian faith requires with rational investigation are part of Thomas Reid's reflection, no matter how distant this reflection is from Aquinas's philosophical perspectives and competence in the field of theology. The abovementioned aspects can equally be found in another stream of thought of the Christian theological and philosophical tradition. I am referring to the Franciscan tradition and, more specifically, to its chronologically first source, the *Summa halensis*, to which the whole subsequent Franciscan reflection traces back. The work in question was written by the first Franciscan thinkers, among whom Alexander of Hales (ca. 1185–1245), the first Franciscan friar to hold a university chair, certainly stood out. In this authoritative work, the superiority of the firmness of faith over that of reason clearly anticipates the distinction adopted by Aquinas decades later:

> There is a certitude of intellect and a certitude of affection.... I say, then, that the theological approach is more certain by the certitude of experience, by the certitude of affection, which is by way of taste ... but not more certain as far as intellectual speculation goes, which operates by way of seeing.[2]

The affinity of the "certitude of affection" employed in this passage with the "adhesion" mentioned by Aquinas[3] is striking. This is especially true if one takes into account substantive differences that can be found between the Franciscan tradition and the "Dominican" one,[4] more specifically that of Aquinas.

---

[2] Alexander of Hales et al., *Doctoris irrefragabilis Alexandri de Hales Ordinis minorum Summa theologica* (Quaracchi, Florence: Collegii S. Bonaventurae, 1924–1948), vol. 1, q. 1, c. 4, a. 2, tr. by Oleg Bychkov, in Oleg Bychkov, "Appendix: Alexander of Hales, The Sum of Theology," *Franciscan Studies* 66 (2008), pp. 63–99. The fact that this work exerted an influence on Aquinas's *Summa* has recently been emphasized. See Lydia Schumacher, *Early Franciscan Theology: Between Authority and Innovation* (Cambridge: Cambridge University Press, 2019), p. 18.

[3] See above, Chapter 3, note 124.

[4] See Eleonore Stump, *Wandering in Darkness: Narrative and the Problem of Suffering* (New York: Oxford University Press, 2010). For more on this, see below, note 88.

Note that the affinity in question is of crucial importance for my purposes. It witnesses to a widespread inclination among Christians to contrast the firmness of faith with the one attained by natural reason. And this inclination is of vital importance to my thesis that there is an unbridgeable gap between a merely epistemological approach and a religious approach to belief. The consequences of such a widespread inclination are worthwhile. If the certitude of faith is different from that achieved by reason, then no criticism can be addressed against the former because it does not conform to the criteria of the latter. But criticisms against the Christian faith have usually been advanced from the viewpoint of reason; therefore, the believers have often been led to respond to these criticisms by cultivating the idea that their beliefs, as well as their own way of thinking, cannot seriously be questioned. Harry Blamires famously said that "thinking Christianly is not the same as thinking about Christian matters" because there is a specifically "Christian mind."[5]

The Christian mind, whose ultimate criteria are other than evidence, cannot boil down to a widespread epistemological conviction, dating back to Socrates and Plato. This conviction can be summarized by citing the following passage:

> I am one of those who are very willing to be refuted if I say anything which is not true, and very willing to refute anyone else who says what is not true, and just as ready to be refuted as to refute; for I hold that this is the greater gain of the two, just as the gain is greater of being cured of a very great evil than of curing the evil in another. For I imagine that there is no evil which a man can endure so great as an erroneous opinion about the matters of which we are speaking; and if you claim to be one of my sort, let us have the discussion out, but if you would rather have done, no matter; – let us make an end.[6]

Plato is depicting Socrates as the perfect philosopher, who is interested in attaining the truth, no matter what that truth is. On the contrary, what matters is that any discussion should be conducted correctly from what I call ME; that is to say, only what is based on sufficient evidence should be considered true.

Note that a sort of moral obligation seems to emerge from the passage here under consideration. Socrates mentions "a very great evil" of which

---

[5] See Harry Blamires, *The Christian Mind: How Should a Christian Think?* (Ann Arbor, MI: Servant Books, 1963), p. 6.
[6] Plato, *Gorgias*, 458 a3–b3, tr. by Benjamin Jowett, in *The Dialogues of Plato* (Cambridge: Cambridge University Press, 2017).

the debaters aim at "being cured," which emphasizes the crucial role that has been ascribed to the search for evidence and justification from the beginning of the history of philosophy. I have already made reference to the proportion between statements and proofs, a proportion that at the dawn of modern age was considered the main feature of correct reasoning by thinkers such as Locke,[7] and was later established by William K. Clifford's celebrated dictum: "It is wrong always, everywhere, and for everyone to believe anything upon insufficient evidence."[8] Consequently, Wolterstorff has spoken of "ethics of belief,"[9] and Plantinga has pointed out that "the fundamental notions of justification ... have been deontological notions, or notions analogically but intimately related to deontological notions."[10]

From the viewpoint of this epistemological and deontological perspective, which spans the whole history of philosophy, no plausibility seems ascribable to the faithful's conviction that they should hold on to their beliefs regardless of opposing arguments.[11]

The same conclusion emerges from a popular philosophical doctrine of our time, such as the so-called relativism. (Of course, relativism consists of clusters of views rather than single theories. For my purposes, however, it is sufficient to take it as the widely accepted conviction that notions like truth, justice, good, and their opposites can be defined only *relatively*, namely, once a framework of assessment has been determined.[12] At any rate, this definition falls into a self-referential contradiction, because, if truth can only be defined relatively, then the truth of this statement is to be defined relatively also.) From the viewpoint of relativism, as Allan Bloom points out, the believers who tenaciously hold on to their faith are not only mistaken but also dangerous:

> The true believer is the real danger. The study of history and of culture teaches that all the world was mad in the past; men always thought they

---

[7] See *An Essay*, IV, xix, 1. See also above, Introduction, note 3.
[8] William K. Clifford, "The Ethics of Belief," in *Lectures and Essays* (London: Macmillan, 1879), p. 186.
[9] See Wolterstorff, *John Locke and the Ethics of Belief*, esp. chapter 1.
[10] Alvin Plantinga, *Warrant: The Current Debate* (New York: Oxford University Press, 1993), p. 188.
[11] This lack of plausibility is usually minimized by those who attempt to provide religious faith with rational arguments. The attempt in question is in itself plausible; they, however, tend to overlook the specificity of faith, from which follows that they put the autonomy of faith from reason in danger.
[12] See Maria Baghramian and Adam J. Carter, "Relativism," in *The Stanford Encyclopedia of Philosophy*, ed. by Edward N. Zalta, https://plato.stanford.edu/archives/sum2017/entries/relativism/, accessed July 1, 2019).

were right, and that led to wars, persecutions, slavery, xenophobia, racism, and chauvinism. The point is not to correct the mistakes and really be right; rather it is not to think you are right at all.[13]

Bloom emphasizes the typically relativistic stance according to which believing "is but one option among others."[14] It follows that, if one thinks that "one is not right at all," then one cannot sensibly claim that religious belief is true. Like the mere epistemologist, therefore, the relativist cannot accept the tenacity of the Christian believers.

The Christian faith, however, seems to require a unique relationship with the employment of cognitive faculties. As I have already said, it seems that there is a specifically Christian mind, and an equally specific Christian way of thinking. The Christian believers may be expected to be responsive to God and not to epistemological criteria elaborated by reasoning. According to John Stackhouse, "Christian thought is supposed to be responsive to God and responsive to the world God created, sustains, loves, and redeems."[15] This gives rise to a striking contrast with the various approaches that epistemologists have usually developed to deal with knowledge. Therefore, surrender and capitulation to current culture become a serious possibility: "Some Christians practice an intentional form of this mode, consciously trying to adapt the Christian tradition to a contemporary ideology of some kind."[16]

Capitulation to the current cultural mainstream might also be encouraged by a sort of inclination to conformity, which seems to play a decisive role in the contemporary academic context. In a book suggestively titled *Academic Freedom in an Age of Conformity*,[17] Joanna Williams makes a point of interest here. She first points out that threats to academic freedom are usually thought of as originating from outside academia, especially from the political terrain. These threats, however, are easily identifiable, and are consequently equally easy to oppose. "More frequent and insidious" are instead those threats "that occur within universities" since they "can often go unnoticed."[18] The author then lists the threats she says are inside academia:

---

[13] Allan Bloom, *The Closing of the American Mind: How Higher Education Has Failed Democracy and Impoverished the Souls of Today's Students* (New York: Simon and Schuster, 1987), p. 26.
[14] This is what Charles Taylor says is a feature of modern age: *A Secular Age* (Cambridge, MA: Belknap Press of Harvard University Press, 2007), p. 3.
[15] John Stackhouse, *Need to Know: Vocation as the Heart of Christian Epistemology* (New York: Oxford University Press, 2014), p. 18.
[16] Ibid., p. 14.
[17] Joanna Williams, *Academic Freedom in an Age of Conformity: Confronting the Fear of Knowledge* (London: Palgrave Macmillan, 2016).
[18] Ibid., p. 2.

> Restricting the terrain of discussion, placing some topics beyond challenge, presenting knowledge as simply individual perspectives and blurring knowledge, beliefs and values all contribute towards the creation of a culture of conformity in academia. Such enforced consensus is the antithesis of academic freedom.[19]

The fact that the faithful stick to their belief against contrary evidence is simply incompatible with the conformity in question. Doing so, they contradict the conviction that no stable truth can be found, a conviction that follows the idea that knowledge is to be taken "as simply individual perspectives."

It may be objected that, since the very conformity under consideration includes the idea that there are topics "beyond challenge," the tenacity of the Christian believers may align with current academic conformism. However, the topics implicitly referred to above, which are considered "beyond challenge," are likely to consist in philosophical or scientific views proposed by way of arguments and evidence, not in religious stances, which are ultimately based on divine revelation. It may still be objected that the faithful here under consideration do not pay attention to contrary evidence only because they are confident that further research will eventually confirm their own beliefs, which is plausible from the viewpoint of ME. However, there are a number of distinctions between the attitude of the believer who holds on to her belief in the face of controversy and the philosopher (or scientist) who, at first sight, acts similarly. Among these distinctions, on which I will focus in the next section, is the fact that the philosopher or scientist is expected to either *suspend* her belief or accept it as a plausible working hypothesis until confirmation by way of argument is provided, whereas this cannot be said of the believer. Otherwise, the believer's religious belief would appear to be grounded in rational arguments, and talking about *faith* – as I take it in the footsteps of Aquinas – would no longer make sense.

In conclusion, the fact that believers should hold on to their beliefs against contrary evidence seems incompatible with ME. Among the believers who reflect on the relationship between faith and reason, some support this incompatibility and consequently oppose faith and reason to each other; there are those who, on the contrary, tend to minimize the incompatibility at hand. The former initiative, which frequently takes shape in various forms of fideism, has often been discouraged. Fideism implies that faith is irrational, from which follows that rational discussions of

---

[19] Ibid., p. 15.

94   God, the Good, and the Spiritual Turn in Epistemology

matters of faith no longer make sense. The latter initiative, on the contrary, has often been encouraged. It is based on a principle that is widely accepted by those who rationally reflect on faith, namely, that there are common aspects between faith and reason. Among the proposals advanced from this perspective, there are the ones I explored (and refuted) in the previous chapter, while referring to scholars committed to interpreting Aquinas's thought.[20] Other attempts, which do not focus on Aquinas, will be considered in the next section. After having argued so far that the typically Christian inclination to persevere in the face of controversy is untenable from the viewpoint of ME, I will explore perspectives according to which such an inclination is shareable by any researchers, unbelievers included, because of its presumed compatibility with ME. These perspectives simply minimize the gap between ME and the way Christians should conduct a rational investigation.

4.2   Refuting the Views That Minimize the Gap between ME and the Tenacity of the Christian Faith

4.2.1   Basil Mitchell on Neutrality and Commitment

Basil Mitchell devoted an extensive reflection to the relationship between the commitment to sticking to one's beliefs and the impartiality to acknowledge the difficulty raised by opposing evidence. It is indicative of the decisive role this subject played in his reflection that, in his inaugural lecture delivered at the University of Oxford in 1968,[21] he focused precisely on the concepts of "commitment" and "neutrality."[22]

According to Mitchell, both concepts are part of scholarly activity. In fact, "any philosopher (and, *mutatis mutandis*, any academic) has this problem of reconciling his neutrality as a philosopher with his commitment as a man."[23] Since philosophy "touches life, at least potentially, at all points,"[24] philosophers are expected to deal with their philosophical arguments as well as with the intuitions and commitments that emerge

---

[20] See above, Chapter 3, Section 3.1.
[21] Basil Mitchell, *Neutrality and Commitment: An Inaugural Lecture Delivered before the University of Oxford on 14 May 1968* (Oxford: Clarendon Press, 1968).
[22] While in the work in question Mitchell makes use of the concept of *neutrality* – which clearly means absence of bias toward every position involved in a debate – he will later use the concept of *impartiality*, taken as the ability to not minimize the difficulty faced by one's thesis (see below, note 32).
[23] Mitchell, *Neutrality and Commitment*, p. 14.   [24] Ibid., p. 10.

from their life experience. Something analogous can also be said of any academics, in proportion to the importance that their life experience has to their scholarly activity.[25] Negative outcomes would follow if they did not pay attention to the needs of both academic research and human experience: "A man who is prepared to accept in everyday life for true nothing which he cannot philosophically defend will either become practically ineffective and humanly incomplete, or else philosophically unadventurous."[26]

In the footsteps of Newman and his criticism against the typically Lockean conviction that a philosopher should proportionate every belief to the available evidence, Mitchell reiterates Newman's idea that our way of reasoning is often "tacit and informal." For him, "in estimating the force of the evidence and in deciding what is to be believed on the strength of it we are rightly influenced by considerations other than those provided by the evidence itself."[27] Consequently, any scholarly activity, in proportion to its ability "to touch life," depends on personal considerations and private assumptions, no matter how questionable they may be.

Like Newman before him, Mitchell shows that the influence exerted by personal assumptions and commitments, whether conscious or not, is inevitable and positive. Without their influence, no progress could be made, although a balance between these assumptions and the need to impartially assess the available evidence is required. Otherwise, a scholar would inevitably be vulnerable to "a double temptation, that of distorting the philosophical arguments so as to bring them into line with his personal commitment, and that of abandoning his personal commitment prematurely when the philosophical going gets difficult."[28]

To highlight the influence exerted by personal assumptions over the rational investigation – both philosophical and scientific – and the positive role they play in searching for truth, Mitchell makes use of the concept of "tenacity." A "principle of tenacity" is a positive component of rational inquiry. It promotes research because all the parties involved, if tenaciously committed to holding on to their view, will do their best to find any

---

[25] In this connection, Plantinga's famous essay "Advice to Christian Philosophers," originally published in *Faith and Philosophy* (see above, Chapter 1, note 31), was later provided with "a special, new preface for Christian thinkers from different disciplines" and published on the website of the journal in question (www.faithandphilosophy.com/article_advice.php, accessed July 5, 2020).
[26] Mitchell, *Neutrality and Commitment*, p. 12.
[27] Basil Mitchell, *Faith and Criticism* (Oxford: Clarendon Press, 1994), p. 14.
[28] Mitchell, *Neutrality and Commitment*, p. 14.

possible argument in support of their position and against the contrary position: "Scientists operate what has been called a 'principle of tenacity,' in virtue of which they do not let go of their fundamental beliefs when things get difficult, but rather persevere in the hope, or – shall we say? – the faith, that the problem will eventually be resolved."[29] But how exactly can the principle under consideration be reconciled with the impartiality to assess the available arguments, which for Mitchell is equally vital to any rational investigation? It is precisely to make this point clear that Mitchell refers to the concluding sentences of *The Origin of Species*, in which Charles Darwin, on the one hand, is confident about the possibility of solving the problems that persist with his theory, and, on the other hand, takes seriously the problems in question.[30] According to Mitchell, "two things are to be noticed here. One is that Darwin does not at all minimize the difficulties. He is, in that sense, open-minded and impartial. The other is that, in spite of fully acknowledging them, he continues to trust his theory. And it is apparent, I think, that both these attitudes are essential to scientific progress."[31] For Mitchell, therefore, one's inclination to not minimize the difficulties faced by one's thesis, which is an obvious indication of impartiality and open-mindedness, can be reconciled with the wish to stick to one's commitments.[32]

While arguing that these two aspects (impartiality and personal assumptions) should align with one another to promote science and philosophy, Mitchell defends those scholars who are also religious believers against the charge of being partial and epistemologically unreliable when they reflect on religion. Based on a well-known and widespread opposition between reason and religious faith that dates back to the Enlightenment, the faithful have usually been seen as unqualified for rational investigations that have to do with their religious faith. Note that this view has been so

---

[29] See Mitchell, *Faith and Criticism*, p. 18.
[30] "A crowd of difficulties will have occurred to the reader. Some of them are so grave that to this day I can never reflect on them without being staggered; but, to the best of my judgement, the greater number are only apparent; and those that are real are not, I think, fatal to my theory" (Charles Darwin, *Origin of Species* [London: John Murray, 1859], p. 171, cit. in Mitchell, *Faith and Criticism*, p. 18).
[31] Mitchell, *Faith and Criticism*, p. 18.
[32] According to Mitchell, "impartiality is a fundamental academic virtue. It requires one to be scrupulous in assembling the evidence, honest in recognizing arguments against one's position, fair in assessing the force of these arguments, sympathetic in representing the position of those with whom one disagrees. Academics all too often fail to satisfy these requirements, but failure nevertheless it is, and the requirements are absolute." Probably more importantly, "impartiality does not imply neutrality." Unlike neutrality, in fact, impartiality can be exhibited "while holding fast to firm convictions of one's own" (Mitchell, *Faith and Criticism*, pp. 24f.).

popular in the last three centuries that Karl Barth, who famously rejected the fundamental claims of the Enlightenment, ended up involuntarily supporting it. According to his well-known "dilemma," in fact, one who is a believer and intends to discuss religion with nonbelievers either blasphemingly gives up on one's faith or dishonestly engages in the discussion.[33]

However, Mitchell does not seem to consider what specifically pertains to religion and, still more specifically, to the Christian faith. While dealing with the abovementioned accusations brought against scholars who are also religious believers, he does not consider the specific way in which faith may lead those believers to approach debates. In the footsteps of Newman, he rather holds that it is the way *reason* functions that needs to be more appropriately investigated and assessed:

> The contention that openness to criticism is incompatible with commitment derives from a certain familiar conception of the way reason works, which associates reason with complete open-mindedness and a readiness at every moment to be swayed entirely by the state of the evidence as it appears at that time.... The inadequacies of this view are exposed by Newman, who notes that we tend to hold on to our central beliefs despite fluctuations in the state of the evidence in all matters of importance.[34]

Consequently, Mitchell's view leads us to minimize the problem, which I have shown in the previous section is typical of the Christian believers who rationally discuss the contents of their faith. Mitchell arguably says that the contents of such a faith and those of philosophy and any other academic discipline involve deeply personal convictions. However, his idea that distinctions between reason and faith should only be seen as due to "differing degrees" is not equally convincing:

> The dilemma in which Christian faith is said to be involved between the need for whole-hearted conviction and the requirements of rational criticism is not unique, but applies to any reflective philosophy of life. Instead of the sharp dichotomy between science and religious faith which is said to generate the dilemma, what we actually find is a continuum in which, in differing degrees, elements of faith and criticism are found at each stage.[35]

The differing degrees in which elements of faith (taken as "whole-hearted convictions") and criticism are found at each stage of the continuum in question are apparently due to the equally differing degrees in which each

---

[33] See Karl Barth, *Church Dogmatics*, tr. by G. T. Thompson and H. Knight (Edinburgh: T & T Clark, 1956), vol. 1, part 1, pp. 93ff.
[34] Mitchell, *Faith and Criticism*, p. 22.   [35] Ibid., p. 67.

stage "touches life." Religion, philosophy, and science occupy different stages, in increasing order of detachment and neutrality.

Mitchell, therefore, minimizes the problem with religion and faith that I have instead highlighted so far. No uniqueness is ascribed to how religious believers engage in debates. Their tenacity in holding on to their beliefs is also ascribed to everyone who may have reasons for sticking to one's convictions. In the same vein, Mitchell argues that, in any field, tenacity is a resource for the best employment of reason. In fact, one's inclination to not overlook contrary evidence, an inclination that is proportionate to the commitment to one's personal assumptions, leads one to employ reason to the best of one's abilities. Consequently, it is the commitment in question that may be seen as the ultimate cause of research progress. In other words, the more one sticks to one's personal commitments, the more appropriately one conducts one's research. Debaters will do their best when they "persevere in the hope, or – shall we say? – the faith, that the problem will eventually be resolved."[36]

However, there is a problem with this attempt to minimize the distinction between, on the one hand, religion and faith, and, on the other hand, any other personal commitment. Mitchell mentions hope, tenacity, and perseverance to show that they successfully participate in the rational debate, and must therefore be seen as indispensable components of scholarly investigation. On closer inspection, however, it emerges that their employment is successful only to the extent that it is based on commonly accepted evidence and allows us to uncover new evidence. According to Mitchell, in fact, if debaters persevere in the faith that their thesis will eventually be proven to be true, then it is plausible to expect that they would succeed. Mitchell quotes Stuart Mill, according to whom – in Mitchell's words – "in general, truth is better served by having a variety of systems of belief in vigorous competition with one another than by allowing the expression only of what is currently held to be the truth."[37]

To summarize, if debaters stick to their beliefs even against contrary evidence, this would likely contribute to the advancement of knowledge more than their giving up on the beliefs in question once confronted with opposing arguments. The tenacity against contrary evidence is based on the fact that there is evidence that persevering in the hope of being successful contributes to progress in knowledge more than the attitude of those who give up on their convictions. Mitchell confirms this view:

---

[36] See above, note 29.   [37] Mitchell, *Faith and Criticism*, p. 29.

In the light of these considerations it would seem that the tendency of people to develop persistent convictions which are underdetermined by the evidence is not only a widespread phenomenon, as Newman noted, but one that is justified as a means to discovering truth. Truth is more likely to be found if people join together in developing a set of ideas with a considerable degree of perseverance than if they allow their opinions to fluctuate readily in response to changes in the evidence.[38]

If the tenacity treated by Mitchell "is not only a widespread phenomenon ... but one that is *justified* as a means to discovering truth" (my emphasis), then Mitchell's analysis minimizes the basic distinction that I have argued exists with the tenacity that is typical of the Christian faith. Unlike the one treated by Mitchell, the perseverance that the Christian believers are expected to maintain is not *justified* – it is not based on *common evidence*, and no publicly acceptable explanations can be offered in its support.

It may be objected that Mitchell's account of tenacity does not deny that Christians behave in a certain way *by divine grace*; if divine grace is not against reason, as the Christian tradition usually maintains, then it must be possible to offer plausible explanations in its support also from a rational point of view. This – so the objection might go – is what Mitchell might have tried to do while arguing that the behavior of the faithful is "justified." Furthermore, this is fully consistent with Aquinas's famous conviction that the faithful must be confident that their belief, though mainly due to divine intervention, can be successfully defended using rational arguments.[39]

However, there are at least two reasons for rejecting this objection. First, Mitchell says that philosophers and scientists "persevere in the hope, or – shall we say? – the faith, that the problem will eventually be resolved." The faith or hope at stake does not have anything to do with the *firmness* with which the Christian believers are supposed to hold their beliefs. The faith or hope mentioned by Mitchell is proportioned to the abovementioned evidence that there are cases in which persevering in the face of controversy eventually produces new, satisfactory evidence. In contrast, the firmness of the Christian believers is not proportionate to evidence. Second, the researcher who hopes to find new evidence must continue persevering against the available evidence only within a reasonable period, beyond which her hope should be abandoned. The believers who persevere in the face of controversy might instead be ready to do so for an indefinite time.

[38] Ibid., p. 30. [39] See *Summa theologiae*, I, q. 1, a. 8. See also above, Chapter 3, note 123.

True, like Aquinas and Reid, they can be convinced that reason will sooner or later be able to confirm a certain statement related to their faith; this, however, might happen after the reasonable period mentioned above, beyond which they would be seen as simply unjustified and unreasonably tenacious.

From this it does not follow that I completely reject Mitchell's overall conviction according to which "there is not that sharp dichotomy between scientific explanation and other kinds of explanation which led so many nineteenth-century thinkers to dismiss rational theology as beyond redemption."[40] I find this view acceptable to the extent that it refers to explanations that are offered by both believers and nonbelievers when evidence in support of their theses *can* be provided. In such a case, they are all required to argue in support of their views. Instead, if no evidence in support of one's belief shows up, whereas evidence that opposes one's thesis is available, then nonbelievers are expected to change their mind, whereas believers *qua* believers are expected to be tenacious mainly by way of divine grace, which makes them trust in God.

4.2.2 Faith, Belief in the Face of Controversy, and Practical Rationality

Another way of minimizing the problem with the Christian faith here under consideration emerges from recent investigations conducted on the nature of faith. Those who carry out these investigations focus on a *general* concept of faith, both religious and nonreligious. Daniel Howard-Snyder, for example, believes that the idea that there is something like a religious or Christian faith, as distinguishable from other types of faith, is simply a mistake. He ironically compares such an idea to the conviction that "there's a distinctive form of religious or Christian ingestion and excretion, or pain and pleasure, or belief and desire – which is absurd."[41] This view seems to be echoed by Lara Buchak, according to whom "faith statements

---

[40] Mitchell, *Faith and Criticism*, p. 78.
[41] Daniel Howard-Snyder, "Does Faith Entail Belief?," *Faith and Philosophy* 33 (2016), p. 14. By the same author, see also "Propositional Faith: What It Is and What It Is Not," *American Philosophical Quarterly* 50 (2013), pp. 357–372; and "Schellenberg on Propositional Faith," *Religious Studies* 49 (2013), pp. 181–194. Howard-Snyder's persuasion resembles positions that have often been advanced in regard to the idea of "Christian philosophy," to which I referred in Chapter 3, Section 3.1. According to such positions, Christian persuasions cannot exert any influence on the nature of philosophy. Howard-Snyder seems to rely on the idea that the same is to be said of the nature of faith, which for him does not change if applied to religion. From a merely philosophical point of view – he seems to say – we can only focus on the concept of faith *in general*.

in religious contexts and in more mundane contexts express the same attitude and so share some typical characteristics."[42]

While focusing on the nature of this general notion of faith, Buchak argues that those who have faith commit to acting on the claim that they maintain by faith, no matter if counterevidence is provided;[43] they are consequently able to engage in long-term, risky projects, which may be profitable for them. This is why Buchak says that faith can serve "an important purpose in human life."[44] For her, faith "means *not looking for further evidence* for the specific purpose of deciding whether to act on the proposition, or not basing one's decision on how *the evidence* turns out."[45] This is not irrational at all, because there are circumstances in which the worse strategy, contrary to what is usually believed, consists precisely of looking for more evidence: "There are situations in which, because of the structure of the available acts and the available evidence, it is instrumentally rational – rational *from the point of view of getting what you want* – to act rather than to examine additional evidence."[46]

According to Buchak, therefore, faith in some propositions requires taking risks on those propositions before examining further evidence. Faith can be stronger or weaker along a couple of dimensions. The first one is "how much counterevidence the individual would be willing to tolerate (the tenacity of his commitment)"; the second one is "the size of risk he is willing to take; the bigger risks he is willing to take, the stronger his faith is."[47]

Buchak's view of faith does not align with the concept of religious faith I am focusing on in this book. Buchak maintains that faith "means *not*

---

[42] Lara Buchak, "Can It Be Rational to Have Faith?," in *Probability in the Philosophy of Religion*, ed. by Jake Chandler and Victoria S. Harrison (Oxford: Oxford University Press, 2012), p. 226.

[43] The subject of faith "must care whether the proposition is true, must have a positive attitude towards the proposition, and must not be certain of the proposition on the basis of his evidence alone – his evidence must leave it open that the proposition is false" (Lara Buchak, "Faith and Steadfastness in the Face of Counter-Evidence," *International Journal for Philosophy of Religion* 81 [2017], p. 114).

[44] Buchak, "Faith and Steadfastness in the Face of Counter-Evidence," p. 113.

[45] Lara Buchak, "Rational Faith and Justified Belief," in Callahan and O'Connor, eds., *Religious Faith and Intellectual Virtue*, p. 55, my emphasis.

[46] Buchak, "Faith and Steadfastness in the Face of Counter-Evidence," p. 115.

[47] Ibid., p. 120. See also p. 115: "S has a higher degree of faith in X to the extent that he is willing to take more risks on X without looking for further evidence." Michael Pace partly disagrees with Buchak, since he believes that different degrees of faith cannot be explained only on how big the risk involved by the act of faith is. In his view, Buchak should also make mention of "a degree of confidence, belief, or any other cognitive attitude as even partially constituting faith" (Michael Pace, "The Strength of Faith and Trust," *International Journal for Philosophy of Religion* 81 [2017], p. 142).

looking for further evidence," and makes clear that "in many cases, a decision to eschew further evidence will be based on the evidence one already has: faith need not be 'blind' faith."[48] I agree with her that "faith need not be blind faith,"[49] but from this, it does not follow that not looking for further evidence and sticking to one's faith against opposing arguments "will be based on evidence one already has." Grounding faith into evidence that is already possessed may apply to mundane faith but not to religious faith, at least to the model of faith that I have championed so far, whose ultimate foundation is supposed to be God's grace.

Would the distinction between Buchak's view and my view disappear if my thesis were stated in terms of *practical* rationality? After all, considering the possibility that my thesis be seen in practically rational terms is supported by the fact that religious belief is not just speculative in character, but concerned with questions of action. It is also supported by the fact that, like Buchak's proposal, a view that appeals to practical rationality will in some measure insulate religious belief from fluctuations in evidence. However, again like Buchak's proposal, such a view will rely "on evidence one already has." I mean that, if comparison with rival beliefs shows that these beliefs enjoy a significantly higher amount of evidence than my belief, then (in normal circumstances) it would not be (practically) rational for me to take that belief as a basis for action.

Buchak simply *assumes* at the outset that there is no ultimate difference between religious faith and mundane faith. Evan Fales *argues* in support of the same conviction. In a way that resembles Mitchell's reflection, he says that

> having faith ... may mean simply that, while the evangelist has no effective response to offer to the objections, he or she remains confident that there is such an explanation, compatible with her worldview, even if neither he/she nor anyone else at present knows what it is. And this confidence need not be at all irrational. After all, scientists regularly remain committed to their theories in the face of what Kuhn called anomalies.[50]

I agree with the idea that, while persevering in her belief against contrary evidence, the believer remains confident that evidence in support of her choice will eventually be found.

---

[48] Buchak, "Rational Faith and Justified Belief," p. 55.
[49] For more on this, see Chapter 3, notes 53ff., where I focus on Aquinas's view that, although the object of faith lacks evidentness, the same cannot be said of its signs.
[50] Evan Fales, "Making and Breaking Faith," in Callahan and O'Connor, eds., *Religious Faith and Intellectual Virtue*, p. 130.

I disagree with Fales, however, when he says that *the same* happens to scientists *qua* scientists. While discussing Mitchell's position, I have determined two unbridgeable differences between those who remain confident by faith and those who remain confident by reason. They can be profitably employed in response to Fales's conviction.[51]

In the same book in which Fales's essay is published, John Bishop focuses on the fact that, if it is God in whom the faithful trust, then the trust in question should be taken to the fullest possible extent: "If it really is *God* to whom we are related as person-to-person, an overall practical orientation of trust seems justified to the fullest extent, beyond anything justifiable in human relationships."[52] I agree with the idea that trust in God may be taken beyond any rational justification. This coincides with what I have argued so far, namely, that the steadfastness with which the believers are supposed to hold on to their conviction against opposing evidence is beyond rational justification, and is consequently a problem for debaters. However, one aspect of Bishop's reflection may still pave the way for minimizing the difference between the Christian faith and other motivations or commitments. Bishop mentions *our* trust in God without mentioning that, if "it really is *God* to whom we are related," then we trust in God mainly because of *his* initiative. On closer inspection, this initiative seems to be the only plausible cause of the firmness with which we can believe "beyond anything justifiable in human relationships."

4.2.3 On Disagreement

The concept of disagreement is crucial to the subject here under consideration.[53] Therefore, the research recently carried out on this concept makes a substantive contribution to the reflection I am conducting here. Like debates on faith in the face of controversy, this research minimizes the difference between Christian faith and any other view in regard to rational debates and related disagreement. While depicting some traits of this research, I will show that, when it comes to religious disagreement, those

---

[51] See above, pp. 99f.
[52] John Bishop, "Trusting Others, Trusting in God, Trusting the World," in Callahan and O'Connor, eds., *Religious Faith and Intellectual Virtue*, p. 165.
[53] Discussions on disagreement started with discussions on religious exclusivism, and soon it was understood that exclusivism as well as disagreement may also apply to other areas of human experience like philosophy, politics, and science (see Peter Van Inwagen, "We're Right. They're Wrong," in *Disagreement*, ed. by Richard Feldman and Ted A. Warfield [Oxford: Oxford University Press, 2000], p. 11).

conducting such research take for granted that no attention is to be paid to specifically religious considerations.

Let me start by noting that it may seem commonsensical that the vast majority of the beliefs that people hold are expected to become subject to disagreement and are consequently supposed to be either substantially revised or abandoned. On closer inspection, however, this position, which has been called "conformist" or "conciliatory," is not the only possible one; another is the "nonconformist" or "steadfast."[54] The former, which is held, among others, by David Christensen, Richard Feldman, and Hilary Kornblith, argues that one cannot continue holding on to one's beliefs if one does not have reasons that are not related to the disagreement itself. By contrast, the latter view, which is held, among others, by Thomas Kelly and Richard Foley, argues that one can stick to one's thesis even if one does not have reasons that are independent of the disagreement itself.

Both conformists and nonconformists, as I will show in a moment, support the minimization here at stake. It is true that nonconformists' perspective may at first seem to be in line with the view of Christian faith, which I have championed so far. However, given nonconformists' view that *all* debates can be characterized by disagreement among peers, it seems to minimize the difference between religious and nonreligious debates, since it follows that no unbridgeable gap should be seen between them. (Furthermore, it should be noted that although nonconformists place an emphasis on the value of tenacity, which, again, makes them seem close to my view, they do not endorse the idea, which I endorse, that such tenacity may ultimately be due to factors such as love for God. The commonality they find is based on evidential reasons, which means that religious steadfastness should be adjusted to ME.) With regard to conformists, something more should be said. Christensen claims that one has to *distinguish* areas in which disagreement is not really possible from areas in which it is instead a serious possibility. If this distinction occurred between, on the one hand, any realm of knowledge excluding religion and, on the other hand, religious faith, then it would align with my thesis that, unlike other subjects of debate, religion is an obstacle to agreement. In reality, Christensen proposes a distinction between some areas of knowledge, such as mathematics and sciences "that are not subject to significant peer-to-peer disagreement," and "areas of morality, religion, politics, and economics, and, unfortunately, philosophy which are rife

---

[54] See *The Epistemology of Disagreement: New Essays*, ed. by David Christensen and Jennifer Lackey (Oxford: Oxford University Press, 2013), p. 2.

with disagreement." Therefore, Christensen's distinction confirms the idea that the ways religious contents and other contents generate tenacity and perseverance in the face of controversy are not ultimately different. Following the passage that I have just cited, Christensen puts forward on which ground the distinction he proposes obtains:

> It seems clear that disagreement flourishes when evidence is meager or poorly distributed, or when, due to our emotional or intellectual limitations, we are just not very good at reacting correctly to the evidence. In other words, disagreement flourishes when epistemic conditions are bad. To focus in on my own field, I think that we all should acknowledge that epistemic conditions are not so great in philosophy.[55]

Christensen emphasizes the role of evidence, which is taken as the criterion for agreeing or disagreeing in many fields, including religion. The view I advocate here, instead, takes into consideration those specific circumstances in which other criteria intervene and allow one to continue holding one's thesis though such thesis is less supported by evidence than its competing views.[56] The fact that Christensen does not consider the specificity of certain circumstances, such as religious belief, shows that his view is part of the minimization here under consideration.

After referring to conformism and nonconformism, it should be pointed out that these are only some of the views that can emerge before disagreement. (Note that disagreement can also emerge with regard to debates on disagreement.) For a more complete overview, as Robert Audi has pointed out, a "kind of compromise view" between the views mentioned above and "variants of each" should be considered.[57] In this connection, it can also be said that there are numerous factors of disagreement, a list of which is offered by Bryan Frances and Jonathan Matheson:[58] "Cognitive ability had while answering the question; evidence brought to bear in answering the question; relevant background knowledge; time devoted to answering the question; distractions encountered in answering the question; relevant biases; attentiveness when answering the question; intellectual virtues

---

[55] David Christensen, "Epistemology of Disagreement: The Good News," *The Philosophical Review*, 116/2 (April 1, 2007), p. 214.
[56] For more on this distinction, including its relationship with intellectual humility, see below, Chapter 6, pp. 181f.
[57] See Robert Audi, "Cognitive Disparities, Dimensions of Intellectual Diversity and the Resolution of Disagreements," in Christensen and Lackey, eds., *The Epistemology of Disagreement*, p. 222.
[58] See Bryan Frances and Jonathan Matheson, "Disagreement," in *The Stanford Encyclopedia of Philosophy*, ed. by Edward N. Zalta (https://plato.stanford.edu/archives/spr2018/entries/disagreement/, accessed November 1, 2017).

possessed." While elaborating on the notion of "epistemic peers," Jennifer Lackey mentions these factors. She first says that "A and B are epistemic peers relative to the question whether *p* when A and B are (roughly) equally justified in their beliefs regarding this question."[59] She then offers a definition of "equal justification," which appears to coincide with the factors mentioned above, although the nomenclature she employs is different:

> I suggest that we are justified in thinking two people, A and B, are equally justified in their conflicting beliefs whether *p* when (i) A and B have been thinking about the subject matter in question for a sufficiently long time and in significant detail, (ii) A and B are both sufficiently intellectually virtuous with respect to whether *p*, and (iii) neither A nor B is in sole possession of evidence that both would (after careful consideration) take to be decisive on the claim in question.[60]

Note that these factors are so numerous and deeply rooted in our cognitive structures that a "cognitive disparity," as Audi names it, can easily arise.[61] Moreover, disparity regarding the meaning of those factors can make us consider the definition itself of epistemic peers "opaque."[62] Again, it emerges that disagreement affects our debates because it is complicated to reconcile various proofs with one another. In the case of religious tenacity, instead, the cause of inconclusiveness is different.

Sanford C. Goldberg wonders whether or not the notion of "peer disagreement" applies to religious matters. For him, "it is not clear whether the sorts of disagreements on religious matters should be seen as peer disagreements." Believers may, in fact, hold that nonbelievers lack "some sort of crucial insight"; nonbelievers may instead consider themselves in possession of "what they regard as a deflationary (perhaps psychology-based) account of the origins of religious belief."[63]

This reference to religious peer disagreement draws our attention to the way believers and nonbelievers usually look at each other. My thesis is that believers may have at least one reason for not seeing unbelievers as their

---

[59] See Jennifer Lackey, "Taking Religious Disagreement Seriously," in Callahan and O'Connor, eds., *Religious Faith and Intellectual Virtue*, p. 313.
[60] Ibid., p. 314.
[61] According to him, such a disparity regards not only beliefs but also other "truth-valued attitudes, as well as dispositions to form beliefs" (Audi, "Cognitive Disparities, Dimensions of Intellectual Diversity and the Resolution of Disagreements," pp. 206f.).
[62] See John Hawthorne and Amia Srinivasan, "Disagreement without Transparency: Some Bleak Thoughts," in Christensen and Lackey, eds., *The Epistemology of Disagreement*, p. 14, note 15.
[63] Sanford C. Goldberg, "Does Externalist Epistemology Rationalize Religious Commitment?," in Callahan and O'Connor, eds., *Religious Faith and Intellectual Virtue*, p. 286.

peers. This reason is specifically Christian, in the sense that believers hold that God has granted them the trust in him because of which they continue believing in the face of contrary evidence. Consequently, they are expected to confidently maintain their belief that unbelievers lack "some sort of crucial insight."[64]

Richard Feldman focuses on another aspect of disagreement that deserves attention, that is, the difference between belief and action. According to him, we may act in a way that is not related to our beliefs. Once we come to a fork in the road, we can act in a way (choose either one or the other path) that is not related to our belief (we do not believe the path we chose is necessarily the right one).[65] The example Feldman offers can serve the purpose of minimizing the difference between ordinary and religious belief here under consideration. Nevertheless, although we may indeed choose a path without believing that it is necessarily the right one, it remains true that the faithful, at least according to the perspective I advocate here, are supposed to believe that the path they choose *is* the right one.

Finally, let me mention a proposal to solve the problem of disagreement offered by Linda Zagzebski while discussing religious beliefs. She distinguishes *theoretical* reasons from *deliberative* reasons:

> By *theoretical reasons* for believing *p* I mean facts that are logically or probabilistically connected to the truth of *p*.... Theoretical reasons can be shared with others – laid out on the table, so they are third personal.... In contrast, what I mean by *deliberative reasons* has an essential connection to *me and only to me* in my deliberations about whether it is the case that *p*.... They are irreducibly first personal.[66]

This insightful distinction allows us to consider the typically irreducibly first-person character of the religious belief, which the believer sees as mainly due to the relationship she has with God. However, Zagzebski's

---

[64] Although they do not refer to the specifically religious reasons that I consider here, Plantinga and Peter Van Inwagen confirm this view. According to them, if one has special and incommunicable evidence that other parties lack, then one is within one's right to maintain one's own belief. See Plantinga, *Warranted Christian Belief*, p. 457; Peter Van Inwagen, "It Is Wrong, Always, Everywhere, and for Anyone, to Believe Anything, upon Insufficient Evidence," in *Faith, Freedom, and Rationality*, ed. by Jeff Jordan and Daniel Howard-Snyder (Lanham, MD: Rowman and Littlefield, 1996), pp. 137–154.

[65] See Richard Feldman, "Reasonable Religious Disagreements," in *Philosophers without Gods: Meditations on Atheism and the Secular Life*, ed. by Louise M. Antony (New York: Oxford University Press, 2007), pp. 194–214.

[66] Linda Zagzebski, "Trust, Anti-Trust, and Reasons for Religious Belief," in Callahan and O'Connor, eds., *Religious Faith and Intellectual Virtue*, pp. 232f.

reflection on the first-person character in question also applies to other forms of beliefs. Consequently, it implicitly minimizes the ultimate difference between a religious and a nonreligious approach to intellectual debates and related disagreement.

4.2.4 "Quasi-Fideism" and Its Potential

Like the debates I have considered so far, another treatment of religious belief aims at showing that Christian belief is not ultimately different from nonreligious belief. I am referring to Duncan Pritchard's proposal of a view of the Christian faith that he calls "quasi-fideism."[67] Pritchard argues that faith is grounded on a-rational commitments (i.e., commitments too deep for rational defense and *unresponsive* to rational criteria), and that this is not conducive to fideism. Namely, it does not render faith *extraneous* to epistemological evaluation. In fact, as Pritchard says, a-rational commitments constitute the ground for nonreligious or ordinary belief as well. As a result, there is no reason for considering Christian belief ultimately different from other types of belief.[68]

On the one hand, this leads us to see that religion cannot be reduced to merely intellectual or cognitive considerations; on the other hand, since noncognitive considerations also regard nonreligious matters, Pritchard's proposal ends up equaling religious and nonreligious debates. From this, it follows that his proposal seems to not add anything original to the debates I have taken into consideration in the previous sections. On closer inspection, however, focusing on a-rational matters might imply unexpectedly interesting consequences for my reflection. But let me proceed to briefly present Pritchard's proposal.

He backs up his thesis using Wittgenstein's final notebooks, published as *On Certainty*, and also takes into account Newman's *Grammar of Assent*. In fact, both works point out that the epistemic status of ordinary beliefs is

---

[67] See Duncan Pritchard, "Faith and Reason," *Royal Institute of Philosophy Supplements* 81 (2017), pp. 101–118.

[68] The well-known *parity argument* is therefore applied in a new way. While Plantinga, Alston, and others have used this argument to show that religious belief can be as rational as other kinds of belief ordinarily considered rational, "quasi-fideism takes a more radical line. According to the quasi-fideist, our everyday beliefs that we take to be through-and-through rational in fact presuppose fundamental a-rational commitments – i.e., commitments which are not rationally grounded" (Pritchard, "Faith and Reason," p. 103). In other words, instead of insisting on the shared possession of rationality between faith and reason, it is the a-rational ground of any belief that should be explored.

different from what we ordinarily assume it to be because such beliefs seem often to be rationally groundless.

Pritchard refers to the metaphor of a *hinge* employed by Wittgenstein. For the author of *On Certainty*, "the *questions* that we raise and our *doubts* depend upon the fact that some propositions are exempt from doubt, are as it were like hinges on which those turn."[69] Wittgenstein says that we cannot doubt every belief, because this would "drag everything with it and plunge it into chaos."[70] A similar stance is held by Newman, whose view of the foundation of belief expressed in the *Grammar* may have influenced – so Pritchard hypothesizes – Wittgenstein's view of hinge commitments.[71] Wittgenstein's remarks mentioned above manifestly remind us of Newman's claim about the possibility of universal doubt. The author of the *Grammar* firmly rejects the hypothesis that "we ought to begin with a universal doubt." Ironically, so he argues, this "is of all assumptions the greatest," because "doubt itself is a positive state, and implies a definite habit of mind, and thereby necessarily involves a system of principles and doctrines all its own."[72] Newman's refusal of universal doubt was clearly due to his conviction that religious belief and ordinary belief lack the kind of epistemic support provided by evidence, which Locke had proposed in the fourth book of his *Essay*. Like Wittgenstein, the author of the *Grammar* was convinced that our beliefs seem often to be groundless and at the same time undeniable, which is a conviction accepted by Pritchard, who claims that "it is in the very nature of rational evaluations that they take place relative to hinge commitments which are both groundless and indubitable."[73] As a result, if not only faith but also rational belief lies on a-rational commitments, then there is no reason to see faith as extraneous to the epistemological viewpoint from which ordinary beliefs are usually considered: "If the alleged epistemic defect in religious belief were shown to be found in non-religious belief, then this would not be grounds for scepticism about the epistemology of religious belief, specifically, but rather grounds for a general epistemological scepticism."[74] The a-rational commitments that are of interest to Pritchard are the abovementioned hinge commitments, which are not even beliefs. They

---

[69] Ludwig Wittgenstein, *On Certainty*, ed. by Gertrude E. M. Anscombe and Georg H. von Wright (Oxford: Blackwell, 1969), §§341–343, cited in Pritchard, "Faith and Reason," p. 5.
[70] Ibid., §613, cited in Pritchard, "Faith and Reason," p. 5.
[71] See Duncan Pritchard, "Wittgenstein on Faith and Reason: The Influence of Newman," in *God, Truth, and Other Enigmas*, ed. by Miroslaw Szatkowski (Berlin: DeGruyter, 2015), pp. 197–216.
[72] Newman, GA, IX, 3, 2, 2, p. 294.   [73] Pritchard, "Faith and Reason," p. 105.
[74] Pritchard, "Wittgenstein on Faith and Reason: The Influence of Newman," p. 206.

are unresponsive to rational considerations,[75] as it is manifest when one retains such commitments even in the absence of any reason for regarding the proposition which one supports as true.

This stance seems to be perfectly acceptable from the viewpoint of the Christian faith. Does this mean that Pritchard's view bridges the gap between the Christian faith and religious belief, on the one hand, and ME and ordinary belief, on the other?

My thesis is that the gap remains unbridged. This is shown by the fact that Wittgenstein's hinge commitments, as I said above, "are exempt from doubt," in the sense that no one doubts them. In contrast, the same cannot be said of the Christian faith, whose truths cannot be doubted only by those who have faith at paradigmatic level of firmness.

However, I do not exclude that Pritchard's reflection may reveal unexpected *potential* and lend itself to new interpretations. If not only religious matters but also nonreligious matters imply a-rational motivations an opportunity of arguing that there are deep affinities between religious and nonreligious beliefs may more effectively be regained. This is not surprising. The various attempts to minimize the distance between religious tenacity and ME, attempts that I have already considered, were based on the implicit conviction that the former should be adjusted to the latter. Pritchard's proposal, instead, offers such adjustment in the reverse direction. In this direction, Aquinas's views presented in Chapter 3 might already have offered significant suggestions. Thomas considers the possibility of continuing to reflect on something that denies previous convictions even if conclusive evidence in its support has been provided.[76] He mentions "the honor of God or the good of our neighbor" as motivations, which are *a-rational*, to continue reflecting although contrary evidentness has (even if mistakenly) already been provided. May such a-rational commitment to God and our neighbor, *or something analogous*, play a role – even only partly – in the epistemological discussion? May this reflection on the Christian faith promote a new consideration of how *any* type of belief is debated? May this lead us to propose a more comprehensive epistemological view in which to include ME? To respond to these questions, to which I will devote Part III of this book, I first have

---

[75] This is one of the various interpretations of Wittgenstein's hinges, on the nature of which a well-developed discussion is being conducted. For more on this, see Annalisa Coliva, "Which Hinge Epistemology?," *International Journal for the Study of Skepticism* 6/2–3 (2016), pp. 79–96, especially pp. 84ff.

[76] See *Summa theologiae*, II-II, q. 2, a. 9, ad 2. See also above, Chapter 3, note 103.

to consider the nature and purpose of debates in a new light. This is the aim of the next section.

4.3 Rethinking the Nature and Purpose of Debates for Both Believers and Unbelievers

I have focused so far on various perspectives that, more or less explicitly, minimize the difference between the religious and the nonreligious approach to rational debates and, with the exception of Pritchard's proposal, interpret the former from the viewpoint of the latter. That many scholars and streams of thought seek such minimization should not surprise. As Taylor has pointed out,

> the great invention of the West was that of an immanent order in Nature, whose working could be systematically understood and explained on its own terms, leaving open the question whether this whole order had a deeper significance, and whether, if it did, we should infer a transcendent Creator beyond it. This notion of the "immanent" involved denying – or at least isolating and problematizing – any form of interpenetration between the things of Nature, on one hand, and "the supernatural" on the other, be this understood in terms of the one transcendent God, or of Gods or spirits, or magic forces, or whatever.[77]

Unlike the perspectives I have taken into consideration so far, I intend to argue that the interpenetration between natural and supernatural mentioned by Taylor suggests a more profitable approach to rational debates.

In Chapter 3, I have shown that Christians are expected to conduct intellectual investigations bearing in mind aims that are not merely cognitive. The nature of their interest in such investigations should not be limited to the search for truth.

According to Stackhouse, the aim of the Christians who deal with epistemological matters is not "to provide assured knowledge on every subject for everyone"; God may in fact allow us "to believe things that are not true in order to make us most useful in his service."[78] (Note that this does not contradict Aquinas's view that reason, if appropriately employed, cannot contradict faith. In fact, we may use reason inappropriately, and this would make us believe things that are not true. Furthermore, this does not regard fundamental truths of faith such as God's existence and the lordship of Jesus, which the adopters of the view I advocate here are expected to firmly

---

[77] Taylor, *A Secular Age*, pp. 15f.
[78] Stackhouse, *Need to Know: Vocation as the Heart of Christian Epistemology*, p. 20, note 23.

accept as true. It is hard to see how denying them could make Christians more useful in God's service.) Christians are expected to develop "a vocational understanding of epistemology," which implies their active cooperation with God aimed at attaining the good:

> We cannot ... presume that practicing even the most responsible Christian epistemology guarantees epistemic success, if such success is understood in the normal sense of arriving at warranted truth. We can presume instead, however, that practicing responsible Christian thinking fulfills the will of God and thus corresponds to and cooperates with his overarching good plan for each of us and for the world. Like any other practice of the Christian life, therefore, Christian thinking is undertaken in faith that "God causes all things to work together for good to those who love God, to those who are called according to his purpose."[79]

Stackhouse appropriately quotes Romans 8:28 to emphasize that any action the Christians are expected to undertake, knowing process included, aims to accomplish the good, which is the goal God wishes them to achieve. For them, the good in question is union with God, which regards the whole of the human person[80] and her overall flourishing. According to Aquinas, as Stump points out, the union in question is the ultimate good and the ultimate flourishing of the human person.[81] This union is shown by the desire for what God desires: "God desires the good for all things, insofar as a human person desires the good for herself or for any other persons."[82]

Christians have traditionally emphasized the idea that only by pointing to the good itself, our overall flourishing is possible, and any other good can be satisfactorily achieved. As Lewis famously said, "you can't get second things by putting them first; you can get second things only by putting first things first."[83] This seems to remind us of Augustine's "law of love" (*regula dilectionis*). According to the author of *On Christian Doctrine*,

> no one ought to love even himself for his own sake, but for the sake of Him who is the true object of enjoyment. For a man is never in so good a state as when his whole life is a journey towards the unchangeable life, and his

---

[79] Ibid., p. 86.
[80] Clive S. Lewis perfectly summarized the impossibility for Christians to limit the relationship with God to only one aspect of their life: "If you are thinking of becoming a Christian, I warn you, you are embarking on something, which will take the whole of you" (Clive S. Lewis, *Mere Christianity* [New York: Macmillan, 1952], Bk. 3, Section 2).
[81] See Stump, *Wandering in Darkness*, p. 102. [82] Ibid., p. 100.
[83] As a result, "by valuing too highly a real, but subordinate good, we have come near to losing that good itself" (Clive S. Lewis, *God in the Dock: Essays on Theology and Ethics* [Grand Rapids, MI: Eerdmans, 1994], p. 280).

affections are entirely fixed upon that ... he is better when his mind is fully fixed upon, and his affections wrapped up in, the unchangeable good, than when he turns from that to enjoy even himself.... For this is the law of love (*regula dilectionis*) that has been laid down by Divine authority: "Thou shalt love thy neighbour as thyself"; but, "Thou shalt love God with all thy heart, and with all thy soul, and with all thy mind": so that you are to concentrate all your thoughts, your whole life, and your whole intelligence upon Him from whom you derive all that you bring.[84]

Christians are expected to pay special attention to the participation in God's love. A passage from the *Summa halensis* unsurprisingly reads that theology, which its authors see as the highest among the sciences, "perfects the soul by way of affection, moving it towards the good through the principles of fear and love."[85] Theology should be cultivated by way of love, as also Bonaventure points out: "The rightness of mind is rooted in love."[86] And elsewhere, he claims: "First, it must be said that devotion leads us to know what is true and beneficial.... God grants his gifts to all creatures, but he grants knowledge of true things only to those who act devoutly."[87] Note that this reference to the Franciscan theological and philosophical tradition does not imply any opposition to other Christian streams of thought, Thomism included. Of course, significant distinctions can be found between Franciscans and Dominicans;[88] however, I aim to argue that, beyond those differences, a priority ascribed to the good itself and the will over the truth and the intellect, respectively, should be seen as a sign of every Christian approach to the human experience. Chapter 3 was devoted precisely to arguing that Aquinas's thought is mainly characterized by the will to adhere to God's revelation, which God himself grants to

---

[84] Augustine, *On Christian Doctrine, in Four Books*, tr. by James F. Shaw (Grand Rapids, MI: Christian Classics Ethereal Library, 2005), I, xxii, 21 (www.ntslibrary.com/PDF%20Books/Augustine%20doctrine.pdf, accessed on August 2, 2021).

[85] Alexander of Hales et al., *Doctoris irrefragabilis Alexandri de Hales Ordinis minorum Summa theologica*, vol. 1, q. 1, c. 1.

[86] Bonaventure, *Commentaria in quattuor libros Sententiarum Magistri Petri Lombardi: in librum II*, d. 32, a. 3, q. 1, in *Opera Omnia* 1–4 (Quaracchi, Florence: Collegii S. Bonaventurae, 1885), my translation.

[87] Bonaventure, *Collationes de septem donis Spiritus Sancti*, collatio VIII, n. 5, in *Opera Omnia* 5 (Quaracchi, Florence: Collegii S. Bonaventurae, 1891), my translation.

[88] Such distinctions are of no interest for my purposes, except one aspect marked by Stump. She associates Aquinas and more generally Dominicans with an inclination to think that "knowledge about God, and thus knowledge about the ultimate foundation of reality, could be gotten best through philosophical and theological argument"; on the other hand, she argues that for Franciscans "a personal relationship to Christ or to Christ through relationship to Francis is at the core of the order's mission. According to (*typologically understood*) Franciscan views, then, the good life for human beings has as an essential ingredient living a life in personal connection to a personal God and manifesting that life to others" (Stump, *Wandering in Darkness*, p. 47).

believers. Believers think of God as the good itself and believe that his revelation is true because they have previously been granted love for him. This guides them in any activity they take, including the rational one, and not only when the subject is religion.

In this connection, it is worth referring to a passage that I have already cited and that is usually neglected by the existing literature.[89] In it, Aquinas shows that, while before evidentness, one cannot withhold assent; nonetheless, one *can decide* whether or not to reflect on something already known. Aquinas concludes that the reflection at stake "may be meritorious if it be referred to the end of charity, i.e., to the honor of God or the good of our neighbour." (It could be objected that a contradiction arises here with that which Aquinas says in the same article; namely, that the believer "has not, however, sufficient reason for scientific knowledge, hence he does not lose the merit." From this passage, it seems to follow that there cannot be merit in the case of demonstrative knowledge. However, it is easy to realize that, saying so, Aquinas is not referring to demonstrative knowledge in general, but only to *assent*, which he conceives as not being susceptible to merit or demerit.) Therefore, Aquinas argues that the believer should reason based on a *previous* decision, and emphasizes the connection between arguments, which are *rational motives*, and previous decisions, which are *a-rational commitments*.

Note that the passage under consideration offers thoughts on the epistemic nature of demonstrative knowledge that may also apply to non-believers. But let me proceed gradually to develop this important point.

I have so far focused on whether or not *believers*, while conducting their research, may appeal to factors that are not susceptible to rational treatment. I have concentrated on believers without considering the hypothesis that the same may be effectively explored concerning unbelievers. However, this choice was made because the believer openly refers to motivations that may not be epistemologically explicable, whereas the same cannot be said of unbelievers. *Qua* unbelievers, they traditionally see themselves as animated by reasons that, even if not conclusively demonstrable, can be rationally treated and explained. Nothing prevents them, however, from being animated by motivations nonsusceptible of a rational treatment also, motivations to which Aquinas's passage on assent and consideration seems to point. Aquinas claims that "scientific consideration may be meritorious *if* it be referred to the end of charity, i.e., to the honor of God or the good of our neighbor" (my emphasis). This seems to

---

[89] See *Summa theologiae*, II-II, q. 2, a. 9, ad 2. See also above, Chapter 3, note 103.

imply that the scientific consideration at stake may also be *non*meritorious. In that case, it would not be "referred to the end of charity." Instead, it would be guided by other motivations, which for Aquinas, we can imagine would not be commendable. We can also imagine that not only believers but also unbelievers might be guided by such motivations and might hold on to their belief against contrary evidence. In conclusion, not only believers but also unbelievers might stick to their belief, and their tenacity might be either meritorious (their reflection is aimed toward the good of the neighbor) or nonmeritorious (the reflection at stake is aimed toward something other than the good in question).

Note that this affinity between believers and unbelievers does *not* emerge from those attempts to minimize the gap between ME and the tenacity of the Christian faith that I have taken into consideration in the course of this chapter. Those attempts have been made by reducing the tenacity of religious belief to ME.[90] In contrast, the affinity here under consideration consists in the possession by both believers and unbelievers of *a-rational* commitments. These commitments are *unacceptable* from the viewpoint of ME, and require a different and more comprehensive version of this epistemology.

At any rate, referring to a-rational aspects of the intellectual activity and the role that, in Aquinas's words, the honor of God or the good of our neighbor may place in this activity should surprise only at first sight. Two suggestions emerging from epistemological debates can confirm this.

The first suggestion is put forward by Miriam S. McCormick. This author points out that both beliefs and actions are caused by agency, and that our doxastic practices have an unavoidable *practical* character: "If a world existed where true beliefs and knowledge ceased to be at all helpful in achieving one's goals they would cease to have value.... If we lived in a world where true beliefs had no benefits, then, in my view, a proposition being true would not count at all in favor of its being believed."[91] In other words, practical reasons, that is to say, the search for good and not simply for truth, seem to characterize any engagement in debates, by believers and unbelievers alike.

In this connection, it emerges the second suggestion, which is put forward in the introduction to a book that I have already cited, *Religious Faith and Intellectual Virtue*. Epistemologists have traditionally employed

---

[90] I am referring to those perspectives that I have considered above, in Section 4.2.
[91] Miriam McCormick, *Believing Against the Evidence: Agency and the Ethics of Belief* (New York: Routledge, 2015), p. 45.

words and concepts that apply to both epistemology and ethics, as I have already noted.[92] Epistemologists and ethicists "have both employed 'justified,' applying this to beliefs or acts respectively. They talk about what is 'permissible,' what does or doesn't violate 'rules,' what is or isn't under a person's control, what may or may not be his 'duty,' and what is 'good' or 'bad.'"[93] Considering the nature and aims of rational debates from the viewpoint of those who search for good should, therefore, be seen as necessary on the part of both believers and unbelievers.

In the following chapters, I will investigate how the search for good might relate to and shape rational investigations and debates. In this way, I will explore how exactly the spiritual turn occurs.

---

[92] See above, notes 9f.
[93] Callahan and O'Connor, "Introduction," in Callahan and O'Connor, eds., *Religious Faith and Intellectual Virtue*, p. 10.

PART III

The Spiritual Turn
Why and How to Take It

In this part, I focus on how the spiritual turn (ST) occurs, which is the core of the book's subject. This explains why this part is longer than the previous parts. Also, it explains why I provide it with a longer introduction than the previous parts and place a substantive conclusion at the end of both Chapters 5 and 6.

In the second part of this book, I have argued that the inconclusiveness of debates between unbelievers and believers is due to a-rational commitments. Believers often recognize that such commitments play a crucial role in any activity they engage in, including intellectual activities. Drawing from the Christian doctrine of faith and reason, especially Aquinas's, I have argued that for believers these commitments are grounded in their love for God, which – they believe – God himself grants to them. This love is proportionate to the firmness with which they believe, which means that the more the faithful love God, the more they sustain their faith.

From this follows that, if love for God is love for the good itself, as believers think, the firmness with which they maintain their faith is equally proportionate to their love for the good. As a result, the more they believe and search for further evidence in support of their faith, the more they should aim at doing good and loving their neighbor, including their interlocutors and/or competitors. (Note that I take *the act of doing good* as equivalent to *the good*. As Aquinas says, "the absolute good of man consists in good operation."[1])

Based on Aquinas's doctrine, analogous considerations might be advanced with regard to those who do not believe in God. It is true that they traditionally claim that they adopt a rational stance before religious

---

[1] *Summa theologiae*, I, q. 48, a. 6. In this connection, Aristotle argues that the good in question coincides with happiness, which is "something final and self-sufficient, and is the end *of action*" (Aristotle, *Nicomachean Ethics*, I, 1094 a 18–20 and 1097 b 21, tr. by William D. Ross, in *The Works of Aristotle*, revised by L. Brown [Oxford: Oxford University Press, 2009], my emphasis).

matters. From this follows that, unlike believers, they should be ready to change their mind if their own convictions are shown to be unreasonable. Nonetheless, there is no significant difference between the number of those who by way of study convert to religion and those who convert in reverse order. Also, as I have already shown while focusing on Aquinas's reflection on assent and consideration, the will, which by definition aims at what is believed to be good, plays a decisive role in everyone's research. Consequently, unbelievers, too, may conduct their intellectual investigations on the basis of a commitment to the good.

Conducting investigations on the basis of a commitment to the good is the ST that I intend to argue should be taken in epistemology. It is a turn from ME, according to which the intellectual activity must determine the nature of good and that only once this determination has been made can one proceed to do good.

Note that believers *qua* believers should not be mere epistemologists. Their religious view, at least as I take it here, is not consistent with ME. In contrast, unbelievers are expected to be mere epistemologists. It is customary for them to not believe divine revelation precisely because they have not (yet) found evidence in its support. They exclude from the outset any influence that non-epistemic factors such as a-rational commitments may previously exert on their epistemological conduct. In other words, they are expected to trust only reason, which means that they should rely on the outcomes of intellectual activity and change their mind only by accepting whatever evidence will emerge from debates.

In contrast, taking the ST means that, before launching any initiative, intellectual initiatives included, one is openly committed to the good and to those beliefs that the commitment in question involves. Therefore, this commitment is *a-rational*, since the idea of good that it presupposes has not been attained by way of rational research. (This means that a-rationality stands for a lack of justification, which is typical of those who have not [yet] engaged in debates. However, when one has already conducted rational investigations, a-rationality can still occur, because commitments and beliefs that seem to be too deep for a rational explanation can still show up.)

Two clarifications must now be advanced.

First, before the adopters of the ST can act on the good – so one may object – they presumably need some sort of understanding (with some sort of content) of the nature of the good. In reply, let me draw a distinction between knowledge or justified belief, on the one hand, and belief held *hesitantly*, on the other. On my view, the latter is acceptable, whereas the former is not. I mean that those who believe that evidence in support of a certain view of the nature of the good is necessary for them to do good are *mere epistemologists*. Consequently, their epistemic strategy suffers from the problems that I will show later affect ME. Instead, as I will also show, a reading of how one comes to the Christian faith such as Aquinas's offers a more promising view. Before receiving divine revelation, one can *believe hesitantly* that the good is so and so; this allows one to make sense of the content of divine revelation and to subsequently act in accordance with the view of the good that one will (in some cases firmly) accept from that revelation. (This seems to exclude unbelievers. How can they firmly adhere to the good and do good if they by definition reject the revelation in question? I will show that there are states of affairs and beliefs to which, in contemporary Western society, all seem to commit themselves, however convincing contrary evidence may seem to be.)

Second, shifting from the search for truth to the act of doing good does not mean that the ST is a *moral* turn. Instead, it is *spiritual*; that is to say, the good to do is taken as the ultimate perfection of the whole human person. (As I have already said in the Introduction, "spiritual" stands for this overall perfection, which is why it will not be taken as just "nonphysical" or "religious.") In this connection, note that the merely intellectual perfection requires sufficiently vividly cognitive faculties and the purpose of employing them as effectively as possible. The spiritual enhancement of the self requires much more. The perfection of the whole person involves their whole experience, including the relationship with other people. It often requires personal choices that, in the absence of the ST, one cannot or simply does not want to make.

Showing how the ST takes place and is beneficial to researchers and debaters is the subject of this part of the present book.

CHAPTER 5

The Spiritual Turn
Process and Some Benefits. Divine Hiddenness, No-Fault Unbelief, and Religious Diversity

In this chapter, I first explore the exact meaning of the relationship between the search for truth and the act of doing good, which is essential to understand the meaning of the ST. I then show some of the benefits that the ST can offer to debaters. To this end, I focus on two substantive subjects that have traditionally stimulated debates between believers and unbelievers, that is, the existence of God and the problem of religious diversity. I treat them by considering suggestions that emerge from the Christian tradition regarding the relationship between love and knowledge. While discussing the existence of God, I show that focusing on one's spiritual betterment, which is an indispensable aspect of the ST, prevents both believers and unbelievers from engaging in endless and sterile intellectual oppositions. Moving on to treating religious diversity, I dig into some aspects of Aquinas's reflection on faith and reason. This enables me to show that focusing on one's spiritual betterment puts believers in the best possible condition to employ reason, which is beneficial to researchers and debaters.

5.1 Doing Good *Shapes and Includes* the Search for Truth

How exactly does the ST in epistemology occur? Why should one shift from the search for truth to the act of doing good? What exactly does this shift mean? And which opportunities, if any, may it provide? I will devote this section to answering these questions. I will start my reflection by arguing that the act of doing good is the ultimate end of the search for truth, which means that the former *shapes and includes* the latter.

5.1.1 How Exactly the Act of Doing Good Can Be Related to That of Searching for Truth

An ultimate end implies, by definition, the existence of an intermediate end, where the former does not replace the latter. I take the good as the ultimate end of the search for truth, in the sense that the act of doing good includes the search for truth. The act of doing good, however, does not replace the search in question. If the latter disappeared, there would simply be no reason for us to conduct the present research, which concerns epistemology.

This can be explained by referring to Aquinas's doctrine of the relationship between the acts aimed at attaining some ends and the acts aimed at attaining related means or, which is the same, the acts aimed at attaining superordinate and subordinate ends, respectively. While referring to the second book of *Physics* by Aristotle, Aquinas says that "since every agent acts for an end . . . the principle of this motion lies in the end. And hence it is that the art which is concerned with the end, by its command moves the art which is concerned with the means; just as the 'art of sailing commands the art of shipbuilding' (Phys. ii, 2)."[1]

While treating charity and the ways it informs other virtues, Aquinas argues that a virtue that directs the acts of another virtue gives the form to the latter: "It is charity which directs the acts of all other virtues to the last end, and which, consequently, also gives the form to all other acts of virtue: and it is precisely in this sense that charity is called the form of the virtues."[2]

Someone may object that the search for truth, since it is expected to remain in itself an *intellectual* enterprise, must be separate from the good taken as its ultimate end. Let me respond in two ways. First, an act aimed at attaining a subordinate end does not lose its autonomy. The shipbuilder must put into practice the art of shipbuilding, which implies, among other things, a specific way to shape the various materials that are employed to build a ship. The act of the shipbuilder remains a work whose proper purpose is to build ships. In the case here under consideration, the search for truth remains an *intellectual* act, whose proper purpose is to attain *the truth*. Second, if this act is ultimately aimed at attaining a superordinate end, it cannot be consistently performed without aiming at the end in question. All of the shipbuilder's choices – which materials to employ, for example – inevitably involve the consideration of the ultimate end of her work, which is the act of sailing. When it comes to our case, this means that intellectual activity cannot be appropriately conducted if the agents do

---

[1] *Summa theologiae*, I-II, q. 9, a. 1.
[2] Ibid., II-II, q. 23, a. 8. Why the end gives the form is something Aquinas explains in the previous section of the same work: "Acts are called human, inasmuch as they proceed from a deliberate will. Now the object of the will is the good and the end. And hence it is clear that the principle of human acts, in so far as they are human, is the end" (ibid., I-II, q. 1, a. 3).

not primarily commit themselves to the good, which is the end of any activity they take.[3]

These considerations are of great interest to my argument, since they help us understand that taking the ST in epistemology, namely, carrying out the intellectual activity on the basis of a commitment to the good, does not mean that the aim of attaining the truth is put aside. On the contrary, aiming it at its ultimate end should perfect the knowing process, which would, in this way, be put in a condition to avert any departure from its natural path. If the truth is an intermediate end toward the good seen as the ultimate end, then any departure from the path to the good would involve a departure from the path to the truth. To be more explicit, any departure from doing good would imply a *mistake* from the epistemological viewpoint. This is why it can be said that the act of doing good *includes* that of searching for the truth.

Someone may object that it is in reverse order that the abovementioned relationship occurs. In other words, it is the search for truth that includes the act of doing good, and the latter would be aimed at the former. This is how virtue epistemology works. I will specifically consider some streams of it in the next chapter. For now, let me propose two general considerations.

First, everyone agrees that truth is something good, along with justice, generosity, honesty, and so on. This implies that the good in itself is more valuable than the mere truth, which is good only to the extent that it somewhat takes part in the good itself. As a result, it would be unwise to consider something more valuable (the good) a *means* to attain something less valuable (the truth).

Second, if the good in itself works to attain something good, a contradiction arises, because something that is good and is not the good in itself may oppose other equally good things, and this opposition would not be good. One commendably pursues the truth, and yet this pursuit involves much less commendable choices, such as robbing a bank to financially support one's scholarly research – in this case, the search for truth, which is something good, opposes the commandment that forbids robbery, a commandment that is also something good. As a result, truth, which is something good, gets into conflict with honesty, which is something good also. A memorable "thought" by Pascal makes precisely this point: "We make an idol of truth itself; for truth apart from charity is not God, but

---

[3] In this connection, Aquinas argues that an incomplete grasp of their final ends makes the practice of virtues not completely satisfactory. For more on this, see Chapter 6, note 107.

His image and idol, which we must neither love nor worship."[4] For Pascal, the truth may become an idol, whereas the same cannot be said of that which he considers the ultimate end, charity, which for him coincides with God. What can easily follow from this *pensée* is that truth, since it is something good and not the good itself, can be employed to do something that is not good, whereas the same cannot be said of charity. If charity were employed in a way that is not good (e.g., against other people), then it would simply cease to be charity.

Moreover, if one commits oneself to the good, which is the ultimate end of any action one can take, then any other action will spontaneously be conducted in accordance with its own nature, and will consequently be put in a condition to lead to success. Taking the ST, therefore, means that *the ultimate end must somewhat be attained before starting any possible action*, the intellectual one included. This is what I mean by saying that the commitment to the good *shapes and includes* the search for truth.

Before moving on to reflect on how doing good *shapes and includes* the search for truth, let me point out that my argument does not deny a classical view such as the doctrine of divine simplicity, according to which truth ultimately *coincides* with goodness. As Aquinas says,

> the true and the good, even though when considered in themselves are convertible as far as their supposits are concerned, differ in conception ... inasmuch as the intellect apprehends truth and anything contained in it, the true is a good; hence, the good is under the true; but inasmuch as the will moves, the true is under the good.[5]

Since I am focusing on the act of doing good and its consequences, that is, how the ST shapes the intellectual activity, it follows that here "the true is under the good." Note that elsewhere Aquinas makes this point even more clearly. According to him, "in the order of things desirable, good stands as the universal, and the true as the particular ... from the fact, then, that the true is a kind of good, it follows that the good is prior in the order of things desirable."[6]

5.1.2 Why Does the Question Emerge?

I intend now to elaborate on how doing good shapes and includes the search for truth. To this end, I will concentrate on the reason *why* to

---

[4] Blaise Pascal, *Pensées*, tr. by Alban J. Krielsheimer (New York: Penguin Books, 1995), L926/S755.
[5] Aquinas, *Commentary on the Letter of Saint Paul to the Hebrews*, tr. by Fabian Larcher, in *Opera Omnia: The Latin/English Edition of the Works of St. Thomas Aquinas* (Lander, WY: Aquinas Institute, 2012–), chapter 11, lectio 1, no. 554.
[6] *Summa theologiae*, I, q. 16, a. 4, ad 1.

proceed to such an inclusion. Focusing on the reason *why* to act in a certain way, in fact, offers insights into *the nature* of the act in question, as a long philosophical tradition teaches.⁷

As I have said throughout this book, the inclusion in question, which corresponds to the act of taking the ST, is suggested by the consideration of the inconclusiveness of debates about the truth of religion. Therefore, it may seem that the inconclusiveness at stake causes one to wonder whether or not a more efficient procedure could be found to attain conclusiveness. However, this would mean that the ST is adopted to primarily answer an epistemological question. In other words, focusing on the love for good would be aimed at a more effective search for truth, which I have already said is the approach adopted by some virtue epistemologists and not those who take the ST. Adopting the ST is due to other reasons. It aims to reaffirm an order among human activities, which traces back to the origins of the Christian tradition. This order does not emerge from the need to solve particular problems, such as those pertaining to epistemology. The order in question regards instead the more general problem of flourishing and making sense of human existence. Those who start from this viewpoint, once they are before epistemological issues, are not so much interested in solving such issues. Rather, they wonder how and why those issues should be of interest to them, given that their main concern is for their flourishing. (In this connection, not believing "too much," so to say, may be preferable to unshakable certainties, if lack of such certainties appears to be more helpful to attain one's flourishing. In this view, "the fundamental human problem is not ignorance, a deficiency in the intellect ... It is sin, a defect in the soul." Sin "corrupts the mind just as it corrupts the heart." Because of sin, "we tend to see what we *want* to see, to hear what we *want* to hear."⁸)

Christianity seems to offer an unmistakable picture of how all human activities should relate to the ultimate end of life, which for believers consists of experiencing communion with God.⁹ If God is charity, then

---

⁷ As is known, Aristotle inaugurated the study of the four causes, among which the final one is included, in order to better understand the being of everything. In the first book of his *Metaphysics*, Aristotle "shows why his predecessors could have answered their own questions better by recognizing the four causes" (Terence Irwin, *Aristotle's First Principles* [Oxford: Clarendon Press, 1988], p. 159). In his footsteps, Aquinas shows that it is the final end that gives the form to voluntary acts (see *Summa theologiae*, I-II, q. 9, a. 1. See also above, note 1).
⁸ Stackhouse, *Need to Know: Vocation as the Heart of Christian Epistemology*, p. 21.
⁹ A nonbeliever such as John Schellenberg rightly considers communion with God the highest possible good for humans, given God's existence. It is by focusing on this that he attempts to demonstrate that God does not exist. See below, Section 5.2.

communion with him coincides with the act of becoming charitable,[10] and nothing is worth pursuing and practicing apart from charity, as Paul claims in his hymn to charity.[11] In this view, charity is the end of any initiatives, which is why none of them can be perfected without aiming at charity. It does not follow, however, that those initiatives are *in themselves* deprived of value. On the contrary, if God is the all-powerful, omniscient, and perfectly loving creator of everything, whose becoming incarnate in Christ was aimed at redeeming everything, then everything he created, including our intellectual faculties, should be held in high esteem. The more such faculties are valued, the more are they employed in accordance with their origin and end. To put it otherwise, the more one esteems one's last end (i.e., communion with God), the more one is stimulated to employ one's faculties in the best possible way, which coincides with happiness. Doing the right thing at the right time, in fact, is that which brings with it happiness, because it allows us to achieve the end of action.

5.1.3 An Incidental Question: Is Prior Knowledge of the Ultimate End Paradoxical?

That which I have just said implies that no appropriate employment of created things occurs, and no related happiness is achieved, without previously recognizing their ultimate end. However, the fact that the ultimate end should already be recognized before conducting intellectual activity seems to be paradoxical. At the beginning of our philosophical tradition, Plato memorably dealt with this subject. He showed that, on closer inspection, the paradox is ascribable to the opposite conviction, namely, that we can search for something that we still do not know: "And how will you enquire, Socrates, into that which you do not know? What will you put forth as the subject of enquiry? And if you find what you want, how will you ever know that this is the thing which you did not know?"[12]

---

[10] "Beloved, let us love one another: for love is of God; and every one that loveth is begotten of God, and knoweth God" (1 John 4:7, ERV).
[11] "If I speak with the tongues of men and of angels, but have not love, I am become sounding brass, or a clanging cymbal. And if I have the gift of prophecy, and know all mysteries and all knowledge; and if I have all faith, so as to remove mountains, but have not love, I am nothing. And if I bestow all my goods to feed the poor, and if I give my body to be burned, but have not love, it profiteth me nothing" (1 Cor 13:1–3, ERV).
[12] Plato, *Meno*, 80 D, tr. by Benjamin Jowett, in *The Dialogues of Plato*.

There are disputes about how to interpret the various replies Plato offers to Meno's paradox. Gail Fine collects four of the main interpretative options. According to one of them, the dilemma in question can be solved because *not having knowledge* may simply mean *having true belief*, and having true belief requires the act of inquiring. According to another interpretation, which is more comprehensive, the dilemma is unsound because "it relies on a misguided 'all-or-nothing' model of knowledge," whereas "there are intermediate conditions – such as partial knowledge and true belief – that permit inquiry."[13] Michel Meyer proposed that if we consider the "problematological difference," that is, the difference between questions and answers, then the paradox disappears: "I know what I am looking for insofar it is a *question*, but at the same time I do not know it, *because* it is a question."[14] This seems to confirm that knowledge or at least some sort of understanding that lacks the status of knowledge needs to be present at the beginning of the knowing process, since no questions can emerge from total lack of knowledge.[15]

Various ways of putting this run through the history of philosophy. For Aristotle, not everything is demonstrable, which means that there are things we know immediately.[16] In the modern age, Thomas Reid has pointedly emphasized the importance of common sense knowledge, with which everyone is provided by nature.[17] Although from a different viewpoint, Georg W. F. Hegel, too, emphasized the contradictory attitude of those who do not recognize that, while they are preliminarily attempting to determine the method of knowledge, they are already putting into practice the method in question.[18] Still, from another philosophical perspective,

---

[13] Gail Fine, *The Possibility of Inquiry: Meno's Paradox from Socrates to Sextus* (New York: Oxford University Press, 2014), pp. 91f.
[14] Michel Meyer, *Of Problematology: Philosophy, Science, and Language*, tr. by David Jamison (Chicago, IL: University of Chicago Press, 1995), pp. 91f.
[15] In this connection, Newman argued that even doubt "is a positive state," which "involves a system of principles and doctrines all its own." See above, Chapter 4, note 72.
[16] Against those who "claim that it is possible to demonstrate everything, since they take circular and reciprocal demonstration to be possible," he replies that "not all knowledge, is demonstrative, and in fact knowledge of the immediate premises is indemonstrable. Indeed, it is evident that this must be so; for if we must know the prior things (i.e., those from which the demonstration is derived), and if eventually the regress stops, these immediate premises must be indemonstrable" (Aristotle, *Posterior Analytics*, 72 b 17–26, tr. by Terence Irwin and Gail Fine [Indianapolis, IN: Hackett Publishing Company, 1995]).
[17] See above, Chapter 2, notes 4f.
[18] As is known, Hegel rejects Kant's criticism according to which "we must know the faculty of knowledge before we can know." To Hegel, this is simply circular, "for to investigate the faculties of knowledge means to know them; but how we are to know without knowing, how we are to apprehend the truth before the truth, it is impossible to say." Then Hegel suggestively employs "the old story of the σχολαστικός who would not go into the water till he could swim" (Georg F. W.

Wittgenstein emphasized the hinge commitments, commitments that I have already shown he thought of as undeniable and presupposed to all of our beliefs.[19]

Therefore, from a philosophical viewpoint, it seems plausible that we can start reasoning from commitments, which we implicitly hold and cannot dispense with. We can somehow justify these commitments, as the abovementioned attempts to interpret Plato's reflection show. Things change if we shift from a merely intellectual experience, such as the philosophical one described by the author of *Meno*, to a religious one, in which a relationship with a supernatural being is involved. If a supernatural being exists, nothing impedes him or her from intervening in human experience in ways that we cannot justify. We may find ourselves with a-rational commitments and related beliefs, which may spur us to effectively conduct our intellectual investigations. We may be given a pre-comprehension of the ultimate end of our knowledge, which may improve the related knowing process. This, of course, is not susceptible of justification, and nonetheless from this it does not follow that it is implausible. I will call "supernaturalistic" the assumption that a supernatural being exists and intervenes in our experience.[20] Unlike this assumption, philosophical views should be able to somehow justify their points of departure, as occurs with the interpretations of *Meno*'s passage that I have mentioned above. And nonetheless, as I will show later in this chapter while reflecting on a "naturalistic assumption," this is not always the case. There are cases in which pre-comprehension or prejudice that do not seem to be susceptible to justification seem to heavily influence philosophical perspectives, and not only the religious ones.[21]

5.1.4 Turning Back to Inconclusiveness: For Believers, This Inconclusiveness Can Be a Sign of Spiritual Progress

The faithful believe that *qua* believers they are in possession of the ultimate truth by way of divine grace. Based on their faith, they have strong persuasions about the most fundamental questions, such as the meaning

---

Hegel, *Lectures on the History of Philosophy*, tr. by Elisabeth S. Haldane and Frances H. Simson [London: Routledge and Kegan Paul, 1955], vol. 3, p. 428).

[19] See above, Chapter 4, notes 69ff.
[20] I will deal with two assumptions – "supernaturalistic" and "naturalistic" – later in this chapter.
[21] Those who deny this are often "prejudiced against prejudice," as Hans G. Gadamer has famously argued. See Hans G. Gadamer, *Truth and Method*, 2nd ed., tr. by Joel Weinsheimer and Donald Marshall (London: Continuum, 1989), p. 273.

of life and human eternal destiny. They also believe that, while perfecting themselves religiously and spiritually, they can employ their intellectual faculties in accordance with their (intellectual faculties') nature. It follows – as they believe – that they will effectively develop rational inquiries and successfully uncover the truth, which it is their persuasion that cannot contradict their faith.[22]

Obviously, the faithful are expected to be satisfied with the fact that they possess the fundamental truths of life. Being aware of what the meaning of life consists of and attaining various related truths is of primary importance to them. Communion with God is their main interest, and it is the devotion to this primary end that should first and foremost interest them, not the attempt to increase their body of knowledge. This is shown by the fact that, among those who have faith, some know more details than others, and some of those who do not know many details, might believe with more devotion and firmness than those who know lots. The saints of Old Testament times had faith, and some a very firm faith, though revelation was still unfolding. A devout child, or "simple believer," might only be able to recite the Creed, but might well *believe* it much more firmly and devoutly than those who can give a lecture series on the development of the doctrine of the Trinity or of grace. Therefore, it is the complex of their fundamental beliefs and the firmness with which they are held that is expected to be of main interest to believers.

From this, however, it does not follow that knowing all the rest is of no importance. On the contrary, it is precisely because of their faith, according to which God has created everything for our sake, that believers should be interested in knowing everything is possible.

Among all of the possible questions they may want to ask themselves, there is the question of how to effectively conduct a rational investigation and to remedy the inconclusiveness here under consideration. The answer depends on the content at stake. On the one hand, inconclusiveness regarding the fundamental truths mentioned above, and the related a-rational commitments, cannot be an issue to believers. They consider it fully

---

[22] This emerges from Aquinas's thought, as I have shown in Chapter 3. However, it may easily be found in the thought of other outstanding representatives of the Christian tradition. For example, the first chapter of Anselm's *Proslogion* is a prayer, which the author says is *excitatio mentis* aimed at making humans know what in order to know they have been created (*"ad te videndum factus sum"*). This means that, *as believers*, they are put in the best possible condition to conduct research that, *as humans*, they are naturally led to conduct. Marilyn McCord Adams points out that, especially in his *Proslogion*, Anselm makes fully explicit the divine-human collaboration, which he sees as the basis of intellectual inquiry ("Anselm on Faith and Reason," in *The Cambridge Companion to Anselm*, ed. by Brian Davies and Brian Leftow [Cambridge: Cambridge University Press, 2004], pp. 36f.).

plausible and desirable to stick to such truths even against contrary evidence. On the other hand, when it comes to the rest of human knowledge, including beliefs that are more or less peripherally related to their faith, nothing makes the faithful sure that their investigation will always be consistent with the fundamental truths they already possess. They may be mistaken in regard to both the outcomes of their investigation and the will to stick to them.[23] Mainly, the more they love the fundamental truths, which they consider vital to them, the more they are expected to be aware of the possibility of falling into the mistake mentioned above. If sticking to those truths is due to their love for them as well as for God and their neighbor, then they are expected to scrupulously conduct any further investigation by constantly checking whether any step of this investigation is consistent with the fundamental truths in question.[24] Therefore, a deviation from effective research conduct should be seen as due to a deviation from love for God and the neighbor, whereas success in knowing should be seen as mainly due to their sticking to such a love. A radical difference, therefore, emerges between, on the one hand, sticking to God and his truth, and, on the other hand, sticking to one's own convictions and, what is more, to love for oneself.[25]

From this follows that believers are expected to be interested in remedying *a particular form* of inconclusiveness, and not inconclusiveness in itself. The inconclusiveness that they should remedy has to do with various subjects that are more or less close to the fundamental matters they deeply care about. The other form of inconclusiveness, which regards those fundamental matters, is instead indispensable for them. Actually, they are put in a condition to overcome the former kind of inconclusiveness only because they care about the latter. It is, in fact, only their firm adhesion to their fundamental beliefs, including the conviction that such beliefs are due to their love for God and the neighbor, that allow them to

---

[23] The fact that the faithful firmly hold the Christian beliefs does not exclude that the faithful in question may be wrong. See above, Chapter 3, note 30.

[24] Scrupulosity is for Aquinas one of the main characteristics of religion: "Religion would seem to take its name from reading over those things which belong to Divine worship because we ought frequently to ponder over such things in our hearts" (*Summa theologiae*, II-II, q. 81, a. 1).

[25] As is known, the opposition between love for God and self-love traces back at least to Augustine, who ascribes the "city of God" and that "of men," respectively, to these two kinds of love. Of course, Augustine is also aware that self-love, if taken in accordance with the nature of humans as creatures, does coincide with love for God. As a consequence, seemingly mutually incompatible sentences such as "the primal destruction of man was self-love," "there is no one who does not love himself," and "indeed you did not love yourself when you did not love the God who made you" can be found in his work, as Oliver O'Donovan has appropriately argued (see Oliver O'Donovan, *The Problem of Self-Love in St. Augustine* [New Haven, CT: Yale University Press, 1980], p. vii).

wonder whether or not their intellectual research is shaped by a love for God and the neighbor[26] and to reject the outcomes of the research which may be shaped by self-love and self-interest. In this connection, the inconclusiveness typical of believers can be seen as both *a problem and a solution*. It is a problem when it regards the fundamental truths and, strictly speaking, is a problem only to mere epistemologists. It becomes a solution when it regards the rest of knowledge, with respect to which one is put in the best possible condition to change one's mind. If one aims at promoting oneself spiritually, which means that one aims at freeing oneself from self-love, then one is ready to value one's interlocutors' views and frees oneself of those convictions that one may hold because of self-love.[27]

Therefore, the problem of inconclusiveness is for believers first and foremost *an opportunity* to reflect on their own spiritual progress, which they are expected to value incomparably more than conclusiveness.

If my argument is right, the question here under consideration emerges for believers to the extent that they take their spiritual progress seriously. Crucial to their life should only be their participation in the life of Christ. This communion with God, however, is to be experienced and reinforced *in action*. Among the various kinds of action, intellectual enterprises can be numbered. They can become a way for believers to test and, consequently, enhance their communion with God. This should result in an equally positive intellectual enhancement, which implies that inconclusiveness can, for some aspects, be overcome. And nonetheless this remains a secondary goal, whereas the primary goal will always be the believer's spiritual progress.

Stackhouse provides an interesting example of how believers are expected to relate these two goals to each other. Consider the case that "one's interpretation of Scripture seems to lead to beliefs or actions that do not square with what else one thinks one knows." A Christian believer "will then pray and particularly pray that God will direct her to whatever option will best advance God's purposes in the world." This means that "she will not pray primarily to come to a right conclusion. She may well pray for that – of course she should. But her primary prayer will be

---

[26] Not surprisingly, even some forms of secularism "can be seen as the upshot of distinctively religious convictions"(David Fergusson, *Faith and Its Critics: A Conversation* [Oxford: Oxford University Press, 2011], p. 9.).

[27] Aquinas argues that sin, which emerges from self-love and from lack of love for God and the neighbor, impedes one from satisfactorily employing one's intellectual faculties. See below, notes 129f.

vocational and missional, truly pragmatic."²⁸ (This should not confuse the reader. The fact that "she will not pray primarily to come to a right conclusion" refers to the complex of knowledge about which I am arguing that believers should be open to change their mind and search for conclusiveness. With regard to the fundamental beliefs, instead, it must be said that it is on their firm possession that believers can address God when they pray and entrust themselves to him.) The good in itself, which Christians identify with God, is the ultimate end to which the whole human life, including intellectual activity, should be aimed. As Augustine says, "man has no other reason for philosophizing than that he may be happy."²⁹

My references to various Christian thinkers across the centuries suggest that believers have always been expected to act in the way I have just described, and the ST is not a *new* method to engage in debates and related investigations. Thus, I speak of a "turn" only because the protagonists of philosophical and theological debates on the truth and credibility of the Christian faith are often *unaware* of the crucial role that a spiritual approach to those debates may play. A turn *from their explicit views* seems, therefore, necessary. Not surprisingly, I devoted Chapter 1 of this book to prominent Christian debaters who might have benefited from the spiritual approach in question and nonetheless did not point out its criticality. In Chapter 2, I treated Reid's approach, which partly betrays a form of awareness of the ST in epistemology. I finally focused on Aquinas's thought, in Chapter 3 and partly in Chapter 4, from which the ST seems to emerge quite clearly, though Aquinas does not explicitly formulate it either.

5.1.5 *For Unbelievers and Those Believers Who Are Mere Epistemologists, Inconclusiveness Is Not Expected to Stimulate Any Reflection*

I can now move on to consider nonbelievers as well as believers who act as *mere epistemologists* in debates related to faith and its credibility. Their intellectual activity does not aim at the abovementioned spiritual achievements, which implies that it is not shaped by a-rational commitments. Mere epistemologists intend to deal with any problem by way of reason alone. Of course, they may still want to search for good and pursue spiritual perfection. However, since they reject any pre-comprehension,

---

[28] Stackhouse, *Need to Know: Vocation as the Heart of Christian Epistemology*, p. 152.
[29] Augustine, *De civitate Dei*, xix, 1, tr. by Philip Schaff (Grand Rapids, MI: Christian Classics Ethereal Library, 1890).

they need to rely on mere reasoning to first understand how things are and then decide how to deal with them.³⁰

This attitude is exemplified by Descartes's famous choice to start from the beginning as if nothing were written before. On closer inspection, however, such a choice does not appear to be neutral. On the contrary, it was due to an impressive host of arguments, some of which ended up contradicting Descartes's choice. As is known, the author of the *Discourse on the Method* justified his decision to start any reflection anew from the beginning by claiming that, among all of the things he had studied, only doubts and errors emerged: "I found myself embarrassed with so many doubts and errors that it seemed to me that the effort to instruct myself did not affect other than the increasing discovery of my own ignorance."³¹ On the one hand, Descartes claimed that he could not firmly claim anything; on the other hand, he firmly claimed that a new method should be found to finally remedy the abovementioned doubts and errors. In this connection, Newman argued that Descartes's claim to generate a completely new philosophical method was utterly unjustified. For Newman, those who believe "that we have no right in philosophy to make any assumption whatever, and that we ought to begin with a universal doubt," do not realize that this "is of all assumptions the greatest."³² In a similar vein, Kerr has insightfully highlighted that aiming at being absolutely objective "brought with it the uncanny thought that the only perfect depiction of any reality would have to be from nobody's point of view – or, if there is any difference, from God's."³³

In the next chapter, I will assess to what extent those who explicitly declare that they only rely on natural reason may *implicitly* take the ST. After all, if ME falls into a self-referential contradiction, then their adopters can consistently conduct research only if they are not in line with ME, no matter if they are not aware of this.

---

³⁰ One may object that the principle of noncontradiction as well as beliefs such as that we have two hands are taken for granted and accepted *without any demonstration*. Even in this case, however, a form of evidence is expected to be provided. As is known, in the fourth book of *Metaphysics*, Aristotle offered a demonstration *ad hominem* to show that the principle of noncontradiction cannot be denied. Similarly, while focusing on the belief that we have two hands, Wittgenstein argues that there is *no evidence to deny* such a belief. If one denies that, one should also deny that one's sight functions appropriately, and should in turn end up doubting any other possible belief (see Wittgenstein, *On Certainty*, §250).
³¹ René Descartes, *Discourse on Method*, in *Discourse on Method and Meditations*, tr. by Elisabeth S. Haldane and George R. T. Ross (Mineola, NY: Dover Publications, 2003), Part I, p. 5.
³² Newman, GA, IX, 3, 2, 2, p. 294.
³³ Fergus Kerr, *Theology after Wittgenstein* (Oxford: Basil Blackwell, 1986), p. 24.

For now, I intend to point out that the question of whether or not inconclusiveness might stimulate a reflection that leads to the ST simply does not emerge on the side of mere epistemologists. It is true that inconclusiveness in itself should appear to be of interest to every philosopher. However, a philosopher who is a mere epistemologist typically ascribes it to a mistaken employment of reason, which consequently stimulates a search for remedies. This has been done throughout the history of epistemology. Philosophers have always engaged in more or less successful attempts to understand how people should reason to avoid mistakes and attain the truth. Especially from such thinkers as Locke and Spinoza and those later on, all of these attempts have been made from a viewpoint that the thinkers in question considered merely rational. The conviction, which no one has ever openly expressed, was formed that every subject matter, including the religious one, needed to be explored without considering the hypothesis that a supernatural being may exist and exert an influence on human life and understanding. Let me refer to this conviction as a "naturalistic assumption" (NA). Because of the NA, the idea that spiritual progress, taken as mainly due to the relationship with a supernatural and all-perfect being, should be seen as an aim that is already known and pursued before any process of knowledge starts has never been considered. I will call the assumption of this idea a "supernaturalistic assumption" (SA). Needless to say, the SA is seen as unacceptable by those accustomed to believing that the rational approach is the only way to attain the truth and eventually do good.

From this, it does not follow that they do not consider the role that spiritual regeneration may play in every human activity, including intellectual activities. They might be ready to believe that doing good constitutes both the aim and the promotion of knowledge. However, such supporters of reason alone would want to convince us that, before embracing any view of morality and spirituality, this view should be first assessed by way of reason. ("By way of reason" has a general meaning. It applies not only to knowledge properly said but also to justified beliefs, whose level of justification determines proportionally the firmness with which one commits oneself to the truth of certain propositions.) This is ME, which coincides with the NA when it comes to religion. (According to the NA, one first argues in support of the existence of a supernatural being and then believes in divine revelation. According to ME, one first understands what the good is, and then does good.) Among those who exerted great influence on modern thought, Locke held this view while arguing that one can believe in divine revelation if one has good arguments for stating that God authored such a revelation.³⁴ Analogously, Spinoza claimed that "love for God springs from knowledge of Him, and knowledge of Him should be derived from general ideas, in themselves certain and known."³⁵

Later in this book, I will focus on how those who *in principle* adhere to ME might *in practice* participate in the ST. But before I do that, I need to show how exactly the ST takes place. This can be explored mainly using believers' convictions – believers offer reflections that, more or less implicitly, contain the ST. I will consider two prominent topics in contemporary debates on religion. They are the existence of God, more precisely the idea that there may be nonresistant unbelievers, and the problem of religious diversity.

Before proceeding, let me note that, in the case of religious matters, the ST coincides with the SA. (As I have said above, an analogous relationship is between ME and the NA.) Adopting the SA means that one somewhat knows of God and proceeds to worship him before finding evidence in support of his existence and related beliefs. This cannot be said of unbelievers and those believers who stick to ME and the NA. They exclude from the outset the possibility to take the ST and making it a reality.³⁶

5.2 Reflecting on *No-Fault Unbelief* as an Opportunity of Spiritual Enhancement

An insightful strategy aimed at arguing that God does not exist has been proposed in the course of the last decades. I am referring to the so-called divine hiddenness problem and the related conviction that there are those whose unbelief is a "no-fault" one. The problem in question has matched the problem of evil as a prominent argument for atheism. Among the several versions that have been collected, the divine hiddenness argument (DHA) championed by Schellenberg³⁷ has often been seen as "the most widely discussed articulation of the problem."³⁸

---

[34] See *An Essay*, IV, xix, 10f. See also above, Chapter 1, note 8.
[35] Baruch Spinoza, *Tractatus theologico-politicus*, IV, 61, tr. by Robert H. M. Elwes (London: Bell, 1883).
[36] For believers this may be counterproductive. According to Michael Buckley, Christian response to the development of modern atheism, being exceedingly based on philosophical and scientific reasons, led to atheism's further development, which is why "atheism is essentially parasitic" and "depends upon theism for its vocabulary, for its meaning, and for the hypothesis it rejects" (Michael Buckley, *At the Origins of Modern Atheism* [New Haven, CT: Yale University Press, 1987], p. 15).
[37] See John Schellenberg, *Divine Hiddenness and Human Reason*, 2nd ed. (Ithaca, NY: Cornell University Press, 2006).
[38] Michael Rea, "Divine Hiddenness, Divine Silence," in *Philosophy of Religion: An Anthology*, ed. by Louis Pojman and Michael Rea (Boston: Wadsworth/Cengage, 2013), p. 275.

According to the DHA, if God exists, he would be an all-loving, all-powerful, and totally perfect being. Consequently, he would be able to grant us an opportunity to have a reciprocal relationship of love with him. (This would obviously be the greatest possible good for us, given the existence of such a perfect being.) To this end, God would make his existence so evident that there can be no reasonable or inculpable lack of belief in him.[39] However, belief in God's existence seems sometimes to be accompanied by reasonable doubt. According to the DHA, there are those who do not believe though they do not resist divine revelation. They are "inculpable," which implies that God is "culpable," because, though he is omnipotent and omniscient, he does not provide them with the opportunity to believe and consequently achieve the greatest possible good. If he exists, however, God is a perfectly good being; consequently, God does not exist. On Schellenberg's view, therefore, the lack of sufficient evidence – not only rational but also experiential – is, in itself, proof of God's nonexistence, although this has been acknowledged only in recent times.[40]

Some thinkers have opposed the DHA with numerous and intellectually penetrating reasons why God does not make his existence more evident.[41] Some have pointed out that God may ensure our happiness and ultimate well-being in a way that is, at first sight, incomprehensible to us. For Paul Moser and Daniel Howard-Snyder, for example, "the Jewish-Christian God hides at times for a range of reasons, not all of which seem clear to humans."[42]

Here I intend to focus on Schellenberg's proposal that there are reasonable and inculpable unbelievers (I call this view "no-fault unbelief," NFU). It frontally opposes the view, which believers have traditionally held, that unbelief is either unreasonable, because it is due to intellectual mistakes, or culpable, because is due to moral flaw (I call this view "fault unbelief," FU). In the footsteps of various Christian thinkers, I will focus on FU,

---

[39] Schellenberg refers to the evidence "sufficient" to believe. However, the notion of "sufficient," as he employs it, needs to be determined more precisely. On the one hand, it seems to correspond to "undeniable," because evidence that is not undeniable gives rise to doubt and, consequently, is expected to be refused by Schellenberg. On the other hand, Schellenberg states that he does not refer to "incontrovertible reasons" (see Schellenberg, *Divine Hiddenness and Human Reason*, pp. 212f.).

[40] See John Schellenberg, "Divine Hiddenness," in *A Companion to Philosophy of Religion*, ed. by Charles Taliaferro, Paul Draper, and Philip Quinn (Oxford: Blackwell, 2010), p. 509.

[41] See John Schellenberg, *The Hiddenness Argument: Philosophy's New Challenge to Belief in God* (Oxford: Oxford University Press, 2015), pp. 133–139, where an impressively long bibliography of what has been published on the DHA is provided.

[42] Daniel Howard-Snyder and Paul Moser, "Introduction," in *Divine Hiddenness: New Essays*, ed. by Daniel Howard-Snyder and Paul Moser (New York: Cambridge University Press, 2002), p. 2.

which only contributes to increase endless inconclusiveness and mutual opposition between debaters. I will then show that believers – and also unbelievers, although to a lesser extent – can avoid getting stuck in this opposition by shifting attention from their interlocutors to themselves and their own spiritual growth. This shift of attention can be seen as the first step for those who want to take the ST.

5.2.1 A Depiction of the FU, That Is, Unbelief Is Unreasonable and Culpable

Numerous examples of how unbelievers have throughout history been blamed for their unbelief quickly come to mind. Psalm 53 famously reads: "Fools say in their hearts, 'there is no God.' They are corrupt, they commit abominable acts; there is no one who does good."[43] Equally famously, St. Paul reproaches

> those who by their wickedness suppress the truth. For what can be known about God is plain to them, because God has shown it to them.... So they are without excuse; for though they knew God ... they exchanged the glory of the immortal God for images resembling a mortal human being or birds or four-footed animals or reptiles.[44]

Though less pointedly, all of the debates and arguments developed by great philosophers and theologians like Augustine, Anselm, and Aquinas in defense of the reasonableness of faith support the conviction that there is something morally and/or intellectually wrong with unbelievers. At the dawn of the modern age, Calvin manifestly accuses them of being mentally insane and morally corrupt. For him, all human beings, not only those who are able to develop sophisticated rational arguments, have been provided with a *sensus divinitatis*, which consequently renders them inexcusable if they do not believe: "This conviction, namely, that *there is some God*, is naturally inborn in all, and is fixed deep within, as it were in the very marrow."[45] If all have been provided by nature with the conviction at stake, God's existence and revelation can be denied only because of mental insanity or moral culpability. Following in the footsteps of Calvin, Plantinga has argued that sin and moral corruption can impede the correct functioning of cognitive faculties, and has proposed the concept of "warranted Christian belief." On the basis of this concept, it can be said that, if

---

[43] Psalm 53:1.   [44] Romans 1:18–23.
[45] Calvin, *Institutes of the Christian Religion*, Bk. 1, chapter 3, pp. 43f.

God exists, then it is highly probable that we all are provided with cognitive faculties able to lead us to believe in him. A considerable obstacle in this direction, however, is sin, which can deform the appropriate employment of our intellectual faculties: "Sin induces in us a *resistance* to the deliverances of the *sensus divinitatis*, muted as they are by the first factor; we don't *want* to pay attention to its deliverances."[46]

Those who – like Calvin and Plantinga – support the FU manifestly take for granted that God is a perfectly loving being. Accordingly, they believe that he cannot be faulted for permitting some to not believe and consequently to miss the opportunity to be related to him, which is the best possible good for humans, given his existence.[47] More pointedly, Aquinas claims that, if God grants us some good, this is due to his mercy; if he does not grant us anything, this is due to his justice.[48]

John Greco has proposed a new approach to this subject.[49] He argues that the traditional way to explain unbelief that constitutes the FU "looks for the explanation of non-belief only in the atheist." By contrast – so he maintains – the explanation at hand might also be found in the social environment and in believers themselves, that is to say, in the way their personal relationships and their communities may end up promoting nonbelief instead of belief.[50]

Unlike Greco, I do not intend to investigate any "social turn" in religious epistemology; like him, I assume that believers would do well to shift attention from unbelievers to themselves. This is the first step to take in the direction of the ST.

Taking the ST in epistemology, in fact, consists first and foremost in avoiding merely intellectual fights and in promoting the act of doing good. This means that one takes advantage of research and debates to reflect *on oneself* so as to see how to promote *one's own ability* to do good.

---

[46] Plantinga, *Warranted Christian Belief*, p. 205.
[47] Analogously, God cannot be faulted for lack of appropriate belief on the part of the faithful. In this connection, Moser distinguishes "people *passively* open to belief in God and people *actively* open to belief in God" (Paul Moser, "Cognitive Idolatry and Divine Hiding," in Howard-Snyder and Moser, eds., *Divine Hiddenness: New Essays*, pp. 142f.).
[48] See *Summa theologiae*, II-II, q. 2, a. 5, ad 1; Aquinas relies on Augustine's passages such as *De correptione et gratia*, 7, xiv.
[49] See John Greco, "No-Fault Atheism," in *Hidden Divinity and Religious Belief*, ed. by Adam Green and Eleonore Stump (Cambridge: Cambridge University Press, 2016), pp. 109–125. Greco employs the word "atheism," though he is well aware that not only atheists but also agnostics are involved in the discussion of the subject. However, he does not turn "flawed atheist response" into "flawed nonbeliever response" or "no-fault nonbelief," because the employment of nonbelief is "not nearly as catchy" (p. 109, note 2). Therefore, I am using "unbeliever" instead of "nonbeliever."
[50] See Greco, "No-Fault Atheism," p. 109.

Before the idea that unbelief can be held reasonably and/or inculpably, which implies God's blameworthiness, the believer who takes the ST does not simply espouse the FU. Of course, she firmly maintains her belief in God, since God for her is the good itself, and this can cause the FU. However, the believer will especially wonder how her will to do good and to love the neighbor, including the supporters of the NFU, can allow her to take advantage of the NFU in order to spiritually grow.

The same may be said of the unbelievers who support the NFU, though this similarity only applies if the NFU enables them to do good and to promote their own spirituality. This, however, does not emerge from Schellenberg's proposal, which limits itself to intellectual controversies aimed at showing that *others*, that is, God, are blameworthy. At any rate, I will show that, if supporters of the DHA and the NFU focused on their views while paying more attention to themselves than to others, significant consequences would follow in terms of progress in knowledge and spiritual betterment.

5.2.2 Unbelievers and the NFU

Let me start by noting that the assumption of the NFU is consistent with both

(1) there is no God

and

(2) there is a God who (at least in some cases) is responsible for religious unbelief.

Clearly enough, item (1) manifestly strengthens the idea that one cannot be charged with a cognitive deficiency or moral culpability if one does not believe. The same can be said of item (2). If, at least in some cases, God is responsible for religious unbelief, then there really are unbelievers who cannot be charged with either mental insanity or moral blameworthiness.

If we now consider (1) and (2) more closely, we may notice that both of them lead us to advance more remarkable insights. From (1) it follows that:

(1a) unbelievers can hold that there is moral and/or intellectual failure in believers.

On the other hand, (2) can be developed as follows:

(2a) there is a God who, since he (at least in some cases) is responsible for religious unbelief, *is evil*

or

(2b) there is a God who, though (at least in some cases) is responsible for religious unbelief, *is good*.

What is of interest for our purposes is that from (1) and (2a) it follows that unbelievers are entitled to hold that the believers, *qua* believers, suffer from moral and/or intellectual flaws. Only such flaws can explain belief in and reliance on a God who is evil, not to mention a God who simply does not exist. Unsurprisingly, accusations intended to highlight the flaws in question have regularly and frequently been voiced against believers over the last centuries. To name but a few, Hume, Freud, Russell, and, in our time, Harris have famously adopted this stance. Hume placed in the same boat "Stupidity, Christianity, and Ignorance" and saw all three as limits into which the English nation was "relapsing fast."[51] According to Freud, religion is a psychological disease, "the universal obsessional neurosis of humanity."[52] For Russell, religion originated in barbaric ages and "has been and still is the principal enemy of moral progress in the world." It is therefore "no wonder if cruelty and religion have gone hand in hand."[53] Finally, Harris seems to sum up all of these attacks on religion and especially to the Christian faith by saying that it is now necessary "to demolish the intellectual and moral pretensions of Christianity."[54]

The fact that unbelievers put themselves in a position to ascribe both intellectual and moral flaws to believers somewhat absolves the believers who do the same in the reverse direction from the accusation of being offensive. Or, more precisely, this fact leads to the awareness that this is the way both believers and unbelievers sometimes look at each other. (I say "sometimes" because I am aware that it may not apply to all cases. An unbeliever, for example, might depict religious belief not as blameworthy but as a quasi-natural disposition with some positive practical outcomes,

---

[51] David Hume, Letter 272 (April 6, 1765), in *The Letters of David Hume*, ed. by John Y. T. Greig (Oxford: Clarendon Press, 1932), vol. 1, p. 498.
[52] Sigmund Freud, *The Future of an Illusion*, tr. by James Strachey (London: Hogarth Press, 1927), p. 43.
[53] Bertrand Russell, "Why I Am Not a Christian," in *The Basic Writings of Bertrand Russell*, ed. by Robert E. Egner and Lester E. Denonn (London: Allen and Unwin, 1961), pp. 595f.
[54] Sam Harris, *Letter to a Christian Nation* (New York: Knopf, 2006), p. ix.

even though this results in false beliefs. The unbeliever in question may, therefore, look at belief without lapsing into a superior judgmentalism, though it cannot be excluded that also in this case a kind of intellectual failure may be ascribed to believers.)

This is an unexpected and significant outcome for unbelievers. The assumption of the NFU has been motivated by the impression that accusing unbelievers of being intellectually and/or morally disturbed is in some respect unacceptable. If the assumption in question leads unbelievers to employ the same attitude in the reverse direction, then nothing has changed, except the fact that now unbelievers, and not believers, are responsible for adopting a stance that is usually perceived to be offensive.

Needless to say, this outcome can be avoided by unbelievers if, instead of arguing for their nonculpability, which can also lead them to argue for the culpability of others, they look at themselves, promote self-criticism, and are not afraid of being blamed. This attitude, however, can only follow one's commitment to doing good, no matter what consequences, in terms of personal success, this may lead to. One, therefore, should stick to the commitment to spiritually perfecting oneself and to the related beliefs. Among these beliefs, it does not seem possible to include the one that God does not exist. This belief does not lead to one's spiritual perfection if, as it occurs with the DHA and the NFU, it is grounded in the conviction that the unbelievers are inculpable and reasonable, whereas God is culpable (and believers are unreasonable). I by no means claim that unbelievers cannot take the ST. Actually, in the next chapter I will argue how they can. What I mean, instead, is that they cannot take the ST as supporters of the DHA and the NFU.

Let me now consider (2b), from which follows that unbelievers are prevented from an opportunity to have a positive relationship with God. This positive relationship must be seen as the greatest possible good for humans to the extent that God exists and is good. Consequently, it seems that exclusion from communion with him through no fault of their own, together with lack of understanding of the reasons why this occurs, should cause unbelievers to suffer tremendously.

Since this view is the center of the DHA,[55] I will consider (2b) while focusing on the DHA. According to the DHA, as I said above, the

---

[55] For Howard-Snyder, Schellenberg's fundamental idea "is that if there is a God, there are no reasonable non-believers, or inculpable non-believers, or non-resistant non-believers (all of these terms have been used); but there are, and so there's no God" (Daniel Howard-Snyder, "Divine Openness and Creaturely Non-Resistant Non-Belief," in Green and Stump, eds., *Hidden Divinity and Religious Belief*, p. 126).

existence of people who, through no fault of their own are unable to believe in God and attain the good, demonstrates that God does not exist. An omnipotent and perfectly loving being, in fact, should not permit that his creatures miss their greatest good through no fault of their own.

Note that Schellenberg has recently pointed out that the employment of words such as "culpable" and "blameworthy" dates to the period when he began to develop the hiddenness argument. Further reflection led him to conclude that focusing on culpability and inculpability is a mistake.[56]

However, if the claim that God would be responsible for the failure of those who are nonresistant unbelievers becomes an argument for atheism, this is due to the fact that being responsible for unbelief is evil, which cannot be ascribed to God. As a result, those who are not responsible for their unbelief can appropriately be said to be "blameless" or "inculpable." (There is, furthermore, one more reason for looking at the employment of "inculpability" – as well as "reasonableness" – as totally appropriate to Schellenberg's argument. By having recourse to both adjectives, this argument can frontally oppose the FU.)

Let me now turn back to the suffering that should affect these people. Focusing on one's suffering reveals a shift of attention from others to oneself, which is possible to the extent that one takes the ST. I mean that, once demonstrated that God does not exist, the unbeliever who doesn't take into consideration the ST feels satisfied and doesn't need to continue reflecting on God's existence and communion with him. She has demonstrated that others are unreasonable and – if her atheism is based on the DHA – that God is culpable, whereas she is reasonable and inculpable. However, if she continues reflecting and wonders what, in terms of suffering, the outcome of her demonstration may cause, this reveals that her primary aim is not the mere attainment of the truth. On the contrary, this shows that she is primarily interested in the communion with God, the spiritual perfection it implies, and the tremendous suffering its absence may cause. Clearly, this is not the attitude that seems to characterize the supporters of the DHA and the NFU. Here I only intend to *hypothesize* what consequences for them may emerge if they shifted their attention from the DHA and the NFU to the ST.

The argument that these hypothetical supporters of the ST may present is short and straightforward. God, if he exists, is the maximally great good. As a consequence, the unbelievers in question are expected to suffer because of their nonbelief, which prevents them from thriving. If they

---

[56] See Schellenberg, *The Hiddenness Argument*, pp. 54f.

suffer, however, they cannot consider themselves unbelievers. One cannot suffer from not having been given a certain good if one believes that the good in question has never existed. On the other hand, if they do not suffer, and do not believe that an opportunity of flourishing has been denied to them, they cannot consider God blameworthy (and this means that they cannot conclude that there is no God).

Two noticeable objections, however, can be raised against this argument.

First, one may suffer from one's lack of belief in God and at the same time may not believe in God's existence. It seems that there are numerous ways in which people can and do hold religious belief to be good, even very good, while they themselves do not believe that God exists. There are the cases of nonbelievers who admire greatly the service commitment shown by and the sense of peace exhibited by religious believers. Some would like to be believers, but they just cannot quite seem to achieve the state, even though they have attempted by promoting many spiritual practices for years. Thus, they don't believe that God exists and nevertheless find the belief in him extremely desirable. As a result, the argument that one cannot suffer from a lack of belief in God if one does not believe that God exists fails.

In reply, let me notice that, according to this objection, the unbelievers in question find the belief in God extremely desirable because they see extremely desirable dispositions and actions that *some* believers hold and perform, respectively. These unbelievers, however, are likely to also ascribe noncommendable qualities and reprehensible actions to *other* believers. Without going too far back in history, recent scandals – for example, the ones related to sex-abused children by some clerics –testify that those who are (or at least declare to be) believers do not necessarily exhibit admirable commitments to doing good individually as well as socially. Furthermore, unbelievers tend more often than not to *accuse* believers of not being coherent with the high spiritual and moral teaching that they – the believers – declare to follow. Not surprisingly, such a lack of coherence is frequently included by unbelievers among the reasons that prevent them from believing.[57] As a consequence, the unbelievers in question do not have sufficient evidence to attribute *to the belief in God* the commitment to the good that some believers exhibit and that they – the unbelievers – admire.

---

[57] See above, notes 51ff., especially note 53, where I cite Russell and his work eloquently titled "Why I Am Not a Christian."

As a counter-reply, one may still claim that the unbelievers here under consideration do not admire some dispositions and attitudes that some believers show. Rather, they admire *the religious belief in itself*. In this way, my response that believers may act not only admirably but also deplorably would appear to be neutralized, because our unbelievers look at the belief in itself, not at the believers.

In response, I notice that, at least in the case of the Christian belief, it is hard for unbelievers to say in what exactly the belief in question consists. Believers simply defer to sources of authoritative teaching – first of all, the Bible or, more precisely, those books that the denominations to which they adhere authoritatively consider part of the Bible – and are ready to see as Christian belief that which those sources define as such.[58] Nothing comparable can be said of unbelievers. They may enthusiastically adhere to some aspects of the belief in question – for example, the equal dignity of all human beings – and may equally strongly reject others such as authority and obedience, to which especially some denominations – for example, Catholicism – ascribe a crucial role in the life of the believers.

The second objection I intend to consider runs as follows: one *may not suffer* from lack of belief in God, and nonetheless such a lack is something evil if God exists. My friend Marc, for example, has never been a believer. He does not even conceive of what religious belief is and what benefits the relationship with God may bring with it. He, therefore, does not suffer from not being a believer, though it remains true that, if God exists, there are goods whose lack in his life is an evil that God should not permit.

Before replying to this objection, it should be said that, in line with it, Schellenberg agrees that hiddenness need not (and often does not) cause any subjectively experienced suffering on the part of unbelievers. But he thinks that this in no way weakens the DHA and that to think otherwise may be to confuse the DHA with the problem of suffering. Therefore, such a confusion should accurately be avoided, as Schellenberg has argued in several places.[59] The DHA does not seem to have any direct bearing on issues of suffering. There seem to be possible worlds in which the problem

---

[58] For Aquinas, "as regards the primary points of articles of faith, man *is bound* to believe them." In regard to the other points of faith, "man is not bound to believe them explicitly, but only implicitly, or to be *ready to believe* them, in so far as he is prepared to believe *whatever is contained in the Divine Scriptures*. Then alone is he bound to believe such things explicitly, when it is clear to him that they are *contained in the doctrine of faith*" (*Summa theologiae*, II-II, q. 2, a. 5, my emphasis).

[59] He argues that, although various interesting relations can be seen between the hiddenness problem and the problem of evil, "none suggests that the former ... is subsumable under the latter" (John Schellenberg, "The Hiddenness Problem and the Problem of Evil," *Faith and Philosophy* 27 [2010], p. 60).

of divine hiddenness is a good argument for atheism but not the problem of evil, and vice versa.

The objection under consideration is precisely aimed at showing that the DHA cannot be confused with the problem of suffering. As has been said, for Schellenberg, according to Veronika Weidner, "there is at least one type of nonbelief which clearly does not involve any form of pain or suffering. Here Schellenberg is thinking of a so-called isolated nontheist who has never mentally engaged with or heard of the idea of God."[60] Marc is expected to exemplify this kind of nontheist.

Let me distinguish between what can be said from the viewpoint of the unbeliever – Marc – and that which an external observer can say. Marc is not aware of what he could enjoy had he a relationship with God. As a consequence, he has no reason for suffering and for blaming God.

It may be objected that, on closer inspection, he does suffer, in the sense that he suffers "implicitly." In other words, while some goods are in fact available, Marc has not had an opportunity to enjoy them. His implicit suffering is therefore a form of deprivation, regardless of the fact that he is unaware of it.

A reply should point out that the concept of "implicit suffering" seems a bit arbitrary. According to the *Merriam-Webster Dictionary*, the concept of suffering "implies conscious endurance of pain or distress."[61]

For the sake of argument, however, I accept the idea that Marc suffers implicitly. I am interested in arguing that the evil, which may make Marc suffer, can only be seen *by an external observer*. And saying that Marc suffers "implicitly" is equivalent to saying that he is *unaware* of the fact that something good, which he might have enjoyed, was denied to him. It is only from the observer's viewpoint, therefore, that what occurs to Marc can be said to be evil.

The observer in question, however, can consider Marc's lack of religious belief a form of unfair deprivation only on the basis of the belief that God exists. Let me remind the reader of the objection here under consideration that Marc may not suffer (explicitly) for his lack of religious belief, and nonetheless such condition remains a deprivation that God, *if he exists*, should not permit. In other words, only if God exists it makes sense to say that the condition in question is a deprivation.

---

[60] Veronika Weidner, *Examining Schellenberg's Hiddenness Argument* (London: Palgrave Macmillan, 2018), p. 86.
[61] See www.merriam-webster.com/dictionary/suffering, accessed July 25, 2019.

What I have just argued is grounded precisely in the DHA, according to which it is God's existence that renders the lack of religious belief a form of evil. Since God cannot be culpable for this evil – so the DHA runs – then God does not exist, from which also follows that the evil in question disappears, or, more clearly, what was considered evil in conjunction with God's existence can no longer be seen as evil. The conclusion of the DHA is that God does not exist, from which follows that the lack in question can no longer be seen as a form of deprivation. Therefore, the objection here under consideration falls into contradiction. If God does not exist, it cannot be said that those who do not believe in him suffer, even only implicitly, from a form of deprivation.

The subject of this section shows the benefits that supporters of the DHA and the NFU can achieve once they *abandon their stance* and take the ST, the first step of which consists in shifting one's attention from others to oneself. Those who explore their own views, perhaps blaming themselves for adopting such views, reveal a disposition to do good and to change themselves rather than others. They do not focus on the failure of their interlocutors or even on the failure of God, as happens to DHA's adopters. They focus on themselves to see whether or not they are faithful to their commitment to the good. In other words, they do not seem so much interested in understanding and solving *the issues* they explore. Rather, they want to understand if and how the issues in question are of interest *to them*. Do they suffer because of those issues? Are they impeded from committing themselves to the good? This shows that they are interested in their overall flourishing, and not in the mere progress in knowledge. As I have shown so far, while focusing on themselves, those who previously adopted the DHA and the NFU may become aware that they either are believers or, being unbelievers, do not have any reason for proposing the DHA and the NFU. In both cases, spiritual betterment may likely follow. First, if the former proponent of the DHA and the NFU sees that she, too, is a believer, then she is led to change the way she previously looked at believers. Instead of blaming them and focusing on their failures, she is expected to employ good habits, especially docility,[62] and to be disposed to value believers' views. In the same vein, she may likely be put in a condition to take seriously the views of those who, unlike her, continue to support the DHA. Once become aware that she is a believer, she should start valuing religious belief and communion with God and the neighbor; consequently, she may feel compassion toward those who, unlike her, are still

---

[62] For more on the virtue of docility, as Aquinas treats it, see below, notes 111f.

unable to benefit from that belief and related communion. Second, if the former proponent of the DHA and the NFU is aware that she does not have any reason for blaming God, then she will likely stop assuming a judgmental attitude toward God and the faithful. If she does not suffer from unbelief, then they will no longer appear to her as insensitive to her suffering – whereas they should appear so to the extent that they believe in an omnipotent, omniscient, and perfectly loving God who seems to allow people like her to suffer from unbelief. Consequently, while debating with those believers, she can assume a more friendly attitude toward them and develop good habits.

One clarification and one objection are now in place. The clarification regards the fact that the unbelievers here under consideration reveal a disposition to do good, although it is unclear to what this disposition is due. Did they reason to see in what exactly this disposition consists? And what philosophical view allowed them to achieve this outcome? Is it possible that various philosophical views may create confusion regarding the nature of the good and the related assumption of good habits? In reply, let me point out that in the contemporary Western society there are beliefs such as the equal fundamental dignity of all human beings and the unacceptability of discriminations, especially racism, to which all seem to a-rationally commit themselves. This means that it is possible for unbelievers to share in such (widely accepted) commitments to the good. At the same time, it should be acknowledged that believers seem to show an advantage over unbelievers, because those who believe in God possess a well-established and detailed view of how to do good, a view that they believe has been bestowed on them because of their readiness to commit themselves to God. This allows them to judge themselves and ask themselves whether they are faithful to their commitment to such a good. Consequently, their commitment to God and the good is enough for them to see what habits to develop with the aim of doing good.

Let me now deal with the objection mentioned above. It seems that it is the believer, and not the former supporter of the DHA and the NFU, who develops researches such as the one I have conducted so far. If so, the believer seems to conduct this research with the aim of showing that both DHA and NFU are wrong. Consequently, she may consider herself the winner of the dispute, and this would contradict the adoption of the ST, which is primarily aimed at one's spiritual betterment. However, showing what may occur if the supporters of the DHA and the NFU abandon their stance and focus on themselves instead of blaming others is not that which the believer who takes the ST is expected to do. According to the ST, the believers, like the unbelievers, have to focus *on themselves*. Showing what may occur to the former supporters of the DHA and the NFU is instead an initiative of mine, which is a hypothesis aimed at reflecting on the benefits that they may receive from taking the ST.

5.2.3 Believers Who Take the ST before the NFU

I have already shown that those who adopt the DHA and the NFU do not seem to be in a condition to take the ST. I have so far described a hypothesis, which I wanted to advance only to show the fruitful consequences that would follow in case the proponents of the DHA and the NFU abandoned their stance and took the first step in the direction of the ST. By contrast, the believers naturally find themselves with many reasons for taking the ST, which more or less implicitly characterize religious traditions, especially the Christian one. In this section, I will show how, on the basis of suggestions emerging from this tradition, the believers can make the ST a reality. In regard to the DHA, this consists in taking seriously the NFU and wondering whether the believers, and not the unbelievers, really believe in God and do good in full compliance with their faith. In other words, they focus on themselves to understand whether their attitudes and choices are consistent with their commitment to the good.

Let me start by saying that, of the consequences that follow the assumption of the NFU, believers can only accept (2b). In fact, (1) and – at least from the point of view of the theistic world religions – (2a) are incompatible with religious belief. (It is true that [2b], too, is somewhat incompatible with Judaism, Christianity, and Islam, or at least with their main branches. However, [2b] follows from combining theism and the assumption of the NFU. I assume [2b] for my purposes and not because I see it as entirely compatible with the religious views mentioned above.)

While assuming (2b), the faithful are led to take into consideration a worthwhile aspect of their religious experience. It is part of their belief – especially the Christian one – that only rarely do they find themselves satisfactorily provided with the positive relationship and the communion with God that I have mentioned in the previous section. In the Gospel according to Luke, "the apostles said to the Lord, 'Increase our faith!,'"[63] which is a clear indication of their awareness that, however close to him

---

[63] Luke 17:5.

they might have been, they needed to move on to a more satisfactory level of communion. Augustine consecrates himself to God by proclaiming: "I love Thee alone, Thee alone follow, Thee alone seek, Thee alone I am ready to serve." Nonetheless, in the same passage, he also addresses this prayer to God: "Increase my faith, increase my hope, increase my charity."[64] Kierkegaard says to the Christian who practices the sacraments: "You have come here today because you feel drawn to him, but from this it does not follow that you dare to think that he has already drawn you *wholly* to himself." Kierkegaard then concludes by quoting the passage of the Gospel I have mentioned above: "Lord, increase my faith."[65] Aquinas proposes penetrating thoughts on this point while reflecting on religious devotion, which he defines as "the will to give oneself readily to things concerning the service of God."[66] Thomas wonders whether or not this fundamental religious act causes joy in the devotees.[67] In a nutshell, his answer is that, though devotion causes joy because the act of giving oneself to God cannot but produce joy, it also "causes a certain sorrow." In fact – Aquinas goes on to argue – if we consider God's goodness, then we see that those "who do not yet enjoy God fully" suffer from this. If we consider one's own failings, then again we see that one is led to suffer from lack of communion with God. (Note that in the first case Aquinas refers to "those who do not yet enjoy God fully" [*in his qui nondum plene Deo fruuntur*], as if he, Aquinas, was not associable with them. In the other case, instead, Aquinas seems to refer to everyone, including himself, and says: "When one thinks over one's own failings" [*...recogitando proprios defectus*]. It is plausible to hold that in both cases Aquinas includes himself among those who have not yet achieved full communion with God.)

The communion at stake would certainly allow the believers to attain incomparably valuable benefits of any sort. As Schellenberg says, "to be personally related to unsurpassable goodness is a great good in itself."[68] Besides, this would make available ethical benefits, that is, "certain resources for dealing with the moral weakness endemic to humanity."[69] Consequently, believers, and not only unbelievers, as it may seem to be reasonable at first sight, are expected to suffer because of a lack of appropriate communion with God.

---

[64] Augustine, *The Soliloquies* (Boston: Little, Brown, 1910), vol. 1, 1:5.
[65] Sören Kierkegaard, *Practice in Christianity*, ed. by Howard V. Hong and Edna H. Hong (Princeton, NJ: Princeton University Press, 1991), p. 156.
[66] *Summa theologiae*, II-II, q. 82, a. 1.   [67] See ibid., II-II, q. 82, a. 4.
[68] Schellenberg *Divine Hiddenness and Human Reason*, p. 21.   [69] Ibid., p. 18.

It may be objected that this is only a peripheral problem for believers, since lack of full communion with God is expected to concern just those faithful who are equally peripherally involved in religious experience. Those who more passionately devote themselves to God, on the contrary, should not be affected by the problem in question.

In response, it must be noticed that, at least in respect to the Christian faith, the more the believers have faith and adhere to revelation, the more they are expected to ask God to increase their faith. I have already mentioned some passages from various authors that may contribute to support this thesis. Furthermore, I have referred to Aquinas's reflection about the fact that people experience faith at different levels of intensity. This implies the idea that faith in God and love for him are proportionate to a desire to adhere more strictly to his revelation. For Aquinas it is the love for God, which God himself grants to believers, that is not possessed by faithful in equal degree. The more they love God, the more they are ready to believe what he has revealed and to argue in support of such a revelation. Obviously, one who is ready to believe and to reason is also aware of one's need to believe and reason. Therefore, readiness and need to believe are directly proportionate to one another. (This may be echoed in the Gospel according to Luke, where it reads, "from everyone to whom much has been given, much will be required; and from the one to whom much has been entrusted, even more will be demanded."[70])

If my argument is correct, it can be said that from Aquinas's reflection on the different levels of faith it follows that the suffering of the believers is to be considered proportionate to the intensity of their faith. In other words, the more one believes, the bigger is the void one feels the need to fulfill. As a result, the more one believes, the more one wishes to increase one's faith.

This may be confirmed on biblical grounds. Jesus says: "Whoever wishes to become great among you must be your servant,"[71] and, while echoing him, Paul says to the Philippians: "In humility regard others as better than yourselves."[72] This may be explained by saying that the more one loves God, the more is one inspired by love for others, which causes one to value them in a directly proportional way. On the other hand, those who are inspired by such a love should value themselves in an inversely proportional way, because the more one wishes something, the more one feels to be in need of it. If the thing one feels the need of achieving is love for others, then one finds oneself unable to love, however

---

[70] Luke 12:48b. [71] Mark 10:43. [72] Phil 2:3.

exaggerated this impression may seem to be to others. From this, Paul's warning may follow: "If you think you are standing, watch out that you do not fall."[73] In other words, those who cultivate their belief in God should be constantly concerned about their own insufficient level of faith. (This does not mean that faith only causes suffering. According to Aquinas, as I have already shown, the suffering due to the fact that these believers are aware of their defects is proportionate to the joy they experience to the extent that they are sure that God's mercy overcomes their defects. Therefore, being close to him causes more joy than suffering.)

In conclusion, those who take the ST in epistemology are expected to focus on their spiritual life and the wish to increase its level of intensity. The mere opposition of arguments between them and those who oppose their views only leads to inconclusiveness. Both the DHA and the NFU, on the one hand, and, on the other, the FU are representative of this attitude. It is true that, unlike the FU, the DHA and the NFU do not openly blame those who support other views. On the contrary, Schellenberg seems to limit himself to emphasizing the fact that unbelievers may in some cases be nonresistant, reasonable, and inculpable. It remains true, however, that, according to the DHA, the culpability for some forms of unbelief is ascribed to God, whereas no failures ascribable to unbelievers are taken into account. By contrast, taking the ST requires debaters to shift attention from others to themselves because no spiritual growth is possible without taking this step. In this section, I have argued that, once this step is taken before the DHA, the believer and – at least hypothetically – the supporter of the DHA and the NFU can see the DHA as an opportunity to promote their spiritual growth.

I intend now to treat the problem of religious diversity to show how exactly the spiritual growth in question can play a role in epistemology.

5.3 Religious Diversity, Spiritual Progress, and Epistemological Advancement

As is known, religious diversity became a substantive problem for the truth of the Christian religion in the modern age. Animosity and wars among Christians led eventually to the persuasion that a peaceful, tolerant, and respectful coexistence among religions is incompatible with the conviction that one's religion is true. Let me call such a persuasion the "incompatibility problem" (IP).

---

[73] 1 Cor 10:12.

The IP's first expression may be found in Locke's first *Letter Concerning Toleration* (1689). In it, Locke focused on the conflicts and wars that plagued Europe in his time, which were often related to religious intolerance. Locke noted how this was in contradiction with the basic message of peace conveyed by the Gospel. He identified tolerance with "the chief characteristic mark of the true Church"[74] and Christianity with "the most modest and peaceable religion that ever was."[75] Some decades later, Hume concentrated on the relationship between religions and peace. Unlike Locke, he criticized the conviction that only one religion is true. In his *Natural History of Religion* (1755), he argued that from the conviction that only one religion is true inevitably followed conflicts and violence:

> While one sole object of devotion is acknowledged, the worship of other deities is regarded as absurd and impious. Nay, this unity of object seems naturally to require the unity of faith and ceremonies, and furnishes designing men with a pretence for representing their adversaries as profane, and the objects of divine as well as human vengeance.[76]

Hume's conviction has come down to the present times.[77] Thinkers such as Philip Quinn claim that, if believers do not support the superiority of their religion over other religious perspectives, then they will be more tolerant toward those perspectives.[78] Similarly, Robert McKim notes that, confronting religious diversity, one should be open to accepting the hypothesis "that the position one had thought to be correct may be wrong," and that "one of the other positions may be right."[79] In other words, giving up the conviction that only one religion is true would solve IP. It would promote a more inclusive society, based on diversity of opinion.

---

[74] John Locke, *A Letter Concerning Toleration*, tr. by William Popple (Indianapolis, IN: Bobbs-Merrill, 1950), p. 1.
[75] Ibid., p. 11.
[76] David Hume, *The Natural History of Religion*, ed. by H. Root (Stanford, CA: Stanford University Press, 1956), p. ix.
[77] See, for example, Jan Assmann's *The Price of Monotheism*, tr. by Robert Savage (Stanford, CA: Stanford University Press, 2010). According to this famous Egyptologist, religious violence, including among the practitioners of various monotheisms, is grounded in the Mosaic exclusive monotheism. Assmann contrasts monotheism with ancient polytheism, which he finds intrinsically ready to accept otherness.
[78] See Philip Quinn, "Religious Diversity and Religious Toleration," *International Journal for Philosophy of Religion* 50 (2001), pp. 57–80; "Epistemology in Philosophy of Religion," in *The Oxford Handbook on Epistemology*, ed. by Paul Moser (Oxford: Oxford University Press, 2002), pp. 533–537.
[79] Robert McKim, *Religious Ambiguity and Religious Diversity* (Oxford: Oxford University Press, 2001), pp. 154f.

I intend to argue that the IP is the result of what I call a "naturalistic assumption" (NA). Starting with this assumption, religious beliefs and faiths are explored intellectually as if they did not involve any reference to a supernatural being and his revelation. This is confirmed by the fact that the methodology employed by those who hold the IP applies indifferently to religious experience and other experience as well. My thesis is that, when it comes to religious matters, the NA should be abandoned and replaced by a "supernaturalistic assumption" (SA), which is nothing but the ST, once it comes to religion. Assuming the existence of a supernatural being who reveals himself to us and takes part in our religious experience may help us reconcile the two poles of IP. In other words, the SA may promote respect and peace among religions and, at the same time, a firm belief that only one of them is true.

5.3.1 *The IP Implies the NA: Hick's Reasons for Religious Pluralism*

If the IP applies to the religious realm as well as to traditions, cultures, philosophies, and so on, then the IP grounds in the NA, or, put otherwise, it does not take into consideration the SA.

The fact that the IP does not apply only to the religious realm can be demonstrated by taking into consideration the three reasons that Hick – one of the most representative proponents of the IP – brings forth in support of his famous theory of religious pluralism.[80] The first reason is grounded in the idea that all of the world's religions are "transformational"; namely, they provide their followers with "transformation from self-centeredness to Reality-centeredness."[81] This transformation makes them morally better, because they are no longer interested in their individual salvation (as if religion dealt with acquiring a "ticket" to eternal life), but aim to liberate themselves from their desires and to orient their existence around the divine. The normative core of religion is to be transformational, and all major religions can equally be considered salvific. (I have just shifted my attention from religious truth to salvation and ultimate destiny. However, as Hick himself has stated, "the truth-claim and the salvation-claim cohere closely together and should be treated as a single package."[82]) The second reason for supporting religious pluralism is

---

[80] For this individuation of the three reasons in question, I am indebted to David Basinger, "Religious Diversity (Pluralism)," in *The Stanford Encyclopedia of Philosophy*, ed. by Edward N. Zalta, https://plato.stanford.edu/archives/spr2018/entries/religious-pluralism/, accessed July 1, 2018.
[81] John Hick, "The Philosophy of World Religions," *Scottish Journal of Theology* 37 (1984), p. 229.
[82] John Hick, *Problems of Religious Pluralism* (London: Palgrave Macmillan, 1985), p. 46.

that "in the great majority of cases – say 98 to 99 percent – the religion in which a person believes and to which he adheres depends upon where he was born."[83] Evidently, the fact that one was born in a particular part of the world cannot be considered a plausible reason for identifying one's religion with the only true religion. Third, Hick argues that in the present century we have become aware that there are substantially different patterns and not only one to interpret human experience.[84] In this new light, the attitude of those who believe that their own gospel is true "and that other gospels are false in so far as they differ from it"[85] becomes simply untenable.

Hick supports his view of religious pluralism with arguments that could be applied to any realm of human experience, from which follows that he adopts the NA. This is especially evident in the case of the second reason. The fact that one's beliefs may depend on where one was born is not indicative of the truth of such beliefs – whether or not they are religious. The same can be said of the third reason. Once we become convinced that various interpretations can be offered to understand our experience, we should adopt a pluralistic approach to all of our beliefs, and not only the religious ones. Things may seem different in the case of the first reason given by Hick, that is, that all of the world's religions are transformational. This reason, in fact, relates to the existence of a supernatural being and the afterlife, which is why it may seem to be extraneous to the NA. (This reference to a supernatural reality may appear not entirely plausible.[86] My interest, however, is not in the internal coherence of Hick's argument; I am rather interested in establishing whether or not he adopts the NA, however correct the argument he proposes may be.) On closer inspection, however, it is clear that the line of reasoning proposed by Hick in support of "transformational parity" among religions may apply to every human experience. If genuine religion is salvific and transformational, and if there are many transformational experiences, none of them can presume to be the only genuine religion. It is obvious, therefore, that this argument in support of "transformational parity" among religions does not depend on the reference to a supernatural being and the influence they may exert on human experience.

---

[83] John Hick, *God Has Many Names* (London: Macmillan, 1980), p. 44.
[84] See Hick, "The Philosophy of World Religions," p. 232.
[85] Hick, *Problems of Religious Pluralism*, p. 28.
[86] See Graham Oppy, *Reinventing Philosophy of Religion: An Opinionated Introduction* (Basingstoke: Palgrave Macmillan, 2014), p. 12.

5.3.2 Opposing the NA without Employing the SA

Here I intend to focus on the possibility of opposing the NA without having recourse to the SA. I propose two arguments for the claim that the NA, which the IP presupposes, is not applicable to religious matters.

First, a rebutting argument is implicit in what I have argued in the previous section – therefore, presenting this argument will take little time. I showed that the IP applies indifferently to religious and nonreligious subjects. This means that the IP overlooks that which is specific to religion. As a result, the IP may successfully apply to various experiences except the religious one. Not taking into consideration any possible aspect of a particular experience, in fact, is not a favorable viewpoint from which to achieve an understanding of it. The hypothesis that a supernatural being exists and participates in the religious experience of believers might later prove to be untrue. However, the decision to exclude from the outset this hypothesis seems to limit one's understanding of how believers experience their faith and everything related to it, including how they view other religions.

Second, let me propose an undercutting argument. To this end, it is necessary to point out that the NA traces back to Locke's view of faith and reason, according to which assent to propositions comes in degrees and we should proportion our degree of assent to the available evidence.[87] Evidence is public and that which it proves to be true is accepted by everybody. The same cannot be said of that which is believed by those whom Locke calls "enthusiasts," who do not offer any evidence on the basis of which what they believe can be believed by everybody else.[88]

Locke's view of faith and reason implies that a complex of experiences and relevant beliefs, which only the faithful may have, cannot be taken into account, which is precisely what I mean by the NA. Like any other subject, religion can be investigated only by way of rational arguments that *everyone* believes.[89] In formal terms:

---

[87] See *An Essay*, IV, xix, 1. See also above, Introduction, note 3.
[88] See ibid., IV, xix, 11. See also above, Chapter 1, note 9.
[89] "What in principle everybody knows" is the expression that has been used by Ralph McInerny to stress the autonomy of philosophical reflection from the influence of religious belief. To put it in McInerny's own words, "philosophy is a discourse that pins itself to truths that are in the public domain, so that an argument must always be hooked up to the things that in principle everybody knows" (Ralph McInerny, "How I Became a Christian Philosopher," *Faith and Philosophy* 15 [1998], pp. 145f.). Let me add that perhaps Plantinga's words make the meaning of "what in principle everybody knows" clearer: "What we all or nearly all know or take for granted or firmly

(1) Only statements that everyone believes (or follow from what everyone believes) can be employed to attain the truth about human experience, including religion and matters related to it.

However, (1) is not believed by everyone. Religious believers may believe – no matter whether rightly or not – that reason alone is insufficient to achieve an understanding of that which pertains to God and religion. They may believe that a divine revelation, which does not coincide with that which everyone believes, is necessary for them to achieve an understanding of religion and, along with it, of matters such as the existence of only one God, the existence of only one true religion, and how to treat the followers of other religions. Again to put the point formally:

(2) Not everyone believes (1).
(3) From (2) follows that (1) is to be rejected.
(4) Given that (1) is equivalent to the NA, the NA is to be rejected, and the SA is to be adopted.

The SA is to be adopted, since it frontally contradicts the NA. Of course, someone may object that the SA is just an assumption, which is why it cannot solidly support a rational enterprise. Two effective replies, however, can be offered. First, if one has to demonstrate everything, this is due to the NA, which I have already shown is to be refuted. Second, it is true that the SA is an assumption. Adopting it, however, seems fully reasonable, not least because its alternative, the NA, is self-contradictory.

It may also be objected that God's existence and the content of his revelation cannot be treated in the same way. This is especially true for Locke, who was convinced that God's existence, unlike the divine revelation, was knowable by way of demonstration.[90] Nevertheless, the belief that God exists has become more and more debatable in the course of the last centuries.[91] Thus it is no longer seen as a statement that, at least in principle, everyone can know.

---

believe, or what at any rate those conducting the inquiry know or take for granted or believe" (Plantinga, *Warranted Christian Belief*, p. 272).

[90] See *An Essay*, IV, x, 6.

[91] A prominent Catholic historian of philosophy such as Gilson, while asking himself if philosophy alone, without the help of revelation, can allow one to know with certainty that God exists, made reference to contemporary philosophers in these terms: "Some of them say there is no God; others say that there is a God but that His existence cannot be demonstrated; still others say there is a God and they can prove His existence, but their demonstrations fail to carry conviction, or else what they call God in no way resembles the object of our religious worship" (Gilson, "What Is Christian Philosophy?," pp. 180f.).

Note that rejecting (1) and adopting the SA does not coincide with the following:

(5) Commonly accepted rational criteria, including the principle of noncontradiction, must be abandoned when it comes to religion.

In other words, my proposal should not be associated with the one advanced in the course of the last decades by influential scholars such as Hick, Wilfred Cantwell Smith, and Paul Knitter. They have argued that the principle of noncontradiction should not apply to religious beliefs. According to Hick, it is the Aristotelian concept of truth, which is intrinsically related to the principle of noncontradiction, that must be abandoned: it is "a matter of either-or. It is either this or not this: it cannot be both."[92] For Smith, "in all ultimate matters, truth lies not in an either-or but in a both-and."[93] Finally, Knitter denies the employment of the principle of noncontradiction since "all religious experience and all religious language must be two-eyed, dipolar, a union of opposites."[94]

Obviously, the employment of the principle of noncontradiction in any matter, including the religious ones, may seem to be due to the NA. Consequently, its rejection may look similar to the rejection of the NA and the adoption of the SA. To put it otherwise, (4) and (5) would be equivalent to each other, and would both contradict (1).

The similarity in question, however, holds only superficially. It is true that (1) and (5) are two opposite extremes. According to (1), religious statements can only be explored by way of commonly accepted beliefs, including the principle of noncontradiction. According to (5), on the contrary, principles such as the one at stake should be abandoned, which is the view maintained by the scholars mentioned above. However, (4) does not equal (5), and should rather be situated between (1) and (5). (This is ultimately due to the fact that I do not simply deny ME; I intend to offer a more comprehensive view.) In fact, (4) differs from (1) and resembles (5) on the ground that beliefs that are due to a divine revelation may allow us to understand aspects of religion otherwise inconceivable. On

---

[92] John Hick, "The Outcome of Truth: Dialogue into Truth," in *Truth and Dialogue in World Religions: Conflicting Truth-Claims*, ed. by John Hick (Philadelphia: Westminster Press, 1974), pp. 152f.
[93] Wilfred Cantwell Smith, *The Faith of Other Men* (New York: New American Library, 1963), p. 17.
[94] Paul Knitter, *No Other Name? A Critical Survey of Christian Attitudes toward the World Religions* (Maryknoll, NY: Orbis, 1985), p. 221. The persuasion that a "two-eyed" approach to religion should be adopted in place of a "one-eyed" one, which supports exclusivism in religious matters, has been championed by John Robinson, a scholar of the New Testament, in his book *Truth Is Two-Eyed* (Philadelphia: Westminster, 1979).

the other hand, (4) resembles (1) and differs from (5) on the ground that a contradiction between common experience and religious experience should not arise. Aquinas's doctrine of faith, to which I will appeal in the next section while proposing to adopt the SA, includes the conviction that, if God is the author of both faith and reason, no contradiction is acceptable between them: "Since both kinds of truth are from God, God would be the author of error, a thing which is impossible."[95]

Note that neither the undercutting nor the rebutting argument shows in what exactly the stance that opposes the NA consists – this will only emerge in the next section, when I will present the SA. The same can be said of two more arguments, advanced by as many scholars, which – like the arguments I have explored so far – may be taken as attempts to oppose the IP without adopting the SA.

The first argument is the one that Plantinga employs to reject a philosophical view that includes the IP. According to this view, there is something wrong in claiming that, among the existing religions, one is true and the others are not. (As I said, this accusation, which I call "something wrong" [SW], includes the IP. In fact, the IP emphasizes that the claim that there is only one true religion is unacceptable because is incompatible with peace among religions, while SW more generally points out that there is something wrong with the claim in question.) Plantinga argues that, on the contrary, it is SW that is wrong. As he says, if one believes that one possesses knowledge that others do not, one cannot be blamed for being convinced that one's own view is better than others' views. As a result, one would not have any reason for modifying one's conviction. Of course, this is the condition in which those who affirm the exclusive truth of their religion find themselves. What is more interesting, however, is that the detractors of religious exclusiveness find themselves in this condition as well. More precisely, everyone seems to reason in this way. All those who believe that they find themselves, even without any merit of their own, in a condition that is epistemically superior to that of others would end up considering their position better than others' positions and would consequently refuse to exchange it for any other. This regards also those, like Hick, who spoke of the need to put aside Christian exclusivism: "In the light of our accumulated knowledge of the other great world faiths, [Christian exclusivism] has become unacceptable to all except a minority

---

[95] Aquinas, *Super Boetium de Trinitate*, q. 2, a. 3. This matches a widespread philosophical conviction, according to which rejecting the principle of noncontradiction is self-referentially contradictory. See Aristotle, *Metaphysics*, 4, 4, 1006a35ff.

of dogmatic diehards."⁹⁶ Plantinga's conclusion is therefore hard to reject: "The abstemious pluralist who brings charges of intellectual arrogance against the believer is in a familiar but perilous dialectical situation; he shoots himself in the foot, is hoist with his own petard, holds a position that in a certain way is self-referentially inconsistent in the circumstances."⁹⁷

Plantinga's argument shows that those who hold the IP, and claim that it can be solved if religious exclusivism is given up, are exclusivists too. They are not ready to abandon their view either. Plantinga's position is to be numbered among the ones that, in the current debate on disagreement, can be defined "nonconformist" or "steadfast"⁹⁸ and support the conviction that perseverance in the face of controversy is epistemologically plausible. In this, Plantinga is joined by Van Inwagen, for whom, if one has incommunicable evidence that other parties lack, then one is within one's right to maintain one's own belief.⁹⁹

Let me now point out that the argument offered by Plantinga does not provide any reason to solve the IP. It limits itself to show that, if SW is true, then the same may be said of any possible view, including SW's negation. From this follows that Plantinga's argument may even end up reinforcing intolerance and conflicts. If there is nothing wrong with the person who believes that she possesses knowledge that others do not, and accordingly prefers her view – and her religion – to others, then the person in question may reasonably consider herself superior to others, and somewhat morally obliged to force them to accept her views.

The second argument I intend to examine is the one offered by Peter Byrne while considering tolerance and religious diversity.¹⁰⁰ Byrne argues that tolerance as a virtue implies that one holds strong convictions and also welcomes that which one tolerates, opening up the possibility for a reexamination of one's own convictions. In other words, practicing the virtue of tolerance, which Byrne also calls "full tolerance," seemingly reconciles the two poles of the IP. It is plausible to think, however, that the tolerant person in question will not be ready to revise *every* belief and opinion. A Christian believer may be ready to revise many of the views she usually holds. Nevertheless, the fact that there is only one God, that Jesus is the son of God, that he came into the world for our salvation, and so on

---

⁹⁶ Hick, *God Has Many Names*, p. 27.   ⁹⁷ Plantinga, *Warranted Christian Belief*, p. 446.
⁹⁸ See above, Chapter 4, note 54.   ⁹⁹ See above, Chapter 4, note 64.
¹⁰⁰ See Peter Byrne, "Religious Tolerance, Diversity, and Pluralism," in *Philosophy and Religion*, ed. by Anthony O'Hear, Royal Institute of Philosophy Supplement 68 (Cambridge: Cambridge University Press, 2001), pp. 287–309.

are beliefs that even a fully tolerant Christian is not expected to revise. Like Plantinga's argument, therefore, Byrne's does not seem able to dismiss the IP.

5.3.3 The IP Can Be Dismissed If the SA Replaces the NA

It is now time to explore the hypothesis that the introduction of the SA, which can be seen as the ST when it only applies to the Christian faith, may dismiss the IP as not representing a problem. If a supernatural person, who is the good itself, exists and grants religious believers a special relationship with him, they are expected to be first and foremost interested in this relationship. Any other aspect of life may consequently be enlightened, which is why these believers may keep believing that only their religion is true and, at the same time, that they should not consider themselves superior to others.

I will adopt Aquinas's reflection on faith and its propagation. Of course, the way I will use this reflection goes beyond Aquinas's intentions and real claims. I will use thoughts of him that can apply to religious diversity, although Aquinas did not do this. Furthermore, let me point out that nothing prevents us from considering some of Aquinas's thoughts as applicable to other religious traditions. God's omnipotence and love, for example, is shared by at least the major world's religions. Consequently, at least some of the responses to the IP that emerge from Aquinas's thought may apply to other religions as well. (And nonetheless, this does not point in the direction of any religious relativism, as I have already argued.[101])

Some may still object to the adoption of the SA from the viewpoint offered by only one religion. In other words, some may claim that, even if the choice I have just made is temporarily acceptable, our final aim should be to adopt the SA from the viewpoint of all of the existing religions. In reply, let me note that this objection follows either from (1) or from religious traditions. In the former case, the objection should be rejected with (1), since I have shown so far that (1) is to be rejected. In the latter case, the objection at hand can only emerge from *some* of those traditions, because at least the outstanding branches of Christianity, Judaism, and Islam would not accept the idea that truth in religion can only be achieved from a viewpoint that is common to them. As a consequence, the objection ends up confirming my choice and the related thesis that it is from

---

[101] See above, Chapter 3, p. 87.

some religious traditions and not from all of them that we may adopt the ST.

I can now start my investigation of how such adoption may dismiss the IP. (This is exactly the way the ST can take place.) I begin by taking into account Aquinas's reflection on how religious faith should be held, cultivated, and propagated.

Aquinas argues that faith is "an act of the intellect assenting to the Divine Truth at the command of the will moved by the grace of God."[102] It is by way of will moved by divine grace that believers take as true various statements that, for them, are divinely revealed. God is, therefore, "the chief and proper cause of faith."[103] By faith, believers become aware of things that "surpass human reason. Hence, they [the things in question] do not come to man's knowledge unless God reveals them."[104]

It may seem, at least at first sight, that for Aquinas believers are passively involved in the act of faith. An objection raised against Aquinas's view of faith is precisely that, according to Augustine, "faith depends on the believer's will." Aquinas responds that "man's will needs to be prepared by God with grace."[105] After all, only the intervention of God can justify the certainty that for Aquinas characterizes the Christian faith in things that are above nature. Aquinas holds that the certainty at issue – at least in its paradigmatic instantiations – is even superior to that of demonstrative knowledge.[106]

From these considerations emerges that, if the certainty of faith is caused by the omnipotent and omniscient God, who neither errs nor deceives, the believers who find themselves with such certainty will not have any reason to abandon their faith. As Plantinga and van Inwagen argue,[107] the faithful

---

[102] *Summa theologiae*, II-II, q. 2, a. 9.   [103] Ibid., II-II, q. 6, a. 1, ad 1.
[104] Ibid., II-II, q. 6, a. 1. With regard to this employment of the word "knowledge," which I reject, see above, Chapter 3, note 78.
[105] See above, Chapter 3, note 70, which includes reference to Bauerschmidt's observation that, according to Aquinas, God's intervention and human freedom are perfectly compatible with one another. Regarding how exactly this occurs, Stump has proposed the view that the will should be seen as "inactive or quiescent," and not only ready to assent to something or to reject it. If we think that God grants us his grace when the will is quiescent, then we reconcile human freedom and divine grace (see Stump, *Aquinas*, pp. 389ff.). My impression is that such an insightful proposal ends up missing the target. To use Augustine's terminology, Stump seems to focus on God's grace and *liberum arbitrium*, whereas we should focus on and reconcile God's grace and *libertas*. In other words, what we need is an explanation of how to reconcile divine grace with (the merit due to) the human freedom of a good act, not with quiescence, which obviously is not a good act and is not meritorius. For more on this, see Étienne Gilson, *The Christian Philosophy of Saint Augustine*, tr. by L. E. M. Lynch (New York: Vintage Books, 1960), p. 157.
[106] See *Summa theologiae*, II-II, q. 4, a. 8. See above, Chapter 3, note 72.
[107] See above, Chapter 4, note 64.

may consider themselves gifted with knowledge, which others did not receive, and may consequently find that they are right not to want to give it up in the face of controversy and religious diversity.

Once good reasons are found for sticking to one's faith and keeping to believe that one's religion is true, no matter how many other religious traditions exist, what can be said about the need for peaceful coexistence with them? Will this coexistence be at risk, once affirmed the truth of one's faith and the (even relative and partial) falseness of the others?

Aquinas's reflection implicitly offers a reasonable response. Although faith is an intellectual act, its perfection can be achieved only by way of charity, that is, love for God that God himself grants to believers. This is explained by the conviction that "the act of faith is directed to the object of the will, i.e. the good, as to its end: and this good ... is the end of faith, viz. the Divine good." The divine good "is the proper object of charity. Therefore charity is called the form of faith in so far as the act of faith is perfected and formed by charity."[108]

Thus, the commandment of love is the very center of the Christian belief. Based on it, believers must make a commitment to increase their love for God and their neighbor.[109] Given the fact that this love perfects faith, we may also say that increasing such a love is matched by a parallel increase of faith, which is precisely that which Christians are expected to desire: "The apostles said to the Lord, 'increase our faith.'"[110] This presupposes that believers experience both faith and love for God at different levels of intensity.

For Aquinas, it is by way of this inextricable connection between faith and charity that God grants faith to believers. Given this connection, claiming the truth of one's religion does not exclude, and actually implies a peaceful attitude toward other religions. Believers who are guided by love for God and the neighbor should be the best possible candidates to promote that attitude. The love in question, in fact, perfects all virtues. Among them, docility (*docilitas*) plays a crucial role when it comes to the employment of intellectual virtues.[111] As Thomas says, this virtue makes a debater "carefully, frequently and reverently apply his mind to the teachings of the learned, neither neglecting them through laziness, nor despising

---

[108] *Summa theologiae*, II-II, q. 4, a. 3. See above, Chapter 3, note 85.
[109] "And this is my prayer, that your love may overflow more and more" (Phil 1:9).
[110] Luke 17:5.
[111] Docility "is useful for every intellectual virtue" (*Summa theologiae*, II-II, q. 49, a. 3, ad 1).

them through pride."[112] Thus, those who love God and the neighbor are put in a condition to value what the neighbor does and thinks.

At least three decisive considerations follow, which definitely help us move away from the IP.

First, if assent to divine revelation is granted by God and is not due to personal efforts, those who have graciously received it should not feel superior to those who were not equally gifted. While focusing on the pre-Christian era, Aquinas argues that salvation might also have been possible for people who had not received any divine revelation. Some gentiles – so he says – might have accessed eternal salvation because "though they did not believe in Him explicitly, they did, nevertheless, have implicit faith through believing in Divine providence, since they believed that God would deliver mankind in whatever way was pleasing to Him."[113] In other words, they believed the divine revelation "implicitly,"[114] which means that they were "prepared to believe whatever is contained in the Divine Scriptures."[115] In this connection, a famous verse of the Gospel reads: "Tax collectors and prostitutes are entering the kingdom of God before you."[116] This warning, which is addressed by Jesus to the religious leaders at that time in Israel (the Pharisees and scribes), points out that those who have been granted familiarity with God, who the Gospel says is the truth, should not consider themselves better than others.

Second, if it is charity that perfects faith, then firm faith in one's religion is not possible without love for God and the neighbor. The faithful are committed to making progress in their spiritual perfection, which includes proportionate high levels of moral attitude, given the fact that charity consists in love for God and the neighbor as well. They should, therefore, be committed to the dismissal of the IP by promoting a peaceful relationship with other people, including adherents to different religious traditions. Needless to say, such a commitment will be seriously taken only by those who equally seriously intend to perfect themselves spiritually and morally. It follows that, even if some dismiss the IP, the IP remains true for all the remaining believers or, more precisely, remains true in proportion to the lack of believers' spiritual and moral progress.

---

[112] Ibid., II-II, q. 49, a. 3, ad 2.   [113] Ibid., II-II, q. 2, a. 7, ad 3.   [114] Ibid., II-II, q. 2, a. 5.
[115] Ibid., II-II, q. 2, a. 5. As I have repeatedly pointed out so far, being ready to believe whatever is taken to be revealed by God does not exclude the error. See above, Chapter 3, note 30.
[116] Matt 21:31.

Someone may object that Aquinas should be numbered among those believers who lack the progress in question. What he thinks of other religious faiths seemingly aligns with the IP, because neither a peaceful nor a respectful attitude toward adherents of other religions emerges from his conviction that his religion is the true one. For him, heretics, Saracens, Moors, Jews, and pagans commit a grave sin such as the sin of unbelief, which "is greater than any sin that occurs in the perversion of morals."[117] It is true that Aquinas suggests that those who engage in false worship can be tolerated.[118] He also says, however, that heretics deserve "to be severed from the world by death."[119] They "corrupt the faith which weakens the soul," which – so Aquinas's argument goes on – is "a much graver matter ... than to forge money"; consequently, "if forgers of money and other evil-doers are forthwith condemned to death by the secular authority, much more reason is there for heretics."[120]

In reply, it can be said that this seeming lack of peaceful disposition toward those who believe in "false gods" is not relatable to the IP. The IP regards the relationship between peace and *religious doctrines*, whereas what I have just quoted from Aquinas's works regards the ability of religions to meet *social and political needs*. In Aquinas's time, lack of distinction between politics and religion was customary; as a result, every religious doctrine and/or practice other than Christianity was automatically seen as politically and socially dangerous. This required any remedy that appeared to be effective, however unacceptable it may seem from contemporary Western society's viewpoint. In contrast, if we move from Aquinas's political and social perspective and go back to the merely religious doctrinal concern, it is possible to confirm the thesis that Aquinas's account of faith and charity helps to reject the IP. The IP implies that those who believe that their religion is the true one may consider themselves entitled to force the adherents of other religions to convert. This is at odds with Aquinas's conviction that no one should force others to deviate from their conscience, even if there are reasons for believing that the conscience in question is erroneous. Aquinas clearly claims that "every will at variance with reason, whether right or erring, is always evil."[121] Believing in Christ is good in itself, and nonetheless, if reason proposes it as something evil, "the will tends to it as to something evil; not as if it were evil in itself, but because it is evil accidentally, through the apprehension of

---

[117] *Summa theologiae*, II-II, q. 10, a. 3. [118] Ibid., II-II, q. 10, a. 11.
[119] Ibid., II-II, q. 11, a. 3. [120] Ibid., I-II, q. 11, a. 3. [121] Ibid., I-II, q. 19, a. 5.

the reason."[122] In the same vein, Aquinas rejects the view that the children of unbelievers are to be baptized against their parent's will.[123]

Third, if those who are considered to be guided by erroneous conscience in their religious faith cannot be forced to convert, then the only action that should be taken toward them is the "fraternal correction," which is an act of charity because it "is directed to the amendment of the sinner."[124] This correction involves the employment of reason, which Aquinas trusts. If faith is perfected by charity, then those who firmly believe that their religion is true are expected to love God and to value everything he has created, including human reason. For Aquinas, reason is fully reliable and consistent with the Christian faith. He claims that "the contrary of a truth cannot be demonstrated" and that "arguments brought against faith cannot be demonstrations."[125] Of course, Aquinas is aware that "abuse" and "insufficiency of reason" can occur, but "it is possible from the principles of philosophy to refute an error of this kind, either by showing it to be altogether impossible, or not to be necessary."[126] This implies that reason is expected to be valued and used to the best of human abilities. Given this high level of trust, no limits should be imposed on its employment. Not surprisingly, Aquinas relies on the employment of reason when it comes to dialogue among traditions, cultures, and religions that do not have anything else in common.[127] After all, he believes that there are no doctrines that can only be full of errors.[128] If so, it is by way of a patient, optimistic, and open-minded employment of our cognitive faculties that the truth mingled with error can be found. In this connection, Aquinas seems to be in the best possible condition to employ reason in such an open-minded way, given his conviction that no demonstrations can be found against that which he cares most about, that is, his faith.

Furthermore, Aquinas is convinced that believers can crucially contribute to the best possible employment of the cognitive faculties by renouncing certain sins. In his treatise on faith, he focuses on the blindness of mind and the dullness of sense, and claims that they are due to carnal vices, that is, gluttony and lust, which are "pleasures of touch." For Aquinas,

---

[122] Ibid. [123] See ibid., II-II, q. 10, a. 12. [124] Ibid., II-II, q. 33, a. 1.
[125] Ibid., I, q. 1, a. 8. See above, Chapter 3, note 123.
[126] Aquinas, *Super Boetium de Trinitate*, q. 2, a. 3. See above, Chapter 3, note 114.
[127] "Against the Jews we are able to argue by means of the Old Testament, while against heretics we are able to argue by means of the New Testament. But the Muslims and the pagans accept neither the one nor the other. We must, therefore, have recourse to the natural reason, to which all men are forced to give their assent" (Aquinas, *Summa contra Gentiles*, I, 3).
[128] See *Summa theologiae*, I-II, q. 102, a. 5, ad 4. See above, Chapter 3, note 95.

> these are the most impetuous of all pleasures of the body. For this reason these vices cause man's attention to be very firmly fixed on corporeal things, so that in consequences man's operation in regard to intelligible things is weakened, more, however, by lust than by gluttony ... Lust gives rise to blindness of mind, which excludes almost entirely the knowledge of spiritual things, while dullness of sense arises from gluttony, which makes a man weak in regard to the same intelligible things.[129]

Loving God and renouncing the sin, therefore, is expected to improve our cognitive faculties. Abstinence and chastity, virtues that oppose the vices mentioned above and that believers are warmly advised to practice, "dispose man very much to the perfection of intellectual operation."[130]

5.4 Conclusion

In this chapter, I have shown how one can take the ST and what benefits to debaters and researchers follow from taking it. To this end, I have first focused on the relationship between the act of doing good and the search for truth. I have then treated two outstanding subjects in the philosophy of religion and theology: God's existence and religious diversity.

Focusing on the former allowed me to show that one cannot take the ST without shifting attention from others to oneself. Reflecting on one's spiritual growth and one's will to do good is, for both believers and unbelievers, an indispensable aspect of the ST.

Focusing on the latter subject has allowed me to show how exactly taking the ST puts debaters in the best possible condition to satisfactorily conduct investigations and discussions. If one believes that charity perfects faith, which also means that the act of doing good and loving good perfects the search for truth, then one may plausibly be led to firmly hold the truth of one's religious experience; also, one may be led to love other people and to respect their conscience, however erroneous it may be. In this way, the IP is dismissed as no problem. Someone may object that this does not have to do with the ST *in epistemology*. Epistemology should deal with the truth and the way to attain it. What I have described and argued so far, instead, seems only to be a matter of respect and tolerance among religions, no matter how crucial respect and tolerance are seen to dialogue and debates. On closer inspection, however, the IP is ultimately based on the idea that affirming the truth of one's religion can only exclude the truth of other religions, and this *is* a strictly epistemological view.

---

[129] Ibid., II-II, q. 15, a. 3.   [130] Ibid., I-II, q. 15, a. 3.

I have emphasized that taking the ST is an eminently personal process, which must constantly be pursued. As I have shown so far, from the idea that a religious view potentially offers a dismissal of the IP it by no means follows that all of the adherents to that view can dismiss the IP. Instead, this dismissal is possible in proportion to the attempts that those who experience a love relationship with a supernatural and perfectly loving being make to perfect themselves spiritually and morally. Of course, I am referring only to believers who take the ST. In the next chapter, I will also focus on unbelievers.

It is the attempt to spiritually perfect oneself that is of primary interest to those who take the ST, not the solution of epistemological problems. However, since the search for good shapes and includes, among other activities, the search for truth, adopters of the ST are not only expected to be respectful and charitable toward those who believe differently; they are also expected to be capable of employing reason to the best of their abilities. In this way, they generate the best possible condition to participate in intellectual research and debates. This means that taking the ST can, in some cases, substantially benefit the intellectual activity by increasing the possibility of achieving conclusiveness. This possibility is among the subjects that I will treat in the next chapter.

CHAPTER 6

Comparison with Virtue Epistemology and Reinforcement
More Reasons for Believers and Unbelievers to Take the Spiritual Turn

In this chapter, I first compare the ST with perspectives that only seemingly resemble it. I then reinforce my thesis (i.e., the idea that the ST should be taken). I argue that a self-referential contradiction affects ME. By employing the concept of a-rational commitments, which I have explored in Chapter 4, I show that practitioners of ME are a-rationally committed to avoiding any a-rational commitments. I then show that the abovementioned practitioners, like practically everybody in contemporary Western society, implicitly take on various commitments, which regard specific goods and related beliefs that are widely seen as indispensable and undeniable. Consequently, they too may take the ST and find themselves in the best possible condition to improve intellectual investigations and debates, including the ability to achieve conclusiveness.

6.1 More Reasons for Taking the ST

I have already explored how the ST should be taken and some benefits it may bring to the knowing subject. This exploration, however, was prevalently one-sided. It did not sufficiently consider the situation of unbelievers or, more generally, *mere epistemologists*, who think that moral and spiritual aims, if any, must first be established by intellectual investigation. As a matter of fact, given the primary importance that mere epistemologists ascribe to the cognitive faculties and how they should be used, inconclusiveness – and the related question of whether or not the ST is to be taken – is expected to be dismissible as no problem. Once the right way to make use of the cognitive faculties has been found – so Descartes and many others have maintained, and still maintain – solving the problem of inconclusiveness will be possible by simply making the will follow the faculties in question.

In contrast, the Christian tradition offers many suggestions supporting the possibility for intellectual research to be guided by the will and the aim of searching for good. That is why I have so far limited myself to exploring the possibility of the ST based on the Christian tradition. In this chapter, I intend to somewhat remedy this deficiency.

I first concentrate on those epistemologists whose method seemingly resembles the ST. I am referring to virtue epistemologists, more precisely to those among them who focus on *character virtues* and how these virtues might influence intellectual research. On closer inspection, I intend to show that virtue epistemology is a version of ME, though a more sophisticated one. Unlike the latter, virtue epistemology does not simply focus on evidence and the intellectual dimension of the human person; it also considers epistemic emotions and the human person in her entirety, from which a multifaceted view of knowledge emerges.

I then propose three reasons for all debaters, both believers and unbelievers, to take the ST and abandon ME.

One reason is that a self-referential contradiction affects ME. ME is the view that beliefs supported by more evidence must always be preferred to beliefs supported by less evidence – which can also be described by saying that beliefs supported by evidence must always be preferred to beliefs that are due to a-rational commitments. As I have already noted in the Introduction, this view, however, does not seem to be supported by more evidence than its opposite. The belief that *one should* always *prefer beliefs supported by more evidence than beliefs supported by less evidence* is not supported by more evidence than the belief that *one should* not always *prefer beliefs supported by more evidence than beliefs supported by less evidence*. This can be reformulated by employing the concept of a-rational commitment, which I have taken into consideration in Chapter 4. It can be said that mere epistemologists are a-rationally committed to avoiding any a-rational commitments. Furthermore, reliance on reason as the only criterion to evaluate one's intellectual achievements inevitably makes ME fall into circularity.

Another reason to abandon ME is that, in contemporary Western society, there are states of affairs and related beliefs, such as the existence of the equal dignity of human beings and the unacceptability of racism, to which practically all seem to commit themselves, no matter if contrary evidence, at least at first sight, seems to convince them of the contrary. (Mere epistemologists are found among them, which implies a lack of coherence with their epistemological view. However, this is not surprising, since such a view is self-referentially contradictory.) It follows that, to the extent that the beliefs in question promote one's spiritual betterment, those who maintain these beliefs can be seen as adopters of the ST.

One final reason is that, in this view, how debaters conduct investigations and discussions can significantly improve. I mean that, when those who adopt the ST do not focus on the beliefs that they consider undeniable and only discuss the remainder of their noetic structure – which, on closer inspection, is the greatest part of it – they find themselves in the best possible condition to achieve conclusiveness. Therefore, those who take the ST can substantially improve their ability to participate in debates. Although they are not primarily interested in conclusiveness, they end up being more able than mere epistemologists to increase this conclusiveness.

This chapter bears in its title words such as "comparison" and "reinforcement." I *compare* the ST with virtue epistemology to show the fundamental difference between these two seemingly parallel epistemological methods. Unlike virtue epistemology, the ST involves a-rational commitments to beliefs that its supporters consider undeniable, whether or not the available evidence convinces them of the contrary. I then *reinforce* my proposal by showing, in various ways, that the ST, from the epistemological viewpoint, is more beneficial than ME to both believers and unbelievers.

6.2 Virtue Epistemology as a Version of ME

The version of virtue epistemology that may, at first sight, appear to be similar to the ST is called *responsibilist* (as opposed to the version that is called *reliabilist*). My thesis is that this kind of virtue epistemology is, on closer inspection, a kind of ME. I argue this thesis in three steps. First, I look at the origins and aims of virtue epistemology. Second, as a result of this survey, I show what the nature of this epistemological view consists of. Finally, I specifically focus on one intellectual virtue (i.e., intellectual humility).

6.2.1 *Origins and Aims*

This section aims to offer a brief outline of *how* and *why* the responsibilist version of virtue epistemology has developed in the last decades of the twentieth century. I focus on the responsibilist version of virtue epistemology because I am only interested in this version, which deals with the role of *character traits*. The reliabilist one, which regards the *cognitive functions*, is instead of no interest, because only the former may appear to be similar to the ST. Cognitive functions only regard the intellectual dimension of a human being. In contrast, character traits – friendliness, kindness, and so on – are involved in the search for good, which plays a crucial role in the ST. Furthermore, offering the present outline of *how* and especially *why* the responsibilist version of virtue epistemology has developed is due to my conviction, which I have already shown in the last chapter,[1] that it is by focusing on the aims of human actions that the nature of such actions can adequately be shown.

After the publication of the famous two-and-a-half-page article by Edmund Gettier in 1963,[2] several epistemologists, in a bid to solve the problems raised by that article, started shifting their attention from the idea of knowledge as due to *how we form our beliefs* to a new idea of knowledge as due to *how our belief-forming faculties function*. They attempted to show that our beliefs are justified or warranted to the extent that they result from a reliable or properly functioning working of our faculties, and not from the fact that we are internally convinced that they – our beliefs – are justified or warranted.

This turn from the traditional "internalist" view to an "externalist" approach to epistemology was the main attempt (I say "main" because it does not exclude internalists post-Gettier) to solve the so-called Gettier problem.[3] This problem emphasized that a *true justified belief* – which had traditionally been seen as the only definition of knowledge – may still be not knowledge, and may be due to a lucky guess.[4] Solving the problem seemed to be possible by either reconceiving justification[5] or introducing a fourth condition. After decades of debates, in an essay eloquently titled "The Inescapability of Gettier Problems,"[6] Zagzebski argued that any attempt to find the fourth condition was susceptible to Gettier-style counterexamples.[7] This led various scholars to develop a *virtue*

---

[1] See above, Chapter 5, Section 5.1.
[2] See Edmund Gettier, "Is Justified True Belief Knowledge?," *Analysis* 23 (1963), pp. 121ff.
[3] I need to limit myself to just a few words about the problem in question, which in its most recent treatment is said to be still under way (see Stephen Hetherington, "Introduction: Meet the Gettier Problem," in *The Gettier Problem*, ed. by Stephen Hetherington [Cambridge: Cambridge University Press, 2019], p. 10).
[4] As Pritchard points out, almost all epistemologists accept what he calls "*epistemic luck platitude*," that is, the claim that "knowledge excludes luck" (Duncan Pritchard, *Epistemic Luck* [Oxford: Clarendon Press, 2005], p. 1). For more on this, see Duncan Pritchard, "The Gettier Problem and Epistemic Luck," in Hetherington, ed., *The Gettier Problem*, pp. 96–107.
[5] This is the attempt that, among others, Roderick Chisholm famously made in *Theory of Knowledge*, 2nd ed. (Englewood Cliffs, NJ: Prentice Hall, 1977), Chapter 6.
[6] Linda Zagzebski, "The Inescapability of Gettier Problems," *The Philosophical Quarterly* 44 (1994), pp. 65–73.
[7] However, her argument only affects a fourth condition that's independent of the third. It doesn't afflict the anti-luck virtue epistemology proposal championed by Duncan Pritchard, "Anti-Luck Virtue Epistemology," *The Journal of Philosophy* 109 (2012), pp. 247–279.

epistemology, which is sometimes seen as one of the possible versions of the "externalist" move mentioned above, although internalist versions of virtue epistemology have also been proposed.

According to virtue epistemologists, knowledge is achieved if it is the output of a *virtuous* cognitive process. One knows that p only if one's belief is that p is true, and is true because it is the output of a virtuous cognitive process.

However, there is a substantial difference between the two forms of virtue epistemology mentioned above, the reliabilist and the responsibilist forms. The difference depends on what exactly virtue is taken to be. In the former case, virtues are considered *cognitive functions* such as eyesight, hearing, memory, and inferential reason. Ernest Sosa championed this view.[8] In the latter case, virtues are *character traits* such as intellectual courage, generosity, tenacity, and humility, which more properly resemble how the philosophical tradition and contemporary ordinary language speak of "virtue."[9] This view was inaugurated by Zagzebski,[10] based on Lorraine Code's and James Montmarquet's reflection.[11]

Plantinga has participated in this debate by offering an influential view of the intellectual virtues as "cognitive faculties properly functioning in congenial environments."[12] This seems to associate Plantinga's with Sosa's reflection. As Robert Roberts and William Jay Wood point out,[13] however, Plantinga's religious commitment seems to lead the author of *Warranted Christian Belief* to focus on "the deep and character-involving knowledge of God," which is inevitably expected to exert an influence on character traits and appetitive dispositions. This is of interest here since

---

[8] See at least Ernest Sosa, "The Raft and the Pyramid: Coherence versus Foundations in the Theory of Knowledge," *Midwest Studies in Philosophy* 5 (1980), pp. 3–26, and *A Virtue Epistemology* (Oxford: Oxford University Press, 2007).

[9] Unlike faculties and skills, character traits "are dispositions of thinking and/or feeling and/or motivation and/or action that ground normative evaluations of persons as such" (Nathan King, "Intellectual Perseverance," in *The Routledge Handbook of Virtue Epistemology*, ed. by Heather Battaly [New York: Routledge, 2019], p. 259).

[10] See Linda Zagzebski, *Virtues of the Mind: An Inquiry into the Nature of Virtues and the Ethical Foundations of Knowledge* (New York: Cambridge University Press, 1996).

[11] Lorraine Code was probably the first to use the concept of "responsibilism" as opposed to that of "reliabilism" championed by Sosa. See Lorraine Code, *Epistemic Responsibility* (Hanover, NH: Published for Brown University Press by University Press of New England, 1987), p. 44. James Montmarquet emphasizes the importance of "epistemic conscientiousness," which he characterizes as a desire for truth and the avoidance of error (see James Montmarquet, *Epistemic Virtue and Doxastic Responsibility* [Lanham, MD: Rowman & Littlefield, 1993], p. 21).

[12] See Alvin Plantinga, *Warrant and Proper Function* (New York: Oxford University Press, 1993) as well as *Warranted Christian Belief*.

[13] See Robert Roberts and William Jay Wood, *Intellectual Virtues: An Essay in Regulative Epistemology* (New York: Oxford University Press, 2007), pp. 7f.

I too focus on religious tradition to the extent that it offers significant suggestions when it comes to promoting a spiritual impact on epistemology.

Therefore, the responsibilist version of virtue epistemology focuses on the human person *taken in her entirety* and not just considered from the cognitive viewpoint. Its central question regards what makes *a person intellectually good*. Not surprisingly, this kind of virtue epistemology applies aspects of virtue ethics to epistemology.[14] According to Zagzebski, intellectual virtues are, in fact, a subset of moral virtues, as shown by her conviction that the beliefs held by those who are intellectually virtuous are expected to be due to *habituation* and *deliberate choice*.[15]

Zagzebski argues that no difference can be found between intellectual and moral virtues as to three significant aspects of their working: "Both require training through the imitation of virtuous persons and practice in acting virtuously. Both also involve handling certain feelings and acquiring the ability to *like* acting virtuously. Both also have stages in between vice and virtue consisting of *akrasia* and self-control."[16] This – so Zagzebski argues – is confirmed by the crucial role that, in Aristotle's thought, *phronesis*, which is an intellectual virtue, plays regarding the moral virtues.[17]

Aristotle's view of *phronesis*, however, needs some rethinking, and we need to "understand its [*phronesis*'s] connection to the moral and the intellectual virtues differently from the way Aristotle did."[18] Something similar can be said of Aquinas, as Jay Wood has opportunely pointed out. Like Aristotle, Aquinas argues in support of the interconnection between intellect and will.[19] And nonetheless, "to speak of intellectual humility would have struck Aquinas – and strikes some contemporary philosophers – as something of a category mistake." In Aquinas's view, as Jay

---

[14] Unlike deontologism, which is agent-based, and consequentialism, which is outcome-based, virtue ethics is character-based. The persons who possess character traits and act accordingly are *virtuous*. Tracing back to Aristotle's *Nicomachean Ethics*, Gertrude E. Anscombe in her 1958 important paper *Modern Moral Philosophy* famously argued in support of this view.
[15] This may support the view that responsibilists, who focus on character virtues, do not have anything to do with reliabilists, who focus on excellences of faculties. In reality, they cannot divorce each other. See John Greco, "Virtues in Epistemology," in *Oxford Handbook of Epistemology*, ed. by Paul Moser (New York: Oxford University Press, 2002).
[16] Zagzebski, *Virtues of the Mind*, pp. 157f.   [17] See ibid., p. 212.   [18] Ibid.
[19] "The good and the true include one another, since the good is a kind of truth, insofar as it is grasped by the intellect when intellect understands the will to be willing the good or even insofar as it understands that something is good. So too the true is a good of the intellect which thus falls to the will insofar as a man will to understand the true" (Aquinas, *Disputed Questions on Virtue*, a. 6, ad 5, cit. in Wood, "Faith's Intellectual Rewards," p. 40).

Wood points out, "generosity, humility, and courage seek the good, not the true, and thus are the work of the will, not the intellect: two types of truth grounded in two distinct parts of the soul."[20]

At any rate, how faithful the responsibilist version of virtue epistemology is to the ancient and medieval treatment of virtues is beyond my interest here.[21] I have focused on its origins and aims only because this will now allow me to emphasize its seeming similarity and its real difference with the ST.

6.2.2 Virtue Epistemology and the ST

According to the virtue epistemologists mentioned so far, the intellectually good person is especially qualified to know, and knowledge is achieved if *belief arises out of acts of intellectual virtue*.[22] If one is, say, reflective, fair-minded, perseverant, and intellectually careful, then one is more likely than those who lack these qualities to achieve knowledge. Those who possess these traits are better *persons*, and placing emphasis on the human person in her entirety resembles the ST. Those who take the ST focus on their flourishing as human persons, which they expect will imply the development of single virtues and the achievement of specific forms of success, the intellectual one included.

However, there is a substantial difference between the ST and the virtue epistemology here under consideration. Those who take the ST are primarily interested in their human flourishing and *only secondarily* in any other success. In contrast, virtue epistemologists are interested in that particular achievement that is the attainment of knowledge. Of course, one may aim at achieving eudaimonia through intellectual activity and the related solution of epistemological issues. Nothing impedes virtue epistemology from ultimately aiming at the wider project constituted by one's spiritual betterment, and this may seem to render virtue epistemology fully compatible with the ST. On closer inspection, however, conducting an intellectual activity and solving epistemological issues as a precondition to attaining one's spiritual betterment and supporting related beliefs means that the betterment in question and the related beliefs do not play any role in the solution of those issues. In contrast, those who take the ST are

---

[20] Wood, "Faith's Intellectual Rewards," p. 40.
[21] For more on the distance between Aquinas's treatment of virtues and Zagzebski's, see Roberts and Wood, *Intellectual Virtues*, pp. 70ff.
[22] See Zagzebski, *Virtues of the Mind*, p. 271.

expected to keep sight of their spiritual fulfillment and the related beliefs, which they think can lead one to any other accomplishment, including the solution of epistemological issues.

This attitude seems typically championed by Aquinas when he says that, if believers are confronted with arguments that appear to disprove their beliefs, they should reject such arguments and starting reasoning anew. The adhesion to God and the commitment to the related beliefs are seen as the end of one's life. It is on their basis that any other activity, including the intellectual one, needs conducting. Similarly, Anselm, who, like Aquinas, is usually seen as fully representative of the way a religious belief can stimulate and promote rational research, starts his famous investigation contained in his *Proslogion* by asking God to help him: "O Lord my God. Teach my heart where and how to seek you, where and how to find you."[23] For Anselm, God is expected to answer believers' prayers by revealing to them where to seek and find him. In other words, communion with God orients the intellectual research and works as its criterion. Unsurprisingly, at the beginning of another of his famous works devoted to rationally exploring God's existence and attributes, Anselm goes so far as to claim that

> if in this [investigation] I say anything that a greater authority does not teach, I wish to be understood in this way: even if I present a conclusion as necessary on the basis of arguments that seem compelling to me, I mean only that it can *seem* necessary for the time being, not that it is therefore in fact altogether necessary.[24]

I will show later that something similar may be said of those who commit themselves to beliefs such as the equal fundamental dignity of all human beings and related values – universal freedom, fraternity, and so on. In contemporary Western society, those who maintain these beliefs are likely to continue supporting them even if contrary reasons suggested that they change their minds. Among such reasons, there are behaviors of individuals and practices spread among cultures and religions, which may reflect such deplorable attitudes that, from their knowledge, the negation of the existence of a common dignity of human beings may easily follow. Not surprisingly, pointing to such reasons is a familiar strategy for those who

---

[23] Anselm, *Proslogion*, 1, tr. by Thomas Williams, in Anselm, *Monologion and Proslogion* (Indianapolis, IN: Hackett Publishing, 1995).
[24] Anselm, *Monologion*, 1, tr. by Thomas Williams, in Anselm, *Monologion and Proslogion*. As two scholars of Anselm point out, Anselm "is confident that if his rational arguments go astray in some way, Scripture will provide the materials to correct them" (Sandra Visser and Thomas Williams, *Anselm* [New York: Oxford University Press, 2009], p. 17).

support forms of discrimination. However, the people who commit themselves to the beliefs mentioned above will be likely to believe that such reasons are either wrong or not necessary. In this way, they show a-rational commitments, which depend on neither rational investigations nor the solution of related epistemological issues. These people prefer beliefs they may see as supported by less evidence to beliefs that they may consider supported by more evidence.

Those who take the ST, be they believers or unbelievers, commit themselves to states of affairs and the related beliefs, which they consider orientation and criterion of any activity. This is because they look at these states of affairs and beliefs as representing and conveying the good itself, that is, that which cannot cause any form of evil. That God is love and all human beings have the same fundamental dignity, for example, seem to be beliefs from which no evil, unless inconsistently, can follow. Being committed to such beliefs is expected to lead one to successfully conduct related and less fundamental activities – the intellectual one is to be numbered among them since it aims to achieve a particular good, that is, the truth, and not the good in itself. The existence of universal equality of humans, as well as the unacceptability of racism, for example, can be considered among the fundamental beliefs mentioned above. Being committed to these beliefs will plausibly render the person who takes the intellectual activity maximally interested in the good of her opponents. This is likely to lead one to value what one's interlocutors or opponents believe and to give rise to the best possible condition to employ and promote intellectual virtues such as humility, open-mindedness, and the like.

However, practicing these virtues should not lead one to doubt the fundamental beliefs to which one is committed and based on which one promoted the abovementioned virtues. No matter whether or not contrary evidence appears to be sufficient to make them change their mind, those who take the ST should reject this evidence and continue searching for arguments in support of their original convictions. Of course, this does not mean that aspects of the committed belief cannot be rethought and seen in a new light. It only means that, from the viewpoint of the ST, beliefs such as "God is love," "Jesus is the son of God," "no one should be discriminated because of race or religion," once considered committed beliefs, cannot be given up.

This is a decisive difference between the ST and virtue epistemology. The latter's proponents should not agree to (a-rationally) maintain beliefs against which more evidence is provided. (Let me remind the reader that maintaining beliefs against contrary evidence, as I take it, does not resemble the so-called nonconciliatory stance in case of peer disagreement.[25] This stance regards circumstances in which equal evidence supporting *both* mutually opposing views is available, not circumstances that show more evidence on one side and less evidence or even only a-rational commitments on the other.)

Furthermore, the crucial role played by a-rational commitments regarding the ST does not resemble the fact that epistemic emotions, such as a passion for truth or repugnance at intellectual dishonesty, are essential to intellectual virtues and play a crucial role in virtue epistemology. Motivations and motives[26] have traditionally been seen as components of distinctive intellectual virtues. Michael Brady rightly shows this fact while referring to Aristotle's account of virtue, according to which "the virtuous person is the person with the correct emotional dispositions."[27] For example, the benevolent person is guided to act benevolently by adequate emotions that make her wish for the well-being of others. This is different from the a-rational commitments that are typical of the ST. These are commitments to propositional representations aimed at representing reality *as it is*. Being a-rationally committed to them means that one commits oneself *to their truth*, no matter whether or not evidence is provided in their support and even if the available evidence seems to convince one of the contrary. In contrast, since virtue epistemologists are aware that "emotions could also be the motivational components of epistemic vices,"[28] they claim that "the virtuous thinker will need to possess certain *regulatory* virtues."[29] And regulating epistemic emotions means, among other things, that one abandons a-rational commitments if they can be replaced with evidence. A love for the truth, which is a motivational component of various epistemic virtues, would turn into an epistemic vice if it supports beliefs that the available evidence disproves.

This seemingly shows that virtue epistemology should be preferred to the ST. Between evidence and a-rational commitment, it seems unreasonable to choose the latter and abandon the former, as the ST requires at least with regard to some beliefs.

---

[25] See above, Chapter 4, note 54.
[26] Zagzebski distinguishes motives, "as occurring at a particular moment of time," from motivation, "as a persistent tendency to be moved by a motive of a certain kind" (*Virtues of the Mind*, p. 132).
[27] Michael Brady, "The Role of Emotions in Intellectual Virtue," in Battaly, ed., *The Routledge Handbook of Virtue Epistemology*, p. 50.
[28] Ibid., note 3.   [29] Ibid., p. 54.

However, two problems emerge that render it equally, if not more, unreasonable to adopt virtue epistemology.

First, the view that more evidence must always be preferred to less evidence gives rise to self-referential contradiction, as I have shown while introducing this chapter.

Second, virtue epistemology is affected by circularity. As I have said above, to avoid turning into epistemic vices, epistemic emotions need to be regulated. Tracing back to Aristotle and his doctrine of moral virtues, it may be said that *habituation* and *choice* are necessary to avoid intellectual vices (and develop intellectual virtues). For Aristotle, it is the intellectual virtue of prudence (*phronesis*) that guides choice. In his view, one needs to deliberate well about what is good rather than making choices based on mere appetite or emotions. For the author of *Nicomachean Ethics*, "choice is either desiderative reason or ratiocinative desire,"[30] and the right choice presupposes the right reason. Habituation is learned through an intellectual process (i.e., the deliberative process). Does this cause circularity? It does not in Aristotle's treatment of moral virtues, since for him, we pursue some character traits "not to know what virtue is, but to become good."[31] Things radically change, however, if moral virtues are considered necessary to acquire intellectual virtues. As Zagzebski says, "many moral virtues such as patience, perseverance, and courage are causally necessary for having intellectual virtues."[32] Virtue epistemology seems to fall, therefore, in a circular argument. To acquire intellectual virtues, we need moral virtues; to acquire moral virtues, however, we need intellectual virtues. To put it otherwise, it may be said that according to both virtue epistemology and the ST, better persons improve cognitive processes. However, according to the ST, one is a better person because one is a-rationally committed to the good. This does not cause any circularity between being a better person and improving cognitive processes. In contrast, according to virtue epistemology one is a better person – and consequently improves cognitive processes – because one acquires moral virtues, which, as the abovementioned reference to Aristotle has shown, occurs if one previously improves cognitive processes.

6.2.3 On the Epistemology of Intellectual Humility

Let me now focus in more detail on the difference between the ST and virtue epistemology by concentrating on intellectual humility. Intellectual

---

[30] Aristotle, *Nicomachean Ethics*, 1139b4–5. [31] Ibid., 1103b26–29.
[32] Zagzebski, *Virtues of the Mind*, p. 159.

humility plays a crucial role among intellectual virtues and has attracted considerable attention from virtue epistemologists, who have offered a fair number of possible definitions. As Ian Church and Peter Samuelson point out, "there is no shared or even entirely dominant view of intellectual humility in the literature" and "no consensus regarding what we might be confusing intellectual humility with."[33] Alessandra Tanesini goes so far as to say that intellectual humility "is a cluster of strong attitudes,"[34] whereas others see the virtue in question as partly coincident with open-mindedness.[35] Given that the latter is considered an intellectual virtue par excellence,[36] the partial identification between these two virtues confirms the fundamental role that is usually ascribed to intellectual humility among intellectual virtues.

At any rate, be this identification correct or not,[37] focusing on intellectual humility offers one more profitable opportunity to compare virtue epistemology and the ST, as well as to focus on the problems that affect the former.

Among the numerous definitions that epistemologists have provided of intellectual humility, Julia Driver's seems to constitute an intuitive account. According to her, intellectual humility is "low self-worth," holding oneself in low regard, underestimating self-worth to some extent, despite the available evidence. This, however, does not mean that the intellectually humble person underestimates their abilities, which is why Driver distinguishes humility from modesty. For her, "a humble person, unlike a modest person, can paint an accurate, though perhaps unflattering, picture of herself," whereas "the modest person needs to underestimate."[38]

---

[33] Ian Church and Peter Samuelson, *Intellectual Humility: An Introduction to the Philosophy and Science* (London: Bloomsbury Academy, 2017), p. 30.

[34] Alessandra Tanesini, "Intellectual Humility as Attitude," *Philosophy and Phenomenological Research* 96/2018, p. 399.

[35] According to James Spiegel, intellectual humility is "second-order open-mindedness." Open-mindedness is a first-order attitude toward *one's beliefs*, whereas intellectual humility regards the attitude we take toward *ourselves as believers*. See James Spiegel, "Open-Mindedness and Intellectual Humility," *Theory and Research in Education* 10 (2012), pp. 27–38.

[36] "Open-mindedness seems nothing short of rationality itself" (Wayne Riggs, "Open-Mindedness," *Metaphilosophy* 41 [2010], p. 179).

[37] As Pritchard says, open-mindedness and intellectual humility are not manifestations of one single virtue ("Intellectual Humility and the Epistemology of Disagreement," in *Knowledge and Justification: New Perspectives*, ed. by Rodrigo Borges and Ernest Sosa, in *Synthese*, special issue, 2018, p. 7, note 13).

[38] Julia Driver, *Uneasy Virtue* (Cambridge: Cambridge University Press, 2001), p. 115.

Being intellectually humble, therefore, does not seem to imply ignorance about oneself.[39] Peter Hill points out that intellectual humility requires a sense of security and enduring personal worth.[40] This is necessary to reach self-acceptance, recognition of strengths and limitations, the ability to avoid biases, and freedom from relying on social comparison processes motivated by a concern for social status.

However, a circular argument emerges from this picture. The intellectually humble person is expected to have the ability to give an accurate account of herself. Intellectual humility requires awareness of one's own strengths and limitations. At the same time, the ability to know one's strengths and limitations may presuppose intellectual humility. In fact, the attainment of knowledge is thought to be the output of a virtuous cognitive process. Consequently, since intellectual humility is among those virtues that allow its possessors to know, the virtue of intellectual humility may be seen as the cause of an accurate account of one's capabilities.

One may object that my argument implies that, to provide a fair account of one's capabilities, one must be intellectually humble. As a matter of fact, haughty individuals can have a right estimation of their intellectual capabilities and still fail to be intellectually humble.[41] However, my argument does not imply that intellectual humility is *the only* source of an accurate account of one's capabilities. One may become aware of one's own capabilities and limitations because of one's adoption of *other* intellectual virtues such as intellectual courage, confidence in reason, or intellectual perseverance. However, it is likely that at least in some cases intellectual humility may cause one to be aware of one's limitations, from which circularity would follow. (This circularity parallels the one that characterizes all intellectual virtues, given the responsibilist version of virtue epistemology.[42])

In line with the conviction that intellectual humility does not involve ignorance about oneself, Church and Samuelson provide a "doxastic

---

[39] According to Aristotle, those who are unable to give an accurate account of themselves are foolish, "but no virtuous man is foolish or silly" (*Nicomachean Ethics*, 1123b3–4). In the same vein, contemporary accounts of humility usually exclude ignorance and underestimation. Among them are the view of humility as "low concern," championed by Roberts and Wood, *Intellectual Virtues*, and the one according to which humility is "limitations-owning," proposed by Dennis Whitcomb et al., "Intellectual Humility: Owning Our Limitations," *Philosophy and Phenomenological Research* 94/2017, pp. 509–539.
[40] See Peter Hill et al., "A Few Good Measures," in *Handbook of Humility: Theory, Research, and Applications*, ed. by Everett Worthington, Don Davis, and Joshua Hook (New York: Routledge, 2017), p. 119.
[41] See Tanesini, "Intellectual Humility as Attitude," p. 409.   [42] See above, p. 178.

account" of the virtue in question, according to which intellectual humility consists in valuing one's beliefs *as one ought*. For them, someone "cannot be too humble." Rather, intellectual humility is a mean between, on the one hand, valuing too much one's beliefs and having exaggerated confidence in one's abilities and, on the other hand, undervaluing one's beliefs and overestimating one's failures.[43]

This persuasion that intellectual humility needs to be a mean between opposite extremes (intellectual dogmatism and intellectual timidity) is confirmed by Tanesini based on Aristotle's thought on the subject. As she says, "both vanity and timidity have distorting influences on the relations of dependence that hold among members of epistemic communities."[44]

Church and Samuelson employ this view of intellectual humility in an attempt to solve the problem of disagreement, which seems to be particularly able to test the virtue in question. Especially before cases of "intractable disagreement," as the authors in question call them, those who are intellectually humble cannot simply give up their own beliefs, which would be a sign of self-deprecation. They cannot stick to them either, which would be a sign of vanity and arrogance. Therefore, they are expected "to be vigilant": "We should be extra careful and reflective to make sure we are indeed accurately tracking the positive epistemic status of our beliefs."[45] In other words, "sometimes the right way to handle disagreement is to reflect carefully on your own views and try to put yourself in a position to be receptive to the truth."[46] As they say from the beginning of their book, "the world needs more people who are sensitive to their own intellectual failings, who are more likely to 'think it possible' that their political, religious, and moral beliefs 'may be mistaken.'"[47]

This view, however, makes intellectual humility fall into *a self-referential contradiction*. On the one hand, the intellectually humble people are expected to be "sensitive to their own intellectual failings" and ready to "think it possible that their views may be mistaken." On the other hand, however, they do not seem to be equally ready to consider that this very conviction – that the intellectually humble people are expected to be "sensitive to their own intellectual failings" and ready to "think it possible that their views may be mistaken" – may be mistaken.

---

[43] Church and Samuelson, *Intellectual Humility*, p. 7.
[44] Alessandra Tanesini, "Caring for Esteem and Intellectual Reputation," *Royal Institute of Philosophy Supplement* 84 (2018), p. 48. Let me remind the reader that Aristotle did not include humility in his table of virtues. See his *Nicomachean Ethics*, IV, 3.
[45] Church and Samuelson, *Intellectual Humility*, p. 274.   [46] Ibid., p. 285.   [47] Ibid., p. 4.

Those who take the ST seem to be able to avoid both this self-referential contradiction and the problem of circularity mentioned above. Both problems arise from the view that being humble presupposes the ability to give an accurate account of oneself. (If this seems to be unclear regarding the self-referential contradiction, let me remind the reader that this contradiction emerges from the view that the intellectually humble people are expected to be "sensitive to their own intellectual failings," which makes them ready to "think it possible that their views may be mistaken.") However, the ability to be sensitive to one's intellectual failings is of no interest to those who take the ST, nor is it of interest to those who are expected to cultivate intellectual humility from a religious viewpoint. This is confirmed by two recent publications in the field of theology.

First, Grant Macaskill argues that intellectual humility, if seen from the viewpoint of the New Testament, is not simply "a low level of concern to be well regarded by other people."[48] More importantly, it is due to a commitment to Jesus Christ, to our union with him, which takes the form of "dependency on and submission to God."[49] Giving an account of oneself – the author focuses on the idea of low self-concern/estimate – may perhaps be part of the process that makes one humble. At any rate, "humility is embedded in a thick account that associates it with a thoroughgoing willingness to set aside all of one's self-interests (not just intellectual status) to bring about the good of others."[50] Therefore, it is the commitment to the good itself, which Christians are expected to identify with union with God, love for others, and related beliefs, that mainly makes one intellectually humble. The open-mindedness that believers can show while discussing objections to their view is due to their trust in God's power and the reliable faculties that he grants to them.[51] Believers may, therefore, feel ready to develop debates in any possible direction not because they trust in their own virtues, but because of their confidence that, if they employ their faculties in accordance with God's plan, nothing false can be demonstrated. Therefore, it is their commitment to God and the beliefs that convey such a commitment that, so they maintain, can make them intellectually virtuous.

Second, Kent Dunnington focuses on the view of humility that emerges from ancient Christianity, including desert monastic tradition. He shows

---

[48] Grant Macaskill, *The New Testament and Intellectual Humility* (Oxford: Oxford University Press, 2019), p. 169. The author draws this definition from Roberts and Wood, *Intellectual Virtues*.
[49] Ibid., p. 170. [50] Ibid., p. 169. [51] See above, Chapter 5, notes 125ff.

that this view requires "that we hold loosely to any cherished self-image, always on guard against the ways we use our self-image to insulate ourselves from the call to complete dependence upon God."[52] On this basis, Dunnington argues that humility is to be seen as "no-concern," which he compares with the view of humility as "low-concern." Humility "is the disposition to have no concern to develop, clarify, attain, maintain, or safeguard an ego ideal, because of a trust that one's well-being is entirely secured by the care of God."[53] Unlike low concern, which shows an interest in other goods as the proper motive behind one's concern, "no concern specifies trust in the care of God as the proper motive."[54] While referring to other research on humility from the Christian viewpoint proposed by Robert Roberts and Ryan West,[55] Dunnington maintains that the pride these authors depict as fundamental to human agency is necessary for moral development *but not for consistent moral action*.[56] Proper feelings of pride, so he argues, "are goods, essential to the formation of virtue in our fallen condition, but they are penultimate goods."[57] Instead, what leads us to act virtuously is mainly love: "The *no concern* view of Christian humility that I am trying to reclaim and defend takes it as axiomatic that the proper Christian motive of virtuous action is not pride, but love."[58] In this view, love for God and reliance on him mainly make us virtuous, and our duty consists primarily in keeping sight of the good itself. For those who take the ST, the act of aiming at doing good and the commitment to the related beliefs shape the search for truth. It is their commitment to the ultimate end, which is the good itself, that allows them to perfect the mean they employ to that end.

These religiously inspired accounts of intellectual humility suggest that, if one is not concerned about the necessity to give an adequate account of oneself, then one avoids both the self-referential contradiction and the circularity that affect the abovementioned intellectual humility accounts.

The outcomes of these theological considerations characterize the ST as well as, at least at first sight, one virtue epistemology account of intellectual humility, which has been proposed by Pritchard. He lists two views of

---

[52] Kent Dunnington, *Humility, Pride, and Christian Virtue Theory* (New York: Oxford University Press, 2018), p. 38.
[53] Ibid., p. 88.   [54] Ibid., p. 89.
[55] See Robert Roberts and Ryan West, "Jesus and the Virtues of Pride," in *The Moral Psychology of Pride*, ed. by Adam J. Carter and Emma Gordon (Lanham, MD: Rowman & Littlefield, 2017).
[56] "I affirm the necessary role of proper pride in moral formation, but I deny the necessary role of proper pride in an ongoing and consistent life of virtuous action" (Dunnington, *Humility, Pride, and Christian Virtue Theory*, p. 123).
[57] Ibid., p. 135.   [58] Ibid., p. 126.

intellectual humility. They are the "ignorance proposal," according to which intellectually humble people "really do imagine that they are somehow 'lesser' than they, in fact, are," and the "accuracy proposal," which involves "a *correct* assessment of the extent of one's achievements and abilities." He then advances his proposal, the "non-egotist proposal":

> Humility involves lacking those characteristic dispositions involved in excessive self-regard, such as conceit, arrogance, haughtiness, and so on. In contrast, on this view, humility involves the essentially *other*-directed dispositions of, for example, helping others behind the scenes without seeking the credit for doing so. This is in contrast to the previous two proposals which are in effect self-regarding stances, in that they are focussed on one's own assessment of one's achievements and abilities.[59]

This citation should help the reader see the originality of Pritchard's proposal and its closeness to the ST. For Pritchard, the first two accounts are both egocentric and perfectly compatible with epistemic arrogance. As he rightly points out, "owning one's limitations," for example, "could be entirely compatible with being dismissive of others" in case one gives an accurate account of oneself and finds oneself intellectually superior.[60] Like the ST, Pritchard's "non-egotist proposal" does not pay attention to oneself and one's own abilities. This account of intellectual humility, therefore, escapes both self-referential contradiction and circularity. Furthermore, again like the ST, the "non-egotist view," if it arises out of appropriate motivational states (e.g., a love for the truth, which is constitutive of a good intellectual character), genuinely promotes a range of behaviors such as "considering the other person's reasons for thinking otherwise" as well as "being willing to respectively discuss the issue further."[61]

However, Pritchard's view remains different from the ST. According to Pritchard, the intellectually humble person must show "the willingness to change her mind if that is demanded by the evidence."[62] This is plausible from the viewpoint of ME but is not acceptable from the perspective of the ST. Those who take the ST commit themselves to beliefs that, no matter whether rightly or wrongly, they are by no means ready to abandon, even if the available evidence appeared to them to be against them.

Pritchard might rightly observe that when he refers to the willingness to change one's mind if the evidence demands that, he refers to beliefs and not to religious convictions, which, at root, are not a matter of belief. He

---

[59] Pritchard, *Intellectual Humility and the Epistemology of Disagreement*, p. 6.   [60] Ibid., p. 10.
[61] Ibid., p. 9.   [62] Ibid.

may agree that one is not obliged to be ready to change one's hinge commitments,[63] which may render his view similar to the ST. These commitments, however, are exempt from doubt *to anybody*. Namely, they cannot genuinely be doubted. Unlike religious convictions, therefore, they are reconcilable with ME.

At any rate, there are beliefs that do not seem to be exempt from doubt and that not only the champions of the ST but also the supporters of the "non-egotist proposal" would never abandon. Among them, the beliefs without which the proposal in question would be unrecognizable: the belief that one's interlocutors should always be treated respectfully as well as the belief that it should always be paid attention to other person's reasons for thinking otherwise. But what happens if the available evidence seems to suggest that such beliefs should be abandoned? What should the virtue epistemologist who champions the "egotist account" do? She should abandon them, but this implies that the account in question is to be also abandoned. Otherwise, she does not abandon them, but this implies that she becomes a champion of the ST, which, again, means that the account in question is to be abandoned.

Before concluding this section devoted to virtue epistemology and intellectual humility, let me consider a possibility to escape the self-referential contradiction that, as I have argued so far, affects intellectual humility. I will mention authors who do not make explicit reference to the self-referential contradiction under consideration here. However, what they say regarding the nature of intellectual humility seems to offer a potential solution.

Such a potential solution emerges from an essay by Allan Hazlett. For him, there are situations in which "one can reasonably believe p" and at the same time "suspend judgment about whether believing p is reasonable for her." According to Hazlett, "this will set the stage for an account of the virtue of intellectual humility, on which humility is a matter of your higher-order epistemic attitudes."[64]

While trying to reconcile open-mindedness and the holding of strong beliefs, Jonathan Adler held a similar view earlier than Hazlett. (Because of a considerable similarity between open-mindedness and intellectual humility, I am taking into account reflections on open-mindedness, no matter

---

[63] See above, Chapter 4, notes 69ff.
[64] Allan Hazlet, "Higher-Order Epistemic Attitudes and Intellectual Humility," *Episteme* 9 (2012), p. 205.

how close to intellectual humility open-mindedness may be.[65]) According to Adler, open-mindedness is "a second-order attitude toward one's beliefs as believed, and not just toward the specific proposition believed."[66] In his essay devoted to open-mindedness, Wayne Riggs explains this view by arguing that what supports the willingness of an open-minded person to take a challenge to one of her beliefs seriously "is not any sudden or latent doubts about the truth of the belief but rather his acknowledgement that, being human, he could always have got things wrong in this case."[67]

From this emerges that, at least the conviction that human beings are fallible, that is, they "could always have got things wrong," must be taken as *undoubtable*. This, however, does not seem to solve the self-referential contradiction here at stake. On the one hand, we should be ready to take into consideration the possibility of changing our mind in regard *to all of our beliefs*; on the other hand, this is possible only to the extent that in regard of one of our beliefs, that we "could always have got things wrong," we should *not* be ready to take into consideration the possibility of changing our mind.

The supporters of this view do not seem to see that higher-order attitudes and the specific propositions that one believes are both part of one's noetic structure, which is the *whole* structure of one's beliefs.[68] They only see a divide between these two groups of epistemic attitudes (higher-order attitudes and specific propositions). Because of this divide, they say that intellectual humility applies only to one of the two groups in question, the group of the higher-order attitudes, and not to the other one, the beliefs that one holds.

That said, the distinction between higher- and lower-order attitudes is not a solution to avoid the self-referential contradiction here under consideration. One more reason can be shown in support of my view. To this end, let me focus on an example advanced by Riggs. It is an example that had previously been offered by Adler and which Riggs defines "a powerful analogy." The following long citation is justified by the importance of this analogy to supporting my view that the distinction between higher- and lower-order attitudes is not a viable candidate to avoid the self-referential contradiction at stake:

---

[65] See above, notes 35ff.
[66] Jonathan Adler, "Reconciling Open-Mindedness and Belief," *Theory and Research in Education* 2 (2004), p. 130.
[67] Riggs, "Open-Mindedness," p. 180.
[68] "S's *noetic structure* is the set of propositions he believes, together with certain epistemic relations that hold among him and them" (Plantinga, *Warrant: The Current Debate*, p. 72).

> Consider the position of a quality-control officer in a factory that makes widgets. The officer knows that the factory is highly reliable, and hence that nearly every widget that comes down the assembly line is nondefective. But, to safeguard against even the occasional defective widget making it to the market, it is the officer's job to inspect one of every ten widgets before it leaves the factory. Suppose the officer selects widget number 30. Before inspecting it, she confidently believes that it will be nondefective. The fact that she is willing to check to see if it really is nondefective does not indicate some doubt about widget 30. It is not insecurity about widget 30 that prompts the check but rather an awareness of the possibility, albeit low, that the factory might produce a defective widget. Consequently, her belief that widget 30 is nondefective is no weaker than her belief that widget 29 is nondefective, even though she checked one but not the other.[69]

My view is that, on closer inspection, this analogy is a double analogy, neither of which work. The first one is between the belief that the factory is highly reliable and the belief that our cognitive faculties are highly reliable. This analogy does not work because, in the case of our faculties, it is precisely their reliability that puts us in a condition to find out when they fail. In the case of the factory, instead, our ability to find out whether some widgets are defective is not due to the reliability of the production process. More relevant to my purpose is the second analogy under consideration here. It is the analogy between the widgets and our beliefs. This analogy does not work because the officer does not know in advance which widget will be defective. In contrast, one knows that some of one's beliefs are harder to give up than others. The officer would be ready to check every widget if this did not delay the production process. In contrast, everyone knows that there are some beliefs that do not need to be checked. The level of confidence in one's beliefs varies depending on their closeness to the center of our noetic structure, where beliefs that are considered undeniable are situated.

All said and done, the theory that we should distinguish between higher- and lower-order attitudes and be ready to change our minds in regard to all of our beliefs is untenable. Not only does it fall into contradiction; it does not account for a common distinction between beliefs that can be subjected to doubt and beliefs that cannot – these beliefs cannot genuinely be doubted because doubting them would imply to doubt, in turn, all of our beliefs. In conclusion, distinctions between first- and second-order epistemic attitudes do not seem to salvage several accounts of intellectual humility from self-referential contradiction.

[69] Riggs, "Open-Mindedness," p. 181.

6.3 Self-Referential Contradiction, Circularity, and ME

I have shown so far that various problems, among which self-referential contradiction and circularity, beset ME, which is one of the reasons why ME should be replaced by the ST.

Let me now refer to two passages, one from Plato's *Gorgias* and one from Aquinas's *Summa theologiae*, which I have already quoted in previous chapters. First, the point Plato makes is that the philosopher should desire to be refuted if she says something untrue.[70] This implies that this very point (i.e., that the philosopher should prefer to be refuted) should not be refuted; that is, the philosopher should not desire it to be refuted. Second, Aquinas claims that one may *want* to continue researching in support of one's beliefs, no matter how convincing contrary evidence is. Various reasons, among which the desire to honor God and do good to the neighbor, may lead one to do so.[71] Both Plato's and Aquinas's passages suggest assumptions and related unjustified beliefs that play a crucial role in the knowing process. Newman openly makes this point while distinguishing assent from inference. According to him, "sometimes assent fails, while the reasons for it and the inferential act, which is the recognition of those reasons, are still present and in force."[72]

Looking at these doctrines and thoughts suggests that we all firmly possess some beliefs, though they are not justified. (When I refer to justified beliefs, I include the ones that we possess intuitively, such as the principle of noncontradiction and the idea that we have two hands. They can be *indirectly* justified by having recourse to demonstrations *ad hominem*.) More importantly, we all seem to firmly hold beliefs that we are not ready to abandon even if more evidence seemed, rightly or not, to support their negation. Instead, we seem to be ready to seek whatever evidence can be found to reaffirm our beliefs.

If so, those who take each belief as the mere outcome of the intellectual activity end up contradicting themselves, and their view falls into a self-referential contradiction. In fact, this very belief – that each belief is the mere outcome of the intellectual activity – is not the outcome of any intellectual activity.

Also, circularity emerges because, if any commitment needs to be first assessed by way of reason, then one ultimately relies on reason. But if

---

[70] See Plato, *Gorgias*, 458 a3–b3. See above, Chapter 4, note 6.
[71] See *Summa theologiae*, II-II, q. 2, a. 9, ad 2. See above, Chapter 3, note 103.
[72] Newman, GA, Bk. VI, §1.

I only rely on reason, this can only be said by way of reason, which is a circular argument. In cases such as Descartes's view, it is *by way of reason* that the correct working of one's *rational* abilities must be evaluated.[73] Descartes falls into a circular argument also when he refers to God's eternal veracity taken as the warrant that allows one to rely on *one's reason*. For Descartes, in fact, we attain God's eternal veracity *by reason*.[74]

This circularity, which is typically attributed to Descartes, might, at first sight, be attributed to Aquinas as well. However, this is incompatible with the thesis that I have advanced so far, that Aquinas's thought supports the ST. Taking the ST implies a-rational commitments to doing good, whereas the circularity under consideration emerges when no a-rational views are accepted, and every view must first be determined via an intellectual enterprise. Thus, to continue holding my thesis that Aquinas's thought offers adequate support to the ST, I need to explore and reject the idea that the circularity in question may apply to Aquinas's reflection.

While focusing on Aquinas's epistemology, Stump reacted against the conviction, which is often ascribed to Aquinas, that his epistemology is foundationalist and internalist.[75] In doing so, Stump argued for the presence in Aquinas's thought of "a species of externalism, with reliabilist elements." The externalism in question is grounded on theological views: We rely on our cognitive faculties since we believe that God designed them to put us in a condition to know. This allows us to see why we may consider Aquinas both optimist and fallibilist. In Thomas's view, we are creatures affected by the limitations that are typical of the post-fall condition. This means that we cannot be certain regarding the incontrovertible truth of the principles of science and the consistency of the demonstration processes. At the same time, we can cultivate optimism because God, who is the omnipotent, omniscient, and perfectly loving creator of everything, has granted us cognitive faculties to allow us to attain the truth. As a consequence, "when we use sense and intellect as God designed them to be

---

[73] Michael Losonsky notes that "the idea that the mind needs to be improved and that its improvement requires the mind's reliance on its own devices is a guiding idea of modern philosophy from Descartes to Kant" (Michael Losonsky, *Enlightenment and Action from Descartes to Kant: Passionate Thought* [Cambridge: Cambridge University Press, 2001], p. 12).

[74] See above, Chapter 2, pp. 30 and 37.

[75] See Eleonore Stump, "Aquinas on the Foundations of Knowledge," *Canadian Journal of Philosophy*, suppl. vol. 17 (1992), p. 150. The author reacted to Plantinga's and Wolterstorff's attribution of foundationalism to Aquinas. See Plantinga, "Reason and Belief in God," p. 48. See also Wolterstorff, *Reason within the Bounds of Religion*, p. 30.

used in the environment suited to them," we should consider those faculties fully reliable.

A question, however, emerges before this reading of Aquinas's perspective. Is this perspective caused by reason or faith? Aquinas in fact argues that we can affirm the truth of theism either by faith or by philosophical demonstration:

> Even as regards those truths about God which human reason could have discovered, it was necessary that man should be taught by a divine revelation; because the truth about God such as reason could discover, would only be known by a few, and that after a long time, and with the admixture of many errors.... It was therefore necessary that besides philosophical science built up by reason, there should be a sacred science learned through revelation.[76]

Similarly, our reliabilist view, according to which God has granted us effective cognitive faculties, should be affirmed either by faith or by philosophical demonstration. In the latter case, however, such a view falls into a vicious circle: we rely on our cognitive faculties to affirm the truth of theism and at the same time we rely on what we know of theism to affirm the reliability of our cognitive faculties. To avoid the circularity in question, therefore, our reliabilist view needs to be grounded on Christian faith.

Note that, for Stump, "because God has designed our cognitive capacities in such a way as to make us cognizers of the truth, it is only in our post-fall condition that error, deception, mistake, or even false opinion is a possibility at all." She makes reference to a well-established Christian conviction, based on which it is sin that makes us reject God and fail to know. It remains unclear, however, whether or not she is really talking about the Christian faith. Rather, she seems to refer to theism from a merely rational viewpoint. Furthermore, she claims that "it is plausible ... that a theory of knowledge at least similar to Aquinas's can form part of a non-theistic worldview."[77] In addition, Stump does not mention the Christian faith nor does she label "theological" the externalism she champions, except on the last page of her essay.

At any rate, if it is grounded on a merely rational theism, this reliabilist view, as I have argued so far, falls into circularity. This leads me to

---

[76] *Summa theologiae*, I, q. 1, a. 1. That is what Aquinas teaches throughout his works, as Ralph McInerny emphasized (see Ralph McInerny, "On Behalf of Natural Theology," *Proceedings of the American Catholic Philosophical Association* 54 [1980], p. 64).

[77] Stump, "Aquinas on the Foundations of Knowledge," p. 150.

conclude that Thomas's theism, on which Stump bases her proposal, should be seen as stemming from a-rational commitments to God in faith. If so, Aquinas's epistemology does not fall into any circularity, and his view supports one in taking the ST from ME.

6.4 Nowadays, Most People, Including Those Who in Theory Adhere to ME, Can Take the ST

The circularity that has emerged so far is due to the conviction, which mere epistemologists typically hold, that our cognitive faculties are expected to justify all our beliefs, including those that regard *the way these faculties work*. This omni-pervasive role ascribed to the cognitive faculties and the justification not only causes the circularity under consideration; it also causes the self-referential contradiction that affects ME. On the one hand, ME is based on the conviction that every belief should be justified, be this justification indirect (when it regards beliefs possessed only by way of intuition) or direct (when it regards beliefs that can be acquired by way of demonstration). On the other hand, this very conviction is not based on any justification. It is a mere assumption, and it is similar to numerous other assumptions incoherently adopted by those who in theory adhere to ME.

A number of such assumptions can easily be found in contemporary Western thought. Nowadays, nobody would seriously deny the assumption that there are fundamental rights that all human beings, with no exception, should be put in a condition to exercise, regardless of race, religion, political orientation, and the like. From this fundamental assumption, many others follow. Nobody would seriously affirm that the force of law and the punishment of those who have committed crimes should resemble violence or revenge. In the same vein, nobody would seriously deny that some forms of freedom, such as those regarding speech, information, and sexual orientation, must be promoted. Note that saying that we would never seriously deny such beliefs means that we are likely to stick to them, no matter how convincing contrary evidence may appear to us to be. Obviously, from this, inconclusiveness of debates follows.

Someone might object that these commonly accepted assumptions are grounded at least partly in the Christian religion.[78] If so, the idea that they are held and promoted by not only believers would seem no longer

---

[78] In regard to human rights, John Witte and Christian M. Green notice the special role played by Christianity in the definition of such rights and liberties. According to them, various Asian and

sustainable. I will concentrate below on the fact that at least some of the assumptions under consideration are often considered a Christian inheritance.[79] For now, I am interested in highlighting that the assumptions in question belong to contemporary Western culture. They are accepted by not only believers but also unbelievers, be these assumptions grounded in the Christian religion or not. In this connection, let me recall the famous words that Maritain uttered in response to the question of how people belonging to various traditions and religions could widely accept a definitive list of human rights: "Yes, we agree about the rights *but on condition no one asks us why.*"[80] Consequently, even if the commitments at stake were just a Christian inheritance, talking about both believers and unbelievers as adopters of the ST would still be appropriate.

To assess the abovementioned, widely held acceptance, let me now refer to the beginning of the philosophy of history in the eighteenth century.[81] For the first time, thinkers and philosophers started considering history a continuous development toward more and more valuable achievements. Some of these thinkers, such as Johann G. Herder, Gotthold E. Lessing, and Johann F. Schiller, employed the concept of *education of mankind* to insist on the persuasion that throughout history, some ideas were going to improve human beings morally and intellectually.[82] Implied by this view was the conviction that a rational plan, in some cases coinciding with the religious concept of Providence, guided the whole history.[83] Especially relevant to this perspective was the French revolution, seen by Immanuel

---

indigenous traditions "have also maintained a healthy skepticism about modern formulations of human rights, and question whether human rights are truly universal or just the hegemonic creations of Western Christianity and Enlightenment liberalism" (John Witte and Christian M. Green, "Introduction," in *Religion and Human Rights: An Introduction*, ed. by John Witte and Christian M. Green [Oxford: Oxford University Press, 2012], pp. 5 and 17).

[79] According to Wolterstorff, "the recognition of natural human rights is one of the great jewels bequeathed by Hebrew and Christian Scripture to humankind" (Nicholas Wolterstorff, "Christianity and Human Rights," in Witte and Green, eds., *Religion and Human Rights: An Introduction*, p. 54).

[80] Maritain was speaking in the name of the members of the drafting committee that, after the end of the World War II, was commissioned to prepare the abovementioned list by the United Nations Commission on Human Rights.

[81] Speaking of the "beginning of philosophy of history in the eighteenth century" does not mean that any reflections that are crucial to philosophy of history, such as the one Augustine delivers in his *City of God* (413–427), must necessarily belong to the modern age.

[82] The titles of some of their works are eloquent enough: Johann G. Herder, *This Too a Philosophy of History for the Formation of Humanity* (1774); Gotthold E. Lessing, *The Education of the Human Race* (1780); Johann F. Schiller, *Letters upon the Aesthetic Education of Man* (1794).

[83] As has appropriately been noticed, "the belief in a teleology of history, that history has a purpose, either a doom or salvation of humankind, is deeply rooted in religious thinking" (Dmitri Nikulin, *The Concept of History* [London: Bloomsbury, 2017], p. x).

Kant, Johann G. Fichte, and Georg F. W. Hegel, among others, as the event by which history and its rational plan had openly manifested itself. Just a few years after the revolution, Kant said that a plan inscribed into human nature had, in this way, appeared.[84] After Kant, both Fichte and Hegel were going to mention the limits of that event, which they argued were due to the "abstract" philosophy of Enlightenment.[85] This, however, did not spoil the overall worthiness of that event, which emphasized values doomed to become indisputable in our history. The equal fundamental worthiness of all human beings, with no exception, is openly relatable to the famous triad of "freedom, equality, and fraternity" that accompanied that event. From this view, many facts followed (e.g., the abolition of torture), which in contemporary Western society nobody, including mere epistemologists, would seriously question.

This reference to the modern philosophy of history supports my view that mere epistemologists, be they Christian believers or not, more or less implicitly take for granted and stick to several assumptions, no matter how convincing contrary evidence might seem to be at first sight. This allows us to say that, like Christians who are not mere epistemologists, mere epistemologists can be responsible for the inconclusiveness of debates, although this is inconsistent with ME.

Before moving on to elaborate on this, however, I should consider the objection that the assumptions at stake cannot be compared to those I considered while focusing on the Christian revelation. In other words, Christians are expected to firmly maintain certain beliefs against contrary evidence *by way of faith*. In contrast, the assumptions I have considered so far seem to be somehow due to *rational* processes. These assumptions seem to be grounded in a philosophical view of reality and human nature. Consequently, since it can be explained by having recourse to such a view, their adoption cannot be seen as responsible for the inconclusiveness of debates.

Two responses can be offered to this objection. My first response relates to the conviction that history is guided by a rational plan. It is on the basis of this conviction that the abovementioned assumptions, which have been

---

[84] For him, the French revolution had been caused "by anything other than a moral disposition within the human race" (Immanuel Kant, "A Renewed Attempt to Answer the Question: 'Is the Human Race Continually Improving?,'" in *Kant's Political Writings*, ed. by Hans Reiss [Cambridge: Cambridge University Press, 1970], p. 182).

[85] According to Hegel, during the French revolution "purely abstract philosophical principles were set up" (Hegel, *Lectures on the History of Philosophy*, p. 449). Hegel considered Kant's purely formal concept of will among the causes of the fact that the revolution resulted in the Terror.

gained through history, can be seen as gained *rationally*. This conviction, however, is in turn based on a typically Christian view, according to which God, with his reason, directs everything, history included. Because of their faith, Christians were able to see the seemingly chaotic multitude of events that constitute history as many components of a rational plan designed by God. This is confirmed by the fact that pre-Christian philosophers had not considered history a philosophical object. From a strictly rational viewpoint, there are no reasons for maintaining that the historical events are related to one another by a rational plan such as the divine one that God has foreseen for his creation. In contrast, modern philosophers of history have constantly elaborated on the Christian idea of Providence, as Karl Löwith has argued.[86] (At any rate, I have already said that I am only interested in assessing the crucial role that various assumptions widely accepted in contemporary Western society may play in epistemology, regardless of the possibility that they are rooted in the Christian doctrines.)

My second response is that some of the abovementioned assumptions can by no means be seen as rationally justified, be the justification in question *ad hominem* or not. In Chapter 5, I have assumed that adopting the SA should be justified, whereas adopting the NA does not need any justification. This assumption perfectly coincides with the fact that ME is *taken for granted* in the field of religion. Suppose I deny from the outset that a supernatural being may exist and shape the way in which I live my relationship with him or her, and do so because religious belief lacks justification. In that case, I am applying the more general idea that any belief must be justified, including when it regards the religious experience. This idea, however, is self-referentially contradictory, though it is the main assumption of ME. (Let me point out that, given my reply's aim, being self-referentially contradictory is of no interest. I aim at showing that mere epistemologists adopt assumptions *without justification*, whether or not these assumptions are self-referentially contradictory.)

To confirm the view that even mere epistemologists may adopt assumptions without justification, including assumptions that turn them into (implicit) adopters of the ST, let me consider the objection that views such as that racist attitudes are wrong must be somewhat grounded, perhaps in something like the principle of credulity.[87] In this way, the

---

[86] Löwith's renowned thesis is that the various forms of modern philosophy of history developed a secularized Providence. See Karl Löwith, *Meaning in History: The Theological Implications of the Philosophy of History* (Chicago, IL: Chicago University Press, 1949), esp. pp. 201f.

[87] For more on this principle, especially how Reid employed it in epistemology, see above, Chapter 2, note 28.

inviolability of the commitment to the wrongness of racism may be understood to have an epistemic basis, and not to be rooted in the pursuit of the good. I agree that these commitments can be provided with epistemic basis. Those who support the view that racism is wrong may do so simply because they take for granted and believe what (the vast majority of) others say. However, adopters of the ST will be tenacious in sticking to their view, whereas those who rely on epistemic reasons will likely be led to change their mind once more convincing contrary reasons seem to show up. This should especially apply if the principle of credulity is at stake. Becoming aware that the beliefs one holds are supported by the principle of credulity will likely lead one to doubt the beliefs in question or at least to consider them matter for debate.

I can conclude that not only believers but also unbelievers adopt some assumptions because they *want* to and not because they argue in their support. This conclusion is corroborated by Aquinas's reflection on the relationship between assent and consideration, as well as Newman's separation between assent and inference.[88]

Note that adopting some assumptions and sticking to them even against contrary evidence is not necessarily due to the will *to do good*. Of course, since the subject here under consideration is the ST, I only consider the commitment to promoting one's spiritual betterment. However, it is opportune to point out that modern philosophy has not only emphasized the emergence of undeniable values, such as the assumptions mentioned above. It has also determined the other side of the coin (i.e., the existence of bodies of beliefs to which some stick, regardless of contrary evidence, and do so because of various interests, especially economic interests). This is the theory of "ideology," which emerges from Marx's philosophy.[89] Marx did not offer an unambiguous definition of the concept at stake, and his interpreters have to infer definitions from his use of the word. Nevertheless, ideology may plausibly be thought of as a form of reasoning that, as Bhikhu Parekh says, is "systematically biased in its orientation" and "justificatory in its implications."[90]

From this, two substantial considerations follow.

---

[88] See above, Chapter 3, note 103, and Chapter 1, note 53, respectively.
[89] To focus on the concept of ideology, the scholars of Marx usually refer to *The German Ideology*, which Marx wrote in 1845–1846 and was not published in full until 1932.
[90] Bhikhu Parekh, *Marx's Theory of Ideology* (1982) (London: Routledge, 2015), Introduction (no page number). According to Steven Lukes, ideology is "social in origin, illusory in content, and serving class interests" (Steven Lukes, *Marxism and Morality* [Oxford: Oxford University Press,1985], p. 3).

First, when combined with Aquinas's and Newman's reflections, Marx's theory of ideology confirms the thesis that ME falls into a self-referential contradiction. On the one hand, their practitioners declare that one should accept the outcome of the intellectual activity, whatever it shall be; on the other hand, the very statement that one should accept the outcome of the intellectual activity, whatever shall be, is not the outcome of intellectual research. In other words, mere epistemologists' will plays a crucial role in the choices they make, which means that, before contrary evidence, no matter how convincing it seems to be, they will continue reflecting in search of new evidence that can reconfirm their original view.

Innumerable occurrences of this attitude can be found throughout the history of ideas. I have referred to Descartes's attempt to depict reality in a way that is objective, yet also seems to stem from his will to know from God's point of view.[91] I may also mention the innumerable and endless debates on the existence of God. They have been conducted by believers, unbelievers, and mere epistemologists. (As I have already said above, both unbelievers and believers can act as mere epistemologists. Unbelievers openly declare that they act in this way. After all, they are unbelievers precisely because they are not ready to believe any divine revelation that is not [yet] justified. Believers act as mere epistemologists to the extent that they, too, believe that one should only accept religious beliefs that have previously been justified.)

Second, everyone seems to take for granted a-rational commitments and related unjustified beliefs. Marx's reflection on ideology and the debates on the existence of God, which I have mentioned above, are probably the best examples of the fact that the believers who take the ST are not the only ones who want to stick to their beliefs, regardless of contrary evidence.[92] At any rate, one can take the ST to the extent that one's assumptions lead one *to do good and promote one's spiritual betterment*. I have shown so far that significant values have appeared along with modern history. Equality, freedom, and fraternity among all human beings are values whose stable goodness no one would seriously question nowadays. Those who want to stick to these values, no matter how convincing contrary evidence may appear to be, can appropriately be seen as adopters of the ST.

---

[91] See above, Chapter 5, p. 133.
[92] According to Amelie O. Rorty, Descartes was directed to write his *Meditations* by his will to keep "running through the proofs for the existence of God over and over, over and over and over" (Amelie O. Rorty, "Descartes on Thinking with the Body," in *Cambridge Companion to Descartes*, ed. by John Cottingham [Cambridge: Cambridge University Press, 1992], p. 386).

However, adopting the ST implies much more than the adhesion to the abovementioned values and their related beliefs. No matter how sincere such adhesion may be, the values in question are too general, whereas acting on their basis is possible only *in particular circumstances*. Those who commit to the values at stake can consistently take the ST to the extent that they equally commit to a well-structured body of beliefs, which allows them to apply those values to the particular circumstances in which to act. Needless to say, for believers, this is much easier than for unbelievers. Believers enjoy a body of beliefs, which they receive from long and established traditions. By contrast, unbelievers who only rely on the values mentioned above need to locate the more particular occurrences of those values, which is a difficult task.

At any rate, although the task in question requires much less from believers than unbelievers, both of them can successfully take the ST only if they are committed to doing good and promoting their spiritual growth. This commitment is a *personal* choice that depends on one's will to do good. As I have shown while treating religious diversity, the existence of a well-established body of beliefs certainly supports one's choices and facilitates their realization. However, improving one's spirituality and taking the ST does not automatically proceed from one's taking part in a specific tradition. Instead, it first and foremost depends on one's will and determination.

This distinction between adhesion to a body of beliefs and a personal choice corresponds to the distinction between theory and practice. It is because of one's goodwill, not the mere possession of beliefs, that one commits oneself to the good. Like the believer, the unbeliever may superficially (only intellectually) adhere to fundamental tenets, such as the equal dignity of all human beings, without committing herself to them. Consequently, her adhesion will not lead her to cultivate good habits and pursue human flourishing.

6.5 Those Who Take the ST Are in the Best Possible Condition to Achieve Partial Conclusiveness

On the view that I have outlined so far, full inconclusiveness seems to be the only outcome when believers and unbelievers come to discuss the credibility of Christian faith. (Believers may sometimes act as mere epistemologists, although they are coherent with their faith, as I take it here, only when they act as adopters of the ST. In contrast, unbelievers – at least those who reject faith on the ground that there is no sufficient evidence –

are coherent with their lack of faith when they act as mere epistemologists. However, this does not exclude that they may sometimes act as adopters of the ST.)

I have already shown that when believers take the ST, they may also significantly benefit research and debates, which means that inconclusiveness might partly be overcome. Here I intend to show how exactly this occurs with regard both to believers and unbelievers.

First, inconclusiveness depends on the degree of firmness with which the interlocutors who firmly want to stick to their beliefs hold those beliefs. The more they want to stick to them, the more inconclusive their debates will be. Aquinas's argument supports this view. For him, the *actual consideration* of that which is evident is, in some cases, due to love for God and the neighbor.[93] This love perfects faith, and both love and faith can be experienced at various levels of intensity. Therefore, it is possible to conclude that the more the faithful love and trust in God, the more they want to stick to their belief in him. Something analogous can be said of unbelievers. Presumably, everybody will stick to their beliefs in proportion to the love they have for them and what is implied by them. An atheist, who intensely loved his only child, and equally intensely suffered for having involuntarily caused her premature death, may want to firmly stick to his conviction that he is not responsible for what happened and that a perfectly loving God should not have permitted such an evil. A famous atheist, whose books were bestsellers, will presumably love the reputation, success, and money such books provided. It is equally presumable to expect her to stick to atheism in proportion to her love for the reputation, success, and money in question. (Obviously, a believer may behave in a way that is equally not commendable to the extent that her adhesion to religious belief is mainly intellectual. She too may stick to theism in proportion to her love for reputation, success, and money.)

Second, inconclusiveness also depends on where, in one's noetic structure, beliefs are placed.[94] I mean that the more crucial to the noetic structure a certain belief is, the more inconclusive the debate regarding that belief will be. To the bestselling atheist mentioned above, the belief that God does not exist is certainly more important than the belief that the hiddenness argument, for example, is correct. The latter may be useful to support the former; however, it can be replaced by other arguments,

---

[93] See *Summa theologiae*, II-II, q. 2, a. 9, ad 2. See above, Chapter 3, note 103.
[94] See above, note 68.

whereas the former cannot be replaced by theism, unless the atheist in question stops being an atheist.

Before elaborating on the idea that inconclusiveness comes in degrees, let me consider a remarkable objection that may be raised against the two reasons that I have just advanced. Both of them are based on the persuasion that all of us have a noetic structure, constituted by an indefinite number of beliefs. (Strictly speaking, I referred to the noetic structure while advancing *the second* reason. However, the existence of various beliefs is implied by the first reason as well. If one sticks to some beliefs more than others, this implies that one has several beliefs, which one holds at different degrees of certainty.) This persuasion implies that the beliefs in question are distinct from each other and are not subject to evolution, which means that they may be replaced by others and be excluded by one's noetic structure but would nonetheless remain defined once and for all. It follows that, when in ordinary language we say that beliefs evolve, we only mean that the subject who holds them changed her mind and now holds other beliefs, which are more or less slightly different from the ones she held before. This persuasion may appear to be simply obvious, and nonetheless it is based on a theory of truth, which, like the vast majority of philosophical theories, is not unquestionable (i.e., the theory of truth as correspondence between a statement and a certain state of affairs that exist independently of their representations).[95]

Is it, therefore, possible – so the objection at stake may run – that, once the concept of truth adopted has changed, the two reasons that I have advanced above are no longer acceptable? Let me consider the alternative concept of truth that traces back to idealist thinkers.[96] As is known, it was especially Hegel who rejected the concept of truth as correspondence that had been spontaneously adopted in the past. For him, this idea was unacceptable because it implied the conviction that the object, which the subject knows, is separate from the knowing subject. Hegel labeled this conviction "abstract" and took it as due to the "abstract intellect." Unlike

---

[95] I am referring to the classical theory of correspondence, which traces back to Aristotle and his dictum: "To say of what is that it is not, or of what is not that it is, is false, while to say of what is that it is, or of what is not that it is not, is true" (Aristotle, *Metaphysics* 1011b25–28, tr. by William D. Ross, in *The Works of Aristotle*, 2nd ed. [Oxford: Oxford University Press, 1928]).

[96] I am aware that various alternative concepts of truth have been proposed. Here I refer to the antirealist alternative, which traces back to idealism and Kant. For an insightful defense of the correspondence theory, see Richard Fumerton, *Realism and the Correspondence Theory of Truth* (Lanham, MD: Rowman & Littlefield, 2002). That which I am going to say about Hegel's alternative concept of truth coincides with some reasons Fumerton mentions in defense of the correspondence theory. See below, note 98.

"speculative reason," the abstract intellect cannot see that one is strictly related to the things one knows.[97] When we know certain things, these things are the outcome of a relationship that, along with experience and history, has developed between them and us. Therefore, truth should not be taken as the correspondence between us and the things that are allegedly placed before us. Truth should instead *include* the history of our relationship with the things in question and should consequently undergo constant revisions due to the prosecution of the historical process at stake. This, however, seems affected by self-referential contradiction. Once it has been advanced, Hegel's concept of truth, too, seems to be placed before us, as separate from us, and susceptible to being known as something other than us. Furthermore, that which Hegel's followers say about it seems to remain constantly true. Not surprisingly, they constantly re-propose Hegel's theory as the German philosopher proposed it.[98]

Let me now elaborate on the idea that those who adopt the ST can (partly) achieve conclusiveness. One's noetic structure is not only constituted by beliefs that debaters consider undeniable. It is also constituted by beliefs that, in proportion to their remoteness from the beliefs that the debaters consider undeniable, may be replaced by other beliefs. Consequently, once confronted with contrary evidence, every debater will be ready to change her beliefs in proportion to the distance of these beliefs from the center of her noetic structure.

Although the change in question may be possible to all and not only to adopters of the ST, it seems hard to deny that this is especially true for the adopters in question. One who takes the ST promotes the best possible condition to do research and develop discussions, because one's aim is first and foremost one's spiritual betterment. This includes the will and the ability to benefit one's interlocutors, and not the attainment of truth, let alone the demonstration that one's interlocutor is wrong. I have already made this point while addressing how those who take the ST and believe

---

[97] "When Hegel refers to something as abstract, he means that it is being treated as separate, drawn apart from some unity or whole to which it properly belongs.... To conceive a thing abstractly is to conceive it as merely immediate, not mediated by its relation to some larger whole" (Philip Grier, "The Speculative Concrete," in *Hegel, History, and Interpretation*, ed. by Shaun Gallagher [Albany: State University of New York Press, 1997], p. 178).

[98] "Anti-realists invariably either implicitly reintroduce into their own views the category of representation-independent fact their position commits them to rejecting, or their view degenerates into incoherence by becoming inexpressible." In the end, there is no possibility to understand alternative conceptions of truth without reintroducing the correspondence conception: "Indeed, it is through a conception of truth as correspondence that one can coherently capture what truth is suggested by anti-realist positions" (Fumerton, *Realism and the Correspondence Theory of Truth*, p. xi).

that their religion is true may treat the followers of other religions. Benefiting one's interlocutors implies valuing their views, which favors the opportunity to increase mutual understanding. Believers should be guided not only by the love of God but also by the love of one's neighbor. In other words, debaters may take part in the good itself, and put aside any other goods, especially those that could spoil the search for truth: the exaggerated confidence in one's capabilities, the lack of consideration of the opinions of others, the precipitation in coming to conclusions (especially out of the desire to receive rewards for what one has done), and so on.

Something analogous can be said concerning those mere epistemologists who, more or less implicitly and against the main assumption of ME, may take the ST, which means that they may stick to the widespread values that I have mentioned above. If one does research bearing in mind the aim of equality and fraternity among human beings, then one commits oneself to respect one's interlocutors and their views. This means that, given the assumption of equality, one is always ready to learn from others, as I have shown while considering Aquinas's conviction that "no doctrine is so false as not to have some truth mingled with error."[99] Let me point out that substantial evidence is brought to this conviction by another typical aspect of Aquinas's customary way of conducting debates. While replying to objections, he does not usually reject them. On the contrary, he typically highlights their validity, and then shows that the validity in question is only partial and needs reconsidering from a wider perspective.

In a similar vein, bearing in mind the idea of universal fraternity should lead one to conduct research and debates to benefit one's interlocutors. This is likely to guarantee that nothing, including the possession of truth, is used against one's interlocutors. A famous *pensée* by Pascal immediately comes to mind: "We make an idol of truth itself."[100] Although Pascal does not explicitly say that truth can be used against others, he would clearly accept that this is possible. For him, an idol denies charity, which means that an idol, which can sometimes coincide with the truth, leads humans to do evil.

May it be objected that humans are unable to effectively practice virtues apart from charity? After all, Augustine famously claimed that one cannot love things rightly without directing them toward God.[101] If things are not

---

[99] See *Summa theologiae*, I-II, q. 102, a. 5, ad 4. See above, Chapter 3, note 95.
[100] See above, Chapter 5, note 4.
[101] See Jennifer Herdt, *Putting on Virtue: The Legacy of the Splendid Vices* (Chicago, IL: University of Chicago Press, 2008), p. 75.

ordered to God, then they are ordered to self, which is the *superbia*, pride,[102] that Augustine says pervades pagan virtues.[103] In Augustine's footsteps, Luther goes so far as to reject any virtue, not only false virtue. For him, habituation should be replaced by complete passivity before grace.[104] Augustine's view of pagan virtues, however, seems to be significantly more nuanced: "Augustine bequeathed to subsequent Christian thought a positive account of the Christian life as a life of habituation in virtue, where Christ is the ultimate exemplar of virtue."[105] This seems to somewhat prepare Aquinas's view, which "offers an account of pagan virtue as true if imperfect, directed not toward our true final end but at least toward proximate ends capable of being directed beyond themselves to our true final end."[106]

Although Aquinas's view of pagan virtue is not exempt from ambiguity,[107] the idea that it is a balanced one seems convincing. Herdt describes how Aquinas treats gratitude. He appeals to Seneca, according to whom "he that hastens to repay, is animated with a sense, not of gratitude but of indebtedness" and "he that wishes to repay too soon, is an unwilling debtor, and an unwilling debtor is ungrateful." Following Aquinas's treatment, Herdt notices that, from a Christian viewpoint,

> pagan gratitude will fall short of perfect gratitude ... insofar as pagan gratitude is not gratitude to God ... But pagan gratitude to family and community is nevertheless open to being ordered beyond family and community to God; it is not a prideful assertion of self-sufficiency. It is thus true gratitude, not simply a counterfeit, ordered to self, that would undermine even the possibility of choosing virtuous actions for their own sake.[108]

---

[102] Augustine "charges that pagan virtue not only lacks the right conception of the end, but also includes a mistaken conception of the end, because it expresses arrogance (*superbia*)" (Terence Irwin, "Spendid Vices? Augustine For and Against Pagan Virtues," *Medieval Philosophy and Theology* 8 [1999], p. 124).

[103] See Herdt, *Putting on Virtue*, p. 49.

[104] In Luther's view, as Herdt points out, "Christian righteousness requires the complete interruption of ordinary processes of habituation in the virtues and a foundational moment of pure passivity in which human agency is wholly abandoned" (ibid., p. 15).

[105] Ibid., p. 12.   [106] Ibid.

[107] "Aquinas's generous account of pagan virtue relies on distinctions between acquired and infused, moral and theological virtues that prove ambiguous and that thus leave his synthesis vulnerable to later critique" (ibid.). Thus, it is not surprising that "Aquinas's solution is capable of being interpreted in divergent ways ... it might be seen as reinforcing the separation between natural and supernatural already present within scholastic thought.... On a contrasting interpretation ... pagan virtue ... is true but imperfect, resting on an incomplete grasp of our final end" (ibid., p. 76).

[108] Ibid., pp. 78f.

Precisely from a merely Christian viewpoint, it is possible to recognize the legitimacy of virtues practiced by unbelievers. In this connection, debates on how to sincerely and effectively practice the virtues do not regard only unbelievers. Believers, too, should be stimulated to ask themselves if their way of acting is really consistent with their faith. Herdt appropriately notices that "not only does Aquinas carve out conceptual space for true virtue among pagans, but he also recognizes the possibility of merely apparent virtue among Christians."[109] Not surprisingly, early modern debates on these topics occurred in a Christian world, and the severe criticism expressed by Luther was directed against both pagans and Christians, as shown by his attack against both "putting on virtue" and "putting on Christ."[110]

This makes us focus on both believers' and unbelievers' ability to seriously commit themselves to do good and achieve their own spiritual betterment. A body of beliefs and an established tradition certainly help one make the right choice. The love for good and the commitment to acting accordingly, however, is a personal matter. It comes in degrees, which is why the act of taking the ST and the success that this can provide in epistemology (i.e., the partial conclusiveness here under consideration) occurs in proportion to such love and commitment.

The personal nature of the commitment in question also explains why it does not seem possible to verify whether or not conclusiveness is caused by the ST. If conclusiveness is due to the commitment to doing good, and this commitment has a personal nature, then conclusiveness is due to personal motivations. Consequently, demonstrating (i.e., publicly verifying) whether conclusiveness is due to the act of taking the ST or to other circumstances is a hard enterprise. To this end, one should be able to assess what occurs in the interiority of people involved in investigations and debates, which is impossible.

At any rate, the verification at stake is of no interest here. I am only interested in showing that taking the ST provides the best possible conditions to achieve conclusiveness.

Can it be hypothesized that the mutual trust and understanding, which both believers and unbelievers generate by taking the ST, may induce one's opponent to abandon the assumptions that the opponent considers undeniable? After all, this seems consistent with the ST if one is convinced that one's assumptions are true and exclude their negation. In other words, believers should be expected to hope that they will, in the end, be able to

---

[109] Ibid., p. 80.   [110] See ibid., p. 2.

convert unbelievers, and vice versa. A problem, therefore, would emerge. Both believers and unbelievers would be tempted to convince their interlocutors and make of this the ultimate end of their researching and debating. Needless to say, this would contradict the ST. The ST is first and foremost aimed at one's moral and spiritual promotion, which is joined by one's subordination to God in the case of believers. It is clear, therefore, that the desire that one's interlocutors may change their crucial assumptions should not become the end of the ST. This desire should remain a consequence of one's flourishing, and not its antecedent.[111]

6.6 One Final Consideration on the Distinctions between Believers and Unbelievers Once They Take the ST

I have so far argued that both believers and unbelievers can take the ST. It remains to show some distinctions between them. These distinctions are because, unlike unbelievers, believers search for a good that coincides with *someone* and not just *something*.

From this, two substantial differences follow.

First, let me consider the desire to change the mind of one's interlocutors. Believers can serenely engage in debates and hope that their opponents may one day be graciously provided with faith exactly as the believers were gifted in the past. In this sense, believers may promote their intellectual activity, and any other activity as well, by only caring about their own moral and spiritual promotion, which for them consists of subordinating everything to God's will. Furthermore, they may be convinced that God considers their will, not the outcomes of their actions.[112] As a result, they may be persuaded that what they have not yet been able to put into practice will later be realized by God. A less comfortable condition seems instead to be the one in which unbelievers find themselves. Since they do not trust in any superior being who may remedy their limitations, they will likely experience anxiety and suffering before such limitations and the incapability of converting their opponents to their own beliefs.

---

[111] To mistake means for the end is not acceptable, which is the mistake ascribed by Augustine to Pagans. Herdt refers to Augustine's idea that "even the best Romans... fail to recognize that honor and glory 'must be the consequences of virtue not its antecedents'; honor and glory should be put to use in the promotion of virtue, not the reverse" (ibid., p. 49; cit. from *City of God* V, 12).

[112] "Virtue is praised because of the will, not because of the ability: and therefore if a man fall short of equality which is the mean of justice, through lack of ability, his virtue deserves no less praise, provided there be no failing on the part of his will" (*Summa theologiae*, II-II, q. 81, a. 6, ad 1).

Second, a circularity problem seems to emerge regarding believers, and not unbelievers, when we see that believers typically believe that God exists because – so they say – God himself led them to believe. As John Bishop points out, "believers are to accept theological truths on divine authority, yet the truth that *there is such an authority* (historically mediated as the relevant tradition maintains) is amongst those very truths that are to be accepted on divine authority."[113] This is the way the faithful *typically* believe. There is another way for them to accept theological truths, which avoids the circular argument in question. It consists of demonstrating that God exists. This, however, regards only a few of them. Furthermore, even regarding them, it cannot be said that having faith consists in grounding the Christian belief on a previous demonstration.[114]

I intend to propose a solution to the problem in question. Before proceeding, however, let me advance two considerations. First, this subject may seem of peripheral importance here, and the time that I will devote to its treatment may consequently appear to be excessive. In reality, rejecting the idea that the view maintained by believers falls into circularity turns out to be of primary importance for my purposes here. If we did not reject this idea, in fact, we should abandon the identification of the good searched for by believers with *someone*. Consequently, the fundamental distinction between believers, whose ultimate end is God, and unbelievers, whose ultimate end is the good, would disappear. (Note that I am not referring to unbelievers *as such*, that is, as arguing for the nonexistence of God. I am referring to those adopters of the ST whose noetic structure does not include religious belief.) Second, I argue that the circularity problem in question can be dismissed by referring to Aquinas's thought. This is especially effective because Aquinas is often considered a supporter of the abovementioned idea that, before believing, the faithful should ground their belief in demonstrating God's existence, which is a strategy that avoids the circularity in question.

I agree that, for Aquinas, demonstrating God's existence supports faith's reasonableness usefully and meritoriously.[115] However, it does not follow

---

[113] John Bishop, "Faith," in *The Stanford Encyclopedia of Philosophy* (https://plato.stanford.edu/cgi-bin/encyclopedia/archinfo.cgi?entry=faith, accessed on July 15, 2019).

[114] This view would be hard to reconcile with Aquinas's conviction that philosophy is fallible. According to him, "if ... anything is found in the teachings of the philosophers contrary to faith, this error ... is due to an abuse of philosophy" (Aquinas, *Super Boetium de Trinitate*, q. 2, a. 3; see also above, Chapter 3, note 114). Of course, Aquinas claims that God's existence can be demonstrated, and nonetheless having faith only if the preamble in question has been demonstrated would be unacceptable to him.

[115] See *Summa theologiae*, II-II, q. 2, a. 10. See above, Chapter 3, note 97.

that, to believe in God, one needs to previously *demonstrate* the preambles. This would manifestly contradict Aquinas's conviction that, among believers, only a few, and not without mistakes, can attain a demonstration of God's existence.

Guy de Broglie proposed a convincing reading of Aquinas's preambles decades ago.[116] According to de Broglie, when he discusses preambles of faith, Aquinas only refers to propositional faith (i.e., the articles of the Creed). In other words, if faith is taken as a mere intellectual assent to the revealed truths, preambles constitute a necessary logical premise. But how can we look at the relationship between faith and its preambles if we focus on the act of faith taken as an assent that is due to the will to believe, which is in turn due to divine grace?

Aquinas seems to think that we *need* to previously be provided with some preambles, and at the same time that we do not need to believe them *firmly*. Only divine grace can provide believers with the firmness that Thomas argues is typical of paradigmatic faith. Therefore, we may say that, to believe in God, we need *two factors* that are mutually related to one another. On the one hand, we have to possess beliefs that allow us to get a sense of divine revelation, no matter how firmly they are held. We would not even understand that a God is revealing himself to us if we did not already believe that a God may exist. On the other hand, we need divine grace to firmly adhere to the Christian belief, including God's existence.

Not surprisingly, for Aquinas, there is an awareness of the preambles that coincides neither with faith, which regards only believers, nor with natural theology, which regards only educated people. Jenkins refers to a passage from *On Truth* and notes that for Aquinas, "someone can begin to believe what he did not believe before but which he held with some hesitation. Thus, it is possible that, before believing in God (*antequam credat Deum esse*) someone might think that God exists (*extimaverit Deum esse*),"[117] and that this thinking was characterized by hesitation. Consequently, it can be said that

> (H) To believe in God, God's existence is to be believed, *no matter how hesitantly*.

Aquinas seems to offer, in this way, a solution to the abovementioned problem of circularity. God's existence can be believed "in a general and

---

[116] See Guy de Broglie, "La vraie notion thomiste des *praeambula fidei*," *Gregorianum* 34 (1953), pp. 341–389.

[117] This is the passage that Jenkins cites from *On Truth*, q. 14, a. 9, ad 9. See Jenkins, "Faith and Revelation," pp. 216ff.

confused way," as Thomas sometimes claims to support the idea that God's existence does not necessarily need to be held by demonstration or faith.[118] Thus practically every person may be provided with the preambles of faith. As a consequence, (H) may adequately replace both the claim that we can believe preambles only by way of demonstration (D) and the one that we can believe preambles only by way of faith (F). Unlike (D), (H) does not contradict Aquinas's teaching on faith and reason; unlike (F), it does not fall into a circular argument. If faith is both an intellectual assent to revelation and an act that is due to the will, which is, in turn, caused by divine grace, then the following conclusion is entirely plausible. On the one hand, before getting in touch with divine revelation, one needs to be in possession of the preambles, since they enable one to get a sense of the revealed truths, no matter how hesitantly those preambles may be held; on the other hand, one can obtain firm possession of the preambles only by divine grace.

As I have already said, showing that the circularity, which is usually ascribed to the belief in God, can be dismissed as no problem is of great importance here. This frees from inconsistency my assumption that the believer's search is for *someone* who is good and not simply *something* good. This will also allow me to assess one more difference between believers and unbelievers who take the ST. I intend to show this difference in the next section while arguing that for believers, and not for unbelievers, the ST promotes research and debates.

6.7 One More Final Consideration: The ST Promotes Research and Debates

Once they have taken the ST, both believers and unbelievers are expected to see the assumptions, which the ST implies and to which they adhere, as *orientation* and *criterion* for their search for truth. (Of course, the same can be said of mere epistemologists, given the fact that, though only implicitly, they too stick to their beliefs.) *Orientation*, because adopters of the ST are expected to develop their rational activity to confirm their assumptions and clear away objections and criticisms. *Criterion*, because it is based on the

---

[118] "To know that God exists in a general and confused way is implanted in us by nature, inasmuch as God is man's beatitude.... This, however, is not to know absolutely that God exists; just as to know that someone is approaching is not the same as to know that Peter is approaching, even though it is Peter who is approaching" (*Summa theologiae*, I, q. 2, a. 1, ad 1).

agreement or disagreement with such assumptions that they either accept or reject reason's conclusions, respectively.

Beyond orientation and criterion, the assumptions that are implied by the ST can also *promote* research and debates, although in this case a difference emerges between believers and unbelievers.

In Chapter 5, I have shown that Aquinas maximally trusts human reason, which he considers fully reliable and not susceptible to failure if properly employed. True, human beings and their abilities are afflicted by various types of shortcomings. However, these shortcomings are due not to the faculties that God has created, but (at least ultimately) to human *sin*, which makes their employment ineffective. Believers can rely on their intellectual faculties because they believe that these faculties, when properly employed, cannot contradict that which as believers they maximally care about, which is the complex of assumptions that are due to their faith. Consequently, they will be ready to employ reason in any possible direction, with no fear that rational outcomes might end up contradicting the assumptions due to faith.

Of course, from this does not follow that *no aspects* of such assumptions can be changed. Aquinas offers an antidote against the conviction that whatever the faithful believe is correct: they can simply be wrong when they mistake their own opinions for divine revelation.[119] However, it remains true that they will firmly believe that at least those assumptions that surely trace back to divine revelation ("God exists," "Jesus is the Son of God," and suchlike) will never be contradicted by any rational enterprise. If any contradiction arises, then the assumptions at stake will function as a criterion, and one will start reasoning again from the beginning.

For believers, therefore, taking the ST promotes research in any direction, in a way that is optimistic and open-minded.

The same does not seem possible to unbelievers. Unlike believers, they cannot appeal to *someone* who may guarantee that human reason, once appropriately employed, cannot be wrong. Of course, they cannot appeal to rational criteria either, because this would make their argument fall into circularity. They might consequently be fearful of the possibility that the outcomes of their intellectual enterprise might contradict their assumptions, which they firmly adopt and consider indispensable. This will likely limit their freedom in exploring whatever lines of reasoning might be promoted by research and debates.

---

[119] See *Summa theologiae*, II-II, q. 1, a. 3, ad 3. See above, Chapter 3, note 30.

6.8 A Final List of Significant Epistemic Benefits

In this chapter, I have first shown that self-referential contradiction affects ME. Although with some distinctions, I have then argued that both believers and unbelievers can take the ST. I am now able to conclude that significant epistemic benefits can follow from one's taking the ST.

One benefit consists in the fact that the adoption of good habits, which the act of taking the ST brings with itself, along with the persuasion that neither believers nor unbelievers will give up the fundamental assumptions they disagree on, frees both of them from the anxiety to prevail one over the other. Aquinas goes so far as to suggest that, for the sake of a greater good, debaters may sometimes *avoid debates*. While focusing on the circumstances in which debates occur, he wonders "whether those who hear the disputation are instructed and firm in the faith, or simple and wavering." In regard to those who are simple and wavering, Aquinas again distinguishes between those who "are provoked and molested by unbelievers, for instance, Jews or heretics, or pagans who strive to corrupt the faith in them, or else they are not subject to provocation in this matter." In the second case, Aquinas says that "it is dangerous to dispute in public about the faith, in the presence of simple people, whose faith for this very reason is more firm, that they have never heard anything differing from what they believe. Hence it is not expedient for them to hear what unbelievers have to say against the faith."[120]

Another benefit for researchers and debaters is that they can achieve partial conclusiveness. It is partial because it excludes the assumptions mentioned above. It regards the remainder of human knowledge, which, on closer inspection, is the greater part of it. Any discussion involves many beliefs, and not only the fundamental ones on which debaters might

---

[120] *Summa theologiae*, II-II, q. 10, a. 7. Augustine had made the same point while comparing knowledge and ignorance. Although "on one and the same subject we rightly prefer an instructed man to an ignorant one," this is not true when it comes to different subjects, whose *value* is different. This seems to coincide with the circumstance described by Aquinas. The author of the *Summa theologiae*, in fact, seems to refer to people who have different epistemic backgrounds with different value. On the one hand, there are unbelievers who know only *arguments against faith*. On the other hand, there are believers, whose faith, which Aquinas obviously values more than any argument (especially if against faith), probably implies beliefs that are unknown to unbelievers. At any rate, this is Augustine's rhetorical question: "When one man knows one thing, and another a different thing, and when what the former knows is useful, and what the latter knows is not so useful, or is actually hurtful ... who would not, in regard to the things the latter knows, prefer the ignorance of the former to the knowledge of the latter?" (Augustine, *The Enchiridion; or, On Faith, Hope, and Love*, chapter 17, tr. by James F. Shaw [Chicago, IL: Henry Regnery, 1961]).

endlessly continue disagreeing. Consequently, regarding the beliefs that are not the fundamental ones, the debaters in question may achieve conclusiveness to the extent that their knowledge processes are directed by good habits. The partial conclusiveness under consideration is indeed possible to all, not only to adopters of the ST. However, adopters of the ST are put in the best possible condition to achieve this conclusiveness. From this follows that, although taking the ST is primarily aimed at one's spiritual betterment rather than success in investigation and debates, it paradoxically turns out to be, from an epistemological viewpoint, preferable to ME.

Another benefit seems to be available only to believers. Both believers and unbelievers see the assumptions that they consider undeniable as orientation and criterion for intellectual activity. Only believers, however, seem to be put in a position to *promote* optimistic and open-minded research. They appeal to *someone* who – so they believe – can assure them that, once appropriately employed, reason cannot be wrong. Consequently, believers will feel free to expand research in any possible direction, without fearing that what they first and foremost care about may be found untrue.

Clearly enough, from this it does not follow that relying on God's existence and his revelation is sufficient for believers to take the ST. It is true that being in possession of a body of beliefs such as consolidated religious doctrines, especially the Christian one, substantially helps to do good and benefits research and investigations. However, doing good and spiritually thriving is first and foremost due to one's will and personal motivations. Being part of a venerable tradition does not automatically make one take the ST and improve one's research and investigations.

Conclusion

In Chapter 6 I have shown that, according to a believer such as Aquinas, one should not dispute about faith in public, "in the presence of simple people," because this may be "dangerous." The simple people in question, in fact, "have never heard anything differing from what they believe," and, hence, "it is not expedient for them to hear what unbelievers have to say against the faith."

This might seem utterly incomprehensible given Aquinas's view that our cognitive faculties, once used appropriately, cannot disprove religious belief. He devoted his entire life to intellectual activity. Why, therefore, does he say that the faithful should miss an opportunity to rationally support the belief in question? The response is that, since for Aquinas the commitment of the faithful to God and the related beliefs is of primary importance, to avoid discussions that may render that commitment less firm is highly advisable.

Of course, this only regards those circumstances in which people who cannot adequately conduct intellectual investigations and debates are involved. Therefore, no direct relations can be established with the subject of this book, which regards those who are familiar with research and debates.

However, an idea that plays a fundamental role in this book emerges from what I have just said. It is the conviction that commitments exist, which are so vital that the intellectual activity, even if it is aimed at supporting them, should be avoided in case it might reduce the firmness with which they are taken on. To put it otherwise, those commitments should, in some circumstances, stand alone, though it remains true that they can successfully inspire rational debates.

In this book, I have employed suggestions like this to argue the importance of taking the ST from ME, namely, devoting oneself to someone or something, including beliefs, that are seen as able to perfect the whole human person. This act of ordering oneself to God and/or the good is expected to promote the assumption of good habits and consequently perfect any human enterprise, the intellectual activity included.

At the end of this research, let me list several final considerations.

1. Taking the ST in epistemology promotes a more comprehensive view than ME or, which is the same, a moderate version of it. ME, taken as the view that *one should always prefer beliefs supported by more evidence to beliefs supported by less evidence*, is seemingly incompatible with the ST, which is based on the readiness to maintain some beliefs even if the available evidence seems to disprove them. However, no incompatibility emerges if we adopt the abovementioned moderate version of ME, according to which *one should*, with some exceptions, *prefer beliefs supported by more evidence to beliefs supported by less evidence*.
2. Adopting a moderate version of ME improves epistemology. First, it avoids the self-referential contradiction into which ME inevitably falls. Its moderate version can apply to itself, whereas the same cannot be said of the original one. Saying that *one should* always *prefer beliefs supported by more evidence to beliefs supported by less evidence*, which is the original version in question, is not supported by more evidence than its opposite, which is the belief that *one should* not always *prefer beliefs supported by more evidence to beliefs supported by less evidence*. Second, a moderate and more comprehensive version of ME, unlike the original version, accounts for inconclusiveness. The moderate version, in fact, is the view that, in some cases, debaters may steadfastly stick to their own beliefs even if the available evidence seems to convince them of the contrary.
3. Inconclusiveness is not only due to commitments to human flourishing. Sticking to one's original views regardless of contrary evidence might often be due to intellectual as well as moral vices. Why, therefore, not devote part of this book to this negative component of inconclusiveness? The answer is that not every cause of inconclusiveness is the subject of this book. I only intended to focus on those causes – the commitments to one's spiritual betterment – that can benefit the intellectual activity. Furthermore, focusing on vicious causes would have been superfluous. If ME is widely assumed, this is precisely due to the equally wide assumption that not to be ready to change one's mind in the presence of contrary evidence is not only epistemically wrong but also morally culpable.
4. I have identified the causes of inconclusiveness that are the subject of this book while reflecting on relevant suggestions that typically

accompany the Christian belief. Christians are expected to prefer the achievement of spiritual perfection over knowledge. This should lead them to improve the intellectual activity, since committing oneself to one's spiritual betterment should subsequently improve any activity one takes.

5. The ST, therefore, can improve the knowing process, although the ST is not a strictly epistemological enterprise. The main interest of those who take the ST is their commitment to God and the good, not the mere search for truth.

6. The fact that the main interest of those who take the ST is not the search for truth does not imply opposition between the ST and ME. ME might be part of a wider project, such as the search for human flourishing. However, because of the primacy of evidence that it always supports, ME implies that every commitment must first be epistemically justified. Instead, the ST requires that, in some cases, one can first commit oneself to someone or something and only subsequently search for rational support. As I have already said in (1), once adopted a moderate version of ME, the opposition to the ST disappears. According to this version, one can, in some cases, commit oneself to certain beliefs, whether or not the available evidence seems to convince one of the contrary.

7. Although the ST emerges from a religious perspective, it may also regard those who do not believe. Both believers and unbelievers are responsible for inconclusiveness, as shown by the fact that, in the course of debates between believers and unbelievers, the number of believers who stick to their beliefs before contrary evidence is not significantly different from the number of unbelievers who do the same on the other side of the spectrum. Why, then, could unbelievers not commit themselves, at least in some circumstances, to the good and the human flourishing? In Western contemporary culture, there are values such as the equal dignity of all human beings or the unacceptability of racism to which both believers and unbelievers are expected to be ready to commit themselves. Who may reasonably oppose these values or accept the possibility that evidence emerges against them? Before such evidence, many of us would be ready to stick to our beliefs and start researching anew from the beginning with the aim of finding further evidence in support of those values. This means that those who do not believe in God may take the ST while committing to the good. May this also be possible if, *qua* unbelievers, they commit themselves to atheism? Yes, but only if they take atheism

as a view that allows them to promote spiritual betterment, which involves promoting the values in question and the adoption of virtuous behaviors.

8. The ST regards those commitments and beliefs that lead one to adopt virtuous behaviors. It is expected to cause attitudes from which dialogue, mutual understanding, and respect for differences emerge. It follows that achieving conclusiveness, except those circumstances in which this is not possible because debaters are by no means ready to put aside their original views, will be easier than when the ST is not taken.

9. Given the role that religious experience and theological reflection have played so far, it may seem that this book aims to show that the Christian beliefs (as well as other beliefs, which may be seen as somewhat derived from the Christian ones) *are* good. This is not true. In this book, I have not argued *what the good is*. I have argued that believers and unbelievers, to the extent that they firmly hold certain beliefs they take to be spiritually perfecting the human person, may have an opportunity to create the best possible conditions for dialogue and intellectual activity. This regards not only the strictly Christian beliefs held by the faithful. It also regards those beliefs to which I have shown that in contemporary Western society most people commit themselves. In both cases, the beliefs in question seem to reveal a strong commitment to the good, at least because no evil seems to follow from them, unless inconsistently. (I have also argued that this view does not point in the direction of any relativism, precisely because it does not focus on the identification of the good nor does it promote a comparison among different interpretations of it.)

10. I say that believers and unbelievers "*may* have the opportunity" to improve the intellectual activity because the fact that one *proclaims* one's commitment to some values does not assure that one is taking the ST. Taking the ST, in fact, is a *personal* decision and a voluntary engagement, which does not automatically follow from a certain stance.

11. In this connection, there is a distinction between, on the one hand, the *theory* of the ST (i.e., someone *is aware* of the fact that committing oneself to God and/or the good can benefit knowledge) and, on the other hand, its *practice* (i.e., someone *behaves* consistently with the commitment in question). One may support the theory of the ST without being able to commit oneself to God and the good. On the other hand, one may not develop any theory and, nonetheless, be

able to take the ST. This distinction between theory and practice paves the way to explain why the ST is only partly new. The theory is new because, so formulated, nobody has proposed it so far. The practice, however, is not. It would be unbearably arrogant to believe that there have never been people who have at least in some cases benefited the intellectual activity because of their firm commitment to God and/or the good. The first chapter of this book was devoted to Christian thinkers who have not offered substantive suggestions on which to base the ST – no theory of the ST can be based on their works. And nonetheless, they have stuck to the Christian belief, regardless of contrary evidence advanced by their opponents. This might have led them, at least in some cases, to develop forms of the ST while taking part in debates.

12. The ST has the potential to vastly benefit any intellectual activity. This occurs by mainly caring about one's spiritual betterment. As a consequence, it may largely benefit not only philosophers or theologians. In fact, human flourishing regards everybody, which is why everybody is likely to benefit their intellectual activity to the extent that they are really interested in their spiritual betterment. This frontally opposes the view that intellectual activity, as well as the moral and political enterprise, can be promoted only to the extent that one is ready to change one's mind if challenged by contrary evidence. In some cases, this view might not apply, and the successful promotion of those enterprises might depend on one's commitment to one's flourishing and the related adoption of good habits.

Bibliography

Primary Sources

Alexander of Hales et al., *Doctoris irrefragabilis Alexandri de Hales Ordinis minorum Summa theologica* (Quaracchi, Florence: Collegii S. Bonaventurae, 1924–1948), partly tr. by Oleg Bychkov, in Oleg Bychkov, "Appendix: Alexander of Hales, The Sum of Theology," *Franciscan Studies* 66 (2008), pp. 63–99.

Anselm, *Monologion and Proslogion*, ed. and tr. by Thomas Williams (Indianapolis, IN: Hackett Publishing, 1995).

Aquinas, *Commentary on the Letter of Saint Paul to the Hebrews*, tr. by Fabian Larcher, in *Opera Omnia: The Latin/English Edition of the Works of St. Thomas Aquinas* (Lander, WY: Aquinas Institute, 2012–).

Commentary on the Sentences, tr. by Chris Decaen and Beth Mortensen, in *Opera Omnia: The Latin/English Edition of the Works of St. Thomas Aquinas* (Lander, WY: Aquinas Institute, 2012–).

Quodlibetal Questions, tr. by Urban Hannon, in *Opera Omnia: The Latin/English Edition of the Works of St. Thomas Aquinas* (Lander, WY: Aquinas Institute, 2012–).

Summa contra Gentiles, tr. by Anton Pegis, James F. Anderson, Vernon J. Bourke, and Charles J. O'Neil (New York: Hanover House, 1955–1957).

Summa theologiae, 2nd and revised ed., tr. by the Fathers of the English Dominican Province (London: Oates and Washbourne, 1920).

Super Boetium de Trinitate, tr. by Rose E. Brennan (New York: Herder and Herder, 1946).

On Truth, vol. 2, tr. by James V. McGlynn (Chicago, IL: Henry Regnery, 1953).

Aristotle, *Metaphysics*, tr. by William D. Ross, in *The Works of Aristotle*, 2nd ed. (Oxford: Oxford University Press, 1928).

Nicomachean Ethics, tr. by William D. Ross, in *The Works of Aristotle*, revised by L. Brown (Oxford: Oxford University Press, 2009).

Posterior Analytics, tr. by Terence Irwin and Gail Fine (Indianapolis, IN: Hackett Publishing, 1995).

Augustine, *On Christian Doctrine, in Four Books*, tr. by James F. Shaw (Grand Rapids, MI: Christian Classics Ethereal Library, 2005).

De civitate Dei, tr. by Philip Schaff (Grand Rapids, MI: Christian Classics Ethereal Library, 1890).
The Enchiridion; or, On Faith, Hope, and Love, tr. by James F. Shaw (Chicago, IL: Henry Regnery, 1961).
The Soliloquies, tr. by Rose E. Cleveland (Boston: Little, Brown, 1910).
Barth, Karl, *Church Dogmatics*, ed. by Geoffrey W. Bromiley and Thomas F. Torrance, tr. by G. T. Thompson and Harold Knight (Edinburgh: T&T Clark, 1956).
Bonaventure, *Collationes de septem donis Spiritus Sancti*, in *Opera Omnia* 5 (Quaracchi, Florence: Collegii S. Bonaventurae, 1891).
Commentaria in quattuor libros Sententiarum Magistri Petri Lombardi: in librum II, in *Opera Omnia* 1–4 (Quaracchi, Florence: Collegii S. Bonaventurae, 1885).
Calvin, John, *Institutes of the Christian Religion*, ed. by John T. McNeill, tr. by Ford L. Battles (Philadelphia: Westminster Press, 1960).
Descartes, René, *Discourse on Method*, in *Discourse on Method and Meditations*, tr. by Elisabeth S. Haldane and George R. T. Ross (Mineola, NY: Dover Publications, 2003).
Freud, Sigmund, *The Future of an Illusion*, tr. by James Strachey (London: Hogarth Press, 1927).
Gadamer, Hans G., *Truth and Method*, 2nd ed., tr. by Joel Weinsheimer and Donald Marshall (London: Continuum, 1989).
Hegel, Georg F. W., *Lectures on the History of Philosophy*, tr. by Elisabeth S. Haldane and Frances H. Simson, 1896 (London: Routledge and Kegan Paul, 1955).
Hume, David, Letter 272 (April 6, 1765), in *The Letters of David Hume*, ed. by John Y. T. Greig (Oxford: Clarendon Press, 1932).
The Natural History of Religion, ed. by H. Root (Stanford, CA: Stanford University Press, 1956).
Kant, Immanuel, "A Renewed Attempt to Answer the Question: 'Is the Human Race Continually Improving?,'" in *Kant's Political Writings*, ed. by Hans Reiss (Cambridge: Cambridge University Press, 1970).
Kierkegaard, Sören, *Practice in Christianity*, ed. by Howard V. Hong and Edna H. Hong (Princeton, NJ: Princeton University Press, 1991).
Locke, John, *An Essay Concerning Human Understanding* (London: Printed for Awhsham and John Churchil, 1700).
A Letter Concerning Toleration, tr. by William Popple (Indianapolis, IN: Bobbs-Merrill, 1950).
Newman, John H., *Apologia Pro Vita Sua: Being a History of His Religious Opinions*, edited with an introduction and notes by Martin J. Svaglic (London: Oxford University Press, 1967).
An Essay in Aid of a Grammar of Assent, edited with introduction and notes by Ian T. Ker (New York: Oxford University Press, 1985).
The Idea of a University (London: Basil Montagu Pickering, 1873).

Pascal, Blaise, *Pensées*, tr. by Alban J. Kreilsheimer (New York: Penguin Books, 1995).

Plato, *Gorgias*, tr. by Benjamin Jowett, in *The Dialogues of Plato* (Cambridge: Cambridge University Press, 2017).

   Meno, tr. by Benjamin Jowett, in *The Dialogues of Plato* (Cambridge: Cambridge University Press, 2017).

Reid, Thomas, *A Brief Account of Aristotle's Logic, with Remarks*, in *Thomas Reid on Logic, Rhetoric, and the Fine Arts: Papers on the Culture of Mind*, ed. by Alexander Broadie (Edinburgh: Edinburgh University Press, 2004).

   The Correspondence of Thomas Reid, ed. by Paul Wood (Edinburgh: Edinburgh University Press, 2002).

   Essays on the Active Powers of Man, in *The Works of Thomas Reid*, ed. by William Hamilton (Edinburgh: MacLachlan and Stewart; London: Longman, Green, Longman, Roberts, and Green, 1863).

   Essays on the Intellectual Powers of Man, ed. by Derek R. Brookes (Edinburgh: Edinburgh University Press, 2002).

   An Essay on Quantity, in *The Works of Thomas Reid*, ed. by William Hamilton (Edinburgh: MacLachlan and Stewart; London: Longman, Green, Longman, Roberts, and Green, 1863).

   An Inquiry into the Human Mind on the Principles of Common Sense, ed. by Derek R. Brookes (Edinburgh: Edinburgh University Press, 1997).

   "Of Power," ed. by John Haldane, *The Philosophical Quarterly* 51 (2001), pp. 3–12.

   Thomas Reid on the Animate Creation, ed. by Paul Wood (Edinburgh: Edinburgh University Press, 1995).

   Thomas Reid on Practical Ethics. Lectures and Papers on Natural Religion, Self-Government, Natural Jurisprudence and the Law of Nations, ed. by Knud Haakonssen (Edinburgh: Edinburgh University Press, 2007).

   Thomas Reid on Religion, ed. by James Foster (Exeter: Imprint Academic, 2017).

Russell, Bertrand, *The Problems of Philosophy*, 2nd ed. (Oxford: Oxford University Press, 1998).

   "Why I Am Not a Christian," in *The Basic Writings of Bertrand Russell*, ed. by Robert E. Egner and Lester E. Denonn (London: Allen and Unwin, 1961).

Spinoza, Baruch, *Tractatus theologico-politicus*, tr. by Robert H. M. Elwes (London: Bell, 1883).

Wittgenstein, Ludwig, *On Certainty*, ed. by Gertrude E. M. Anscombe and Georg H. von Wright (Oxford: Blackwell, 1969).

Secondary Sources

Adler, Jonathan, "Reconciling Open-Mindedness and Belief," *Theory and Research in Education* 2 (2004), pp. 127–142.

Anstey, Peter, "Thomas Reid and the Justification of Induction," *History of Philosophy Quarterly* 12 (1995), pp. 77–93.
Assmann, Jan, *The Price of Monotheism*, tr. by Robert Savage (Stanford, CA: Stanford University Press, 2010).
Audi, Robert, "Cognitive Disparities, Dimensions of Intellectual Diversity and the Resolution of Disagreements," in *The Epistemology of Disagreement: New Essays*, ed. by David Christensen and Jennifer Lackey (Oxford: Oxford University Press, 2013), pp. 205–222.
Baghramian, Maria, and Carter, Adam J., "Relativism," in *The Stanford Encyclopedia of Philosophy*, ed. by Edward N. Zalta, https://plato.stanford.edu/archives/sum2017/entries/relativism/, accessed on July 1, 2018.
Baker, Deane-Peter, *Tayloring Reformed Epistemology: Charles Taylor, Alvin Plantinga and the De Iure Challenge to Christian Belief* (London: SCM Press, 2007).
Baldwin, Erick, and McNabb, Tyler, *Plantingian Religious Epistemology and World Religions* (Lanham, MD: Rowman and Littlefield, 2018).
Bary, Philip de, *Thomas Reid and Scepticism: His Reliabilist Response* (London: Routledge, 2002).
Basinger, David, "Religious Diversity (Pluralism)," in *The Stanford Encyclopedia of Philosophy*, ed. by Edward N. Zalta, https://plato.stanford.edu/archives/spr2018/entries/religious-pluralism/, accessed on July 1, 2018.
Bauerschmidt, Frederick, *Thomas Aquinas: Faith, Reason, and Following Christ* (Oxford: Oxford University Press, 2013).
Bergman, Michael, "Rational Religious Belief without Arguments," in *Philosophy of Religion: An Anthology*, ed. by Michael Rea and Louis Pojman (Stamford, CT: Cengage Learning, 2015), pp. 609–624.
Bergmann, Michael, "Religious Belief, Epistemology of, Recent Developments," in *A Companion to Epistemology*, 2nd ed., ed. by Jonathan Dancy, Ernest Sosa, and Matthias Steup (Malden, MA: Wiley-Blackwell, 2010).
Bishop, John, "Faith," in *The Stanford Encyclopedia of Philosophy*, ed. by Edward N. Zalta, https://plato.stanford.edu/cgi-bin/encyclopedia/archinfo.cgi?entry=faith, accessed on July 15, 2019.
  "Trusting Others, Trusting in God, Trusting the World," in *Religious Faith and Intellectual Virtue*, ed. by Laura F. Callahan and Timothy O'Connor (Oxford: Oxford University Press, 2014), pp. 159–173.
Blamires, Harry, *The Christian Mind: How Should a Christian Think?* (Ann Arbor, MI: Servant Books, 1963).
Blehl, V. F., "The Role of Education in the Formation of Conscience and the Illative Sense," in *Internationale Cardinal Newman Studien*, Elfte Folge: Achter Newman-Congress Freiburg, ed. by H. Fries, W. Becker, and G. Biemer (Nürnberg: Glock und Lutz, 1980), pp. 143–149.
Bloom, Allan, *The Closing of the American Mind: How Higher Education Has Failed Democracy and Impoverished the Souls of Today's Students* (New York: Simon and Schuster, 1987).

Bolos, Anthony, and Scott, Kyle, "Reformed Epistemology," 2015, https://iep.utm.edu/ref-epis/, accessed on September 24, 2020.

Brady, Michael, "The Role of Emotions in Intellectual Virtue," in *The Routledge Handbook of Virtue Epistemology*, ed. by Heather Battaly (New York: Routledge, 2019).

Broadie, Alexander, "Reid in Context," in *The Cambridge Companion to Thomas Reid*, ed. by Terence Cuneo and René van Woudenberg (Cambridge: Cambridge University Press, 2004), pp. 31–52.

Broglie, Guy de, "La vraie notion thomiste des *praeambula fidei*," *Gregorianum* 34 (1953), pp. 341–389.

Buchak, Lara, "Can It Be Rational to Have Faith?," in *Probability in the Philosophy of Religion*, ed. by Jake Chandler and Victoria S. Harrison (Oxford: Oxford University Press, 2012), pp. 225–247.

"Faith and Steadfastness in the Face of Counter-evidence," *International Journal for Philosophy of Religion* 81 (2017), pp. 113–133.

"Rational Faith and Justified Belief," in *Religious Faith and Intellectual Virtue*, ed. by Laura F. Callahan and Timothy O'Connor (Oxford: Oxford University Press, 2014), pp. 49–73.

Buckley, Michael, *At the Origins of Modern Atheism* (New Haven, CT: Yale University Press, 1987).

Byrne, Peter, "Religious Tolerance, Diversity, and Pluralism," in *Philosophy and Religion*. Royal Institute of Philosophy Supplement 68, ed. by Anthony O'Hear (Cambridge: Cambridge University Press, 2001), pp. 287–309.

Callahan, Laura F., and O'Connor, Timothy, "Introduction," in *Religious Faith and Intellectual Virtue*, ed. by Laura Callahan and Timothy O'Connor (Oxford: Oxford University Press, 2014), pp. 1–26.

Callergard, Robert, "Thomas Reid's Newtonian Theism: His Differences with the Classical Arguments of Richard Bentley and William Whiston," *Studies in History and Philosophy of Science* 41 (2010), pp. 109–119.

Chisholm, Roderick, *Theory of Knowledge*, 2nd ed. (Englewood Cliffs, NJ: Prentice Hall, 1977).

Church, Ian M., and Samuelson, Peter L., *Intellectual Humility: An Introduction to the Philosophy and Science* (London: Bloomsbury Academy, 2017).

Clifford, William K., "The Ethics of Belief," in *Lectures and Essays* (London: Macmillan, 1879).

Code, Lorraine, *Epistemic Responsibility* (Hanover, NH: Published for Brown University Press by University Press of New England, 1987).

Coliva, Annalisa, "Which Hinge Epistemology?," *International Journal for the Study of Skepticism*, 6/2–3 (2016), pp. 79–96.

Copenhaver, Rebecca, "Is Reid a Mysterian?," *Journal of the History of Philosophy* 44 (2006), pp. 449–466.

Christensen, David, "Epistemology of Disagreement: The Good News," *The Philosophical Review* 116/2 (April 1, 2007), pp. 187–217.

Cuneo, Terence, and van Woudenberg, René, "Introduction," in *The Cambridge Companion to Thomas Reid*, ed. by Terence Cuneo and René van Woudenberg (Cambridge: Cambridge University Press, 2004), pp. 1–30.

Daniels, Norman, *Thomas Reid's "Inquiry": The Geometry of Visibles and the Case for Realism* (New York: B. Franklin, 1974).
Dawes, Gregory W., "The Act of Faith: Aquinas and the Moderns," in *Oxford Studies in Philosophy of Religion*, vol. 6, ed. by Jonathan Kvanvig (New York: Oxford University Press, 2015), pp. 58–86.
DeRose, Keith, "Reid's Anti-Sensationalism and His Realism," *The Philosophical Review* 98 (1989), pp. 313–348.
Di Ceglie, Roberto, "Alvin Plantinga and Thomas Aquinas on Theism and Christianity," *Philosophy and Theology* 27 (2015), pp. 235–252.
  Aquinas on Faith, Reason, and Charity (New York: Routledge, 2022).
Driver, Julia, *Uneasy Virtue* (Cambridge: Cambridge University Press, 2001).
Dunnington, Kent, *Humility, Pride, and Christian Virtue Theory* (New York: Oxford University Press, 2018).
Fales, Evan, "Making and Breaking Faith," in *Religious Faith and Intellectual Virtue*, ed. by Laura Callahan and Timothy O'Connor (Oxford: Oxford University Press, 2014), pp. 124–139.
  "Proper Basicality," *Philosophy and Phenomenological Research* 68/2004, pp. 373–383.
Feldman, Richard, "Reasonable Religious Disagreements," in *Philosophers without Gods: Meditations on Atheism and the Secular Life*, ed. by Louise M. Antony (New York: Oxford University Press, 2007), pp. 194–214.
Fergusson, David, *Faith and Its Critics: A Conversation* (Oxford: Oxford University Press, 2011).
  "Reformed Theology in the British Isles," in *The Cambridge Companion to Reformed Theology*, ed. by Paul Nimmo and David Fergusson (Cambridge: Cambridge University Press, 2016), pp. 248–268.
Fine, Gail, *The Possibility of Inquiry: Meno's Paradox from Socrates to Sextus* (New York: Oxford University Press, 2014).
Forster, Greg, *Starting with Locke* (London: Continuum, 2011).
Foster, James, "Editor's Introduction," in *Thomas Reid on Religion*, ed. by James Foster (Exeter: Imprint Academic, 2017).
Frances, Bryan, and Matheson, Jonathan, "Disagreement," in *The Stanford Encyclopedia of Philosophy*, ed. by Edward N. Zalta, https://plato.stanford.edu/archives/spr2018/entries/disagreement/, accessed on November 1, 2017.
Fumerton, Richard, *Realism and the Correspondence Theory of Truth* (Lanham, MD: Rowman & Littlefield, 2002).
Gettier, Edmund, "Is Justified True Belief Knowledge?," *Analysis* 23 (1963), pp. 121–123.
Gilson, Étienne, *The Christian Philosophy of Saint Augustine*, tr. by L. E. M. Lynch (New York: Vintage Books, 1960).
  La philosophie de saint Bonaventure (Paris: Vrin, 1924).
  The Spirit of Mediaeval Philosophy (London: Sheed & Ward, 1936).
  "What Is Christian Philosophy?," in *A Gilson Reader*, ed. by Anton Pegis (Garden City, NY: Doubleday, 1957), pp. 177–191.

Goldberg, Sanford C., "Does Externalist Epistemology Rationalize Religious Commitment?," in *Religious Faith and Intellectual Virtue*, ed. by Laura F. Callahan and Timothy O'Connor (Oxford: Oxford University Press, 2014), pp. 279–298.
Greco, John, "No-Fault Atheism," in *Hidden Divinity and Religious Belief*, ed. by Adam Green and Eleonore Stump (Cambridge: Cambridge University Press, 2016), pp. 109–125.
  "Virtues in Epistemology," in *Oxford Handbook of Epistemology*, ed. by Paul Moser (New York: Oxford University Press, 2002), pp. 287–312.
Grier, Philip, "The Speculative Concrete," in *Hegel, History, and Interpretation*, ed. by Shaun Gallagher (Albany: State University of New York Press, 1997), pp. 169–193.
Grimm, Stephen R., "Cardinal Newman, Reformed Epistemologist?," *American Catholic Philosophical Quarterly* 75 (2001), pp. 497–522.
Harris, Sam, *Letter to a Christian Nation* (New York: Knopf, 2006).
Hawthorne, John, and Srinivasan, Amia, "Disagreement without Transparency: Some Bleak Thoughts," in *The Epistemology of Disagreement: New Essays*, ed. by David Christensen and Jennifer Lackey (Oxford: Oxford University Press, 2013), pp. 9–30.
Hazlet, Allan, "Higher-Order Epistemic Attitudes and Intellectual Humility," *Episteme* 9 (2012), pp. 205–223.
Helm, Paul, "John Calvin, the *Sensus Divinitatis*, and the Noetic Effects of Sin," *International Journal for Philosophy of Religion* 43 (1998), pp. 87–107.
Herdt, Jennifer A., *Putting on Virtue: The Legacy of the Splendid Vices* (Chicago, IL: University of Chicago Press, 2008).
Hetherington, Stephen, "Introduction: Meet the Gettier Problem," in *The Gettier Problem*, ed. by Stephen Hetherington (Cambridge: Cambridge University Press, 2019), pp. 1–10.
Hick, John, *Faith and Knowledge: A Modern Introduction to the Problem of Religious Knowledge*, 1957 (Eugene, OR: Wipf & Stock, 2009).
  God Has Many Names (London: Macmillan, 1980).
  "The Outcome of Truth: Dialogue into Truth," in *Truth and Dialogue in World Religions: Conflicting Truth-Claims*, ed. by John Hick (Philadelphia: Westminster Press, 1974), pp. 140–155.
  "The Philosophy of World Religions," *Scottish Journal of Theology* 37 (1984), pp. 229–236.
  Problems of Religious Pluralism (London: Palgrave Macmillan, 1985).
Higgins-Biddle, John C., "The Reasonableness of Christianity and Its Vindications," in *The Bloosmbury Companion to Locke*, ed. by S. J. Savonius-Wroth, Paul Schuurman, and Jonathan Walmsley (London: Bloomsbury, 2010).
Hill, Peter, et al., "A Few Good Measures," in *Handbook of Humility: Theory, Research, and Applications*, ed. by Everett Worthington, Don Davis, and Joshua Hook (New York: Routledge, 2017).

Hoitenga, Dewey J., *Faith and Reason from Plato to Plantinga: An Introduction to Reformed Epistemology* (Albany: State University of New York Press, 1991).
Howard-Snyder, Daniel, "Divine Openness and Creaturely Non-resistant Nonbelief," in *Hidden Divinity and Religious Belief*, ed. by Adam Green and Eleonore Stump (Cambridge: Cambridge University Press, 2016), pp. 126–138.
  "Does Faith Entail Belief?," *Faith and Philosophy* 33 (2016), pp. 142–162.
  "Propositional Faith: What It Is and What It Is Not," *American Philosophical Quarterly* 50 (2013), pp. 357–372.
  "Schellenberg on Propositional Faith," *Religious Studies* 49 (2013), pp. 181–194.
Howard-Snyder, Daniel, and Moser, Paul, "Introduction," in *Divine Hiddenness: New Essays*, ed. by Daniel Howard-Snyder and Paul Moser (New York: Cambridge University Press, 2002), pp. 1–23.
Irwin, Terence, *Aristotle's First Principles* (Oxford: Clarendon Press, 1988).
  "Spendid Vices? Augustine for and against Pagan Virtues," *Medieval Philosophy and Theology* 8 (1999), pp. 105–127.
Jeffries, Derek, "How Reformed Is Reformed Epistemology? Alvin Plantinga and Calvin's 'Sensus Divinitatis,'" *Religious Studies* 33 (1997), pp. 419–431.
Jenkins, John, "Faith and Revelation," in *Philosophy of Religion: A Guide to the Subject*, ed. by Brian Davies (Washington, DC: Georgetown University Press, 2007), pp. 202–227.
Kenny, Anthony, *The Five Ways* (London: Routledge & Kegan Paul, 1969).
  What Is Faith? (Oxford: Oxford University Press, 1992).
Kerr, Fergus, *Theology after Wittgenstein* (Oxford: Basil Blackwell, 1986).
  "The Varieties of Interpreting Aquinas," in *Contemplating Aquinas: On the Varieties of Interpretation*, ed. by Fergus Kerr (London: SCM Press, 2003), pp. 27–40.
King, Nathan, "Intellectual Perseverance," in *The Routledge Handbook of Virtue Epistemology*, ed. by Heather Battaly (New York: Routledge, 2019).
Knitter, Paul, *No Other Name? A Critical Survey of Christian Attitudes toward the World Religions* (Maryknoll, NY: Orbis, 1985).
Lackey, Jennifer, "Taking Religious Disagreement Seriously," in *Religious Faith and Intellectual Virtue*, ed. by Laura Callahan and Timothy O'Connor (Oxford: Oxford University Press, 2014), pp. 299–316.
Lamont, John R., "Newman on Faith and Rationality," *International Journal for Philosophy of Religion* 40 (1996), pp. 63–84.
Lehrer, Keith, *Thomas Reid* (London: Routledge, 1989).
Lehrer, Keith, and Warner, Bradley, "Reid, God and Epistemology," *American Catholic Philosophical Quarterly* 74 (2000), pp. 357–372.
Lewis, Clive S., *God in the Dock: Essays on Theology and Ethics* (Grand Rapids, MI: Eerdmans, 1994).
  Mere Christianity (New York: Macmillan, 1952).
Losonsky, Michael, *Enlightenment and Action from Descartes to Kant: Passionate Thought* (Cambridge: Cambridge University Press, 2001).

Löwith, Karl, *Meaning in History: The Theological Implications of the Philosophy of History* (Chicago, IL: Chicago University Press, 1949).
Lukes, Steven, *Marxism and Morality* (Oxford: Oxford University Press, 1985).
Macaskill, Grant, *The New Testament and Intellectual Humility* (Oxford: Oxford University Press, 2019).
Mann, William E., "Theological Virtues," in *Routledge Encyclopedia of Philosophy*, ed. by Edward Craig (London: Routledge, 1998).
Maritain, Jacques, *An Essay on Christian Philosophy* (New York: Philosophical Library, 1955).
  "La notion de philosophie chrétienne," *Bulletin de la Société Française de Philosophie* 31 (1931), pp. 59–72.
  Science and Wisdom (London: Sheed and Ward, 1938).
McCabe, Herbert, *Faith within Reason*, ed. by Brian Davies (London: Continuum, 2007).
McCarthy, Gerald, "Newman, Foundationalism, and the Ethics of Belief," *Horizons* 8/1 (1981), pp. 62–79.
McCord Adams, Marilyn, "Anselm on Faith and Reason," in *The Cambridge Companion to Anselm*, ed. by Brian Davies and Brian Leftow (Cambridge: Cambridge University Press, 2004), pp. 32–60.
McCormick, Miriam S., *Believing against the Evidence: Agency and the Ethics of Belief* (New York: Routledge, 2015).
McInerny, Ralph, "On Behalf of Natural Theology," *Proceedings of the American Catholic Philosophical Association* 54 (1980), pp. 63–73.
  "How I Became a Christian Philosopher," *Faith and Philosophy* 15 (1998), pp. 144–146.
  Praeambula fidei: Thomism and the God of the Philosophers (Washington, DC: Catholic University of America Press, 2006).
McKaughan, Daniel, "Authentic Faith and Acknowledged Risk: Dissolving the Problem of Faith and Reason," *Religious Studies* 49 (2013), pp. 101–124.
McKim, Robert, *Religious Ambiguity and Religious Diversity* (Oxford: Oxford University Press, 2001).
Merrigan, Terrence, "Revelation," in *The Cambridge Companion to John Henry Newman*, ed. by Ian Ker and Terrence Merrigan (Cambridge: Cambridge University Press, 2009), pp. 47–72.
Meyer, Michel, *Of Problematology: Philosophy, Science, and Language*, tr. by David Jamison (Chicago, IL: University of Chicago Press, 1995).
Milbank, John, and Pickstock, Catherine, *Truth in Aquinas* (London: Routledge, 2001).
Mitchell, Basil, *Faith and Criticism* (Oxford: Clarendon Press, 1994).
  Neutrality and Commitment: An Inaugural Lecture Delivered before the University of Oxford on 14 May 1968 (Oxford: Clarendon Press, 1968).
Montmarquet, James, *Epistemic Virtue and Doxastic Responsibility* (Lanham, MD: Rowman & Littlefield, 1993).
Moon, Andrew, "Recent Work in Reformed Epistemology," *Philosophy Compass* 12 (2016), pp. 879–891.

Moser, Paul, "Cognitive Idolatry and Divine Hiding," in *Divine Hiddenness: New Essays*, ed. by Daniel Howard-Snyder and Paul Moser (New York: Cambridge University Press, 2002), pp. 120–148.
Murphy, Claudia, "Aquinas on Voluntary Beliefs," *American Catholic Philosophical Quarterly* 74 (2000), pp. 569–597.
Nikulin, Dmitri, *The Concept of History* (London: Bloomsbury, 2017).
Noone, Timothy B., "The Franciscans and Epistemology: Philosophy and Theology on the Issue of Universal Causality," in *Medieval Masters: Essays in Memory of Msgr. E. A. Synan*, ed. by Rollen E. Houser (Houston, TX: University of St. Thomas, 1999), pp. 63–90.
Norton, David F., *David Hume: Common-Sense Moralist, Sceptical Metaphysician* (Princeton, NJ: Princeton University Press, 1982).
  "Hume's Scottish Critics," in *McGill Hume Studies*, ed. by David F. Norton, Nicholas Capaldi, and Wade Robison (San Diego, CA: Austin Hill Press, 1979).
O'Donovan, Oliver, *The Problem of Self-Love in St. Augustine* (New Haven, CT: Yale University Press, 1980).
Oppy, Graham, *Reinventing Philosophy of Religion: An Opinionated Introduction* (Basingstoke: Palgrave Macmillan, 2014).
Pakaluk, Michael, "A Defence of Scottish Common Sense," *The Philosophical Quarterly* 52 (2002), pp. 564–581.
Parekh, Bhikhu, *Marx's Theory of Ideology*, 1982 (London: Routledge, 2015).
Pasnau, Robert, *After Certainty: A History of Our Epistemic Ideals and Illusions* (Oxford: Oxford University Press, 2017).
Penelhum, Terence, "The Analysis of Faith in St. Thomas Aquinas," *Religious Studies* 13 (1977), pp. 133–154.
  God and Skepticism (Dordrecht: D. Reidel, 1983).
Plantinga, Alvin, "Advice to Christian Philosophers," *Faith and Philosophy* 1 (1984), pp. 253–271.
  "Against Naturalism," in *Knowledge of God*, ed. by Alvin Plantinga and Michael Tooley (Malden, MA: Blackwell, 2008), pp. 1–69.
  God and Other Minds: A Study of the Rational Justification of Belief in God (Ithaca, NY: Cornell University Press, 1967).
  "On 'Proper Basicality,'" *Philosophy and Phenomenological Research* 75/2007, pp. 612–621.
  "Reason and Belief in God," in *Faith and Rationality: Reason and Belief in God*, ed. by Alvin Plantinga and Nicholas Wolterstorff (Notre Dame, IN: University of Notre Dame Press, 1983), pp. 16–94.
  Warrant: The Current Debate (New York: Oxford University Press, 1993).
  Warrant and Proper Function (New York: Oxford University Press, 1993).
  Warranted Christian Belief (New York: Oxford University Press, 2000).
Plasger, Georg, "Does Calvin Teach a *Sensus Divinitatis*? Reflections on Alvin Plantinga's Interpretation of Calvin," in *Plantinga's Warranted Christian Belief*, ed. by Dieter Schonecker (Berlin: De Gruyter, 2015), pp. 169–190.

Price, Henry, "Belief 'In' and Belief 'That,'" *Religious Studies* 1 (1965), pp. 5–27.
Pritchard, Duncan, "Anti-Luck Virtue Epistemology," *The Journal of Philosophy* 109 (2012), pp. 247–279.
  Epistemic Luck (Oxford: Clarendon Press, 2005).
  "Faith and Reason," *Royal Institute of Philosophy Supplements* 81 (2017), pp. 101–118.
  "The Gettier Problem and Epistemic Luck," in *The Gettier Problem*, ed. by Stephen Hetherington (Cambridge: Cambridge University Press, 2019), pp. 96–107.
  "Intellectual Humility and the Epistemology of Disagreement," in *Knowledge and Justification: New Perspectives*, ed. by Rodrigo Borges and Ernest Sosa, in *Synthese*, special issue, 2018, open access: link.springer.com/article/10.1007/s11229-018-02024-5.
  "Skepticism," in *A Companion to Atheism and Philosophy*, ed. by Graham Oppy (Hoboken, NJ: Wiley, 2019), pp. 277–290.
  "Wittgenstein on Faith and Reason: The Influence of Newman," in *God, Truth, and Other Enigmas*, ed. by Miroslaw Szatkowski (Berlin: De Gruyter, 2015), pp. 197–216.
Quinn, Philip, "Epistemology in Philosophy of Religion," in *The Oxford Handbook on Epistemology*, ed. by Paul Moser (Oxford: Oxford University Press, 2002), pp. 533–537.
  "Religious Diversity and Religious Toleration," *International Journal for Philosophy of Religion* 50 (2001), pp. 57–80.
Rea, Michael, "Divine Hiddenness, Divine Silence," in *Philosophy of Religion: An Anthology*, ed. by Louis Pojman and Michael Rea (Boston: Wadsworth/Cengage, 2013), pp. 266–275.
Redpath, Peter, "Romance of Wisdom: The Friendship between Jacques Maritain and Saint Thomas Aquinas," in *Understanding Maritain: Philosopher and Friend*, ed. by Deal W. Hudson and Matthew J. Mancini (Macon, GA: Mercer University Press, 1987), pp. 91–113.
Riga, Peter J., "The Act of Faith in Augustine and Aquinas," *The Thomist* 35 (1971), pp. 143–174.
Riggs, Wayne, "Open-Mindedness," *Metaphilosophy* 41 (2010), pp. 172–188.
Roberts, Robert C., and West, Ryan, "Jesus and the Virtues of Pride," in *The Moral Psychology of Pride*, ed. by J. Adam Carter and Emma Gordon (Lanham, MD: Rowman & Littlefield, 2017), pp. 99–122.
Roberts, Robert C., and Wood, William Jay, *Intellectual Virtues: An Essay in Regulative Epistemology* (New York: Oxford University Press, 2007).
Robinson, John A. T., *Truth Is Two-Eyed* (Philadelphia: Westminster, 1979).
Rorty, Amelie O., "Descartes on Thinking with the Body," in *The Cambridge Companion to Descartes*, ed. by John Cottingham (Cambridge: Cambridge University Press, 1992), pp. 371–392.
Rorty, Richard (ed.), *The Linguistic Turn: Recent Essays in Philosophical Method* (Chicago, IL: University of Chicago Press, 1967).

Rysiew, Patrick, "Reid and Epistemic Naturalism," *The Philosophical Quarterly* 52 (2002), pp. 437–456.
Sadler, Gregory B. (ed.), *Reason Fulfilled by Revelation: The 1930s Christian Philosophy Debates in France* (Washington, DC: Catholic University of America Press, 2011).
Schellenberg, John, "Divine Hiddenness," in *A Companion to Philosophy of Religion*, ed. by Charles Taliaferro, Paul Draper, and Philip Quinn (Oxford: Blackwell, 2010), pp. 509–518.
  Divine Hiddenness and Human Reason, 2nd ed. (Ithaca, NY: Cornell University Press, 2006).
  The Hiddenness Argument: Philosophy's New Challenge to Belief in God (Oxford: Oxford University Press, 2015).
  "The Hiddenness Problem and the Problem of Evil," *Faith and Philosophy* 27 (2010), pp. 45–60.
  Prolegomena to a Philosophy of Religion (Ithaca, NY: Cornell University Press, 2005).
Schumacher, Lydia, *Early Franciscan Theology: Between Authority and Innovation* (Cambridge: Cambridge University Press, 2019).
Smith, Wilfred Cantwell, *The Faith of Other Men* (New York: New American Library, 1963).
Sociétè Thomiste, *La philosophie chrétienne: Journée d'etudes de la Sociétè Thomiste* (Juvisy: Éditions du Cerf, 1933).
Sosa, Ernest, "The Raft and the Pyramid: Coherence versus Foundations in the Theory of Knowledge," *Midwest Studies in Philosophy* 5 (1980), pp. 3–26.
  A Virtue Epistemology (Oxford: Oxford University Press, 2007).
Spiegel, James S., "Open-Mindedness and Intellectual Humility," *Theory and Research in Education* 10 (2012), pp. 27–38.
Stacey, Gregory, "Towards a Catholic Epistemology," PhD dissertation, University of Oxford, 2019, https://ora.ox.ac.uk/objects/uuid:0c333fc1-816 a-4ead-98a7-21df48c2ef1a.
Stackhouse, John G., *Need to Know: Vocation as the Heart of Christian Epistemology* (New York: Oxford University Press, 2014).
Stump, Eleonore, *Aquinas* (London: Routledge, 2003).
  "Aquinas on the Foundations of Knowledge," *Canadian Journal of Philosophy Supplement* 17 (1992), pp. 125–158.
  Wandering in Darkness: Narrative and the Problem of Suffering (New York: Oxford University Press, 2010).
Swinburne, Richard, *Faith and Reason*, 2nd ed. (Oxford: Oxford University Press, 2005).
  "Plantinga on Warrant," *Religious Studies* 37 (2001), pp. 203–214.
Tanesini, Alessandra, "Caring for Esteem and Intellectual Reputation," *Royal Institute of Philosophy Supplement* 84 (2018), pp. 47–67.
  "Intellectual Humility as Attitude," *Philosophy and Phenomenological Research* 96/2018, pp. 399–420.

Taylor, Charles, "Philosophy and Its History," in *Philosophy in History: Essays on the Historiography of Philosophy*, ed. by Richard Rorty, Jerome B. Schneewind, and Quentin Skinner (Cambridge: Cambridge University Press, 1984), pp. 17–30.

A Secular Age (Cambridge, MA: Belknap Press of Harvard University Press, 2007).

Te Velde, Rudi, *Participation and Substantiality in Thomas Aquinas* (London: E. J. Brill, 1995).

Tuggy, Dale, "Reid's Philosophy of Religion," in *The Cambridge Companion to Thomas Reid*, ed. by Terence Cuneo and René van Woudenberg (Cambridge: Cambridge University Press, 2004), pp. 289–312.

Van Inwagen, Peter, "It Is Wrong, Always, Everywhere, and for Anyone, to Believe Anything, upon Insufficient Evidence," in *Faith, Freedom, and Rationality*, ed. by Jeff Jordan and Daniel Howard-Snyder (Lanham, MD: Rowman and Littlefield, 1996), pp. 137–153.

"We're Right. They're Wrong," in *Disagreement*, ed. by Richard Feldman and Tedd A. Warfield (Oxford: Oxford University Press, 2000), pp. 10–28.

Verbeke, Gérard, "Aristotelian Roots of Newman's Illative Sense," in *Newman and Gladstone Centennial Essays*, ed. by James D. Bastable (Dublin: Veritas Publications, 1978), pp. 177–195.

Visser, Sandra, and Williams, Thomas, *Anselm* (New York: Oxford University Press, 2009).

Vos, Arvin, *Aquinas, Calvin, and Contemporary Protestant Thought* (Washington, DC: Christian University Press; Grand Rapids, MI: Eerdmans, 1985).

Weidner, Veronika, *Examining Schellenberg's Hiddenness Argument* (London: Palgrave Macmillan, 2018).

Whitcomb, Dennis, Battaly, Heather, Baehr, Jason, and Howard-Snyder, Daniel, "Intellectual Humility: Owning Our Limitations," *Philosophy and Phenomenological Research* 94/2017, pp. 509–539.

Williams, Joanna, *Academic Freedom in an Age of Conformity: Confronting the Fear of Knowledge* (London: Palgrave Macmillan, 2016).

Wippel, John, *The Metaphysical Thought of Thomas Aquinas* (Washington, DC: Catholic University of America Press, 2000).

"The Possibility of a Christian Philosophy: A Thomistic Perspective," *Faith and Philosophy* 1 (1984), pp. 272–290.

"Thomas Aquinas on Philosophy and the Preambles of Faith," in *The Science of Being as Being: Metaphysical Investigations*, ed. by Gregory T. Doolan (Washington, DC: Catholic University of America Press, 2012), pp. 196–220.

"Thomas Aquinas and the Problem of Christian Philosophy," in *Metaphysical Themes in Thomas Aquinas*, ed. by John Wippel (Washington, DC: Catholic University of America Press, 1984), pp. 1–34.

Witte, John, and Green, M. Christian, "Introduction," in *Religion and Human Rights: An Introduction*, ed. by John Witte and M. Christian Green (Oxford: Oxford University Press, 2012), pp. 3–24.

Wolterstorff, Nicholas, "Christianity and Human Rights," in *Religion and Human Rights: An Introduction*, ed. by John Witte and M. Christian Green (Oxford: Oxford University Press, 2012), pp. 42–55.
  John Locke and the Ethics of Belief (Cambridge: Cambridge University Press, 1996).
  "Locke's Philosophy of Religion," in *The Cambridge Companion to Locke*, ed. by Vere Chappell (Cambridge: Cambridge University Press, 1994), pp. 172–198.
  Reason within the Bounds of Religion (Grand Rapids, MI: Eerdmans, 1984).
  Thomas Reid and the Story of Epistemology (Cambridge: Cambridge University Press, 2001).
Wood, William Jay, "Faith's Intellectual Rewards," in *Religious Faith and Intellectual Virtue*, ed. by Laura F. Callahan and Timothy O'Connor (Oxford: Oxford University Press, 2014), pp. 29–48.
Wynn, Mark R., "The Relationship of Religion and Ethics: A Comparison of Newman and Contemporary Philosophy of Religion," *The Heythrop Journal* 46 (2005), pp. 435–449.
  "Religious Faith," in *The Routledge Handbook of Contemporary Philosophy of Religion*, ed. by Graham Oppy (London: Routledge, 2015), pp. 167–179.
Zagzebski, Linda, "The Inescapability of Gettier Problems," *The Philosophical Quarterly* 44 (1994), pp. 65–73.
Zagzebski, Linda (ed.), *Rational Faith: Catholic Responses to Reformed Epistemology* (Notre Dame, IN: Notre Dame University Press, 1993).
  "Trust, Anti-Trust, and Reasons for Religious Belief," in *Religious Faith and Intellectual Virtue*, ed. by Laura F. Callahan and Timothy O'Connor (Oxford: Oxford University Press, 2014), pp. 231–245.
  Virtues of the Mind: An Inquiry into the Nature of Virtues and the Ethical Foundations of Knowledge (New York: Cambridge University Press, 1996).

Index of Names

Adler, J., 185–186
Alexander of Hales, 89, 113n
Alston, W., 16, 108n
Anscombe, G.E., 109n, 173n
Anselm, 52, 129n, 137, 175
Aristotle, 2n, 74n, 117n, 122, 125n, 127, 133n, 158n, 173, 178, 180-181n, 199n
Assmann, J., 152n
Audi, R., 105–106
Augustine, 14, 51–52, 68, 74n, 113n, 130n, 132, 137, 149, 161, 192n, 201–202, 204n, 209n

Baker, D.P., 21n
Baghramian, M., 91n
Baldwin. E., 22n
Barth, K., 97
Basinger, D., 153n
Bauerschmidt, F., 68n
Bergmann, M., 17n
Bishop, J., 103, 205
Blamires, H., 90
Blehl, V.F., 26
Bloom, A., 91–92
Bolos, A., 16n
Bonaventure, 51–52, 113
Brady, M., 177
Bréhier, É., 51, 52n
Broadie, A., 35
Brookes, D., 30
Brunschvicg, L., 51
Buchak, L., 100–102
Buckley, M., 135n
Buffon, 40, 44
Bychkov, O., 89n
Byrne, P., 159–160

Callergard, R., 38n
Calvin, J., 16–18, 20, 137–138
Carter, A.J., 91n, 183n
Chisholm, R., 171n

Christensen, D., 104–106
Church, I., 179–181
Clifford, W.K., 91
Code, L., 172
Coliva, A., 110n
Copenhaver, R., 41–42
Cuneo, T., 35n, 38n, 41n, 42n

Daniels, N., 30
Darwin, C., 96
Davies, B., 2n, 85n, 129n
Dawes, G., 49, 72n
De Bary, P., 30
De Broglie, G., 206
DeRose, K., 30, 32n
Descartes, R., 30, 32, 37, 52, 133, 168, 189, 196
Di Ceglie, R., 18n, 50n
Driver, J., 179
Dunnington, K., 182–183

Fales, E., 18, 19n, 102–103
Feldman, R., 103n, 104, 107
Fergusson, D., 36n, 131n
Fichte, J.G., 193
Fine, G., 127
Foley, R., 104
Forster, G., 14n
Frances, B., 105
Freud, S., 140
Fumerton, R., 199, 200n

Gadamer, H.G., 128n
Gettier, E., 171
Gilson, É., 50–54, 56, 156n, 161n
Goldberg, S.C., 106
Greco, J., 41n, 138, 173n
Green, A., 138n, 141n
Green, C.M., 191n, 192n
Grier, P., 200n
Grimm, S.R., 22n

Index of Names

Haankonssen, K., 38n
Harris, S., 140
Hawthorne, J., 106n
Hazlett, A., 185
Hegel, G.F.W., 7, 127, 193, 199–200
Helm, P., 17
Herder, J.G., 192
Herdt, J., 201–204
Hetherington, S., 171n
Hick, J., 49n, 63n, 71n, 75, 153–154, 157–159
Higgins-Biddle, J.C., 13n
Hilary (St.), 76
Hill, P., 180
Hoitenga, D.J., 15n
Howard-Snyder, D., 100, 107n, 136, 138n, 141n
Hume, D., 28, 30, 32, 34, 140, 152
Hutcheson, F., 39

Irwin, T., 125n, 127n, 202n

Jeffries, D., 17n
Jenkins, J., 2, 11–12, 16n, 57, 206
John of Damascus, 66
Justin (St.), 52

Kant, I., 127n, 193, 199n
Kelly, T., 104
Kenny, A., 22n, 58n, 59
Kerr, F., 50, 133
Kierkegaard, S., 149
King, N., 172n
Knitter, P., 157
Kornblith, H., 104

Lackey, J., 104n, 105n, 106
Lactantius, 52
Lamont, J., 23
Lehrer, K., 30–31
Lessing, G.E., 192
Lewis, C.S., 112
Locke, J., 1–2, 9–27, 57–58, 91, 109, 134, 152, 155–156
Losonsky, M., 189
Löwith, K., 194
Lukes, S., 195
Luther, M., 72, 202–203

Macaskill, G., 182
Mandonnet, P., 50–56
Mann, W., 72n
Maritain, J., 50–56, 192
Marx, K., 195
Masnovo, A., 52n
Matheson, J., 105

McCabe, H., 85
McCarthy, G., 23n
McCord Adams, M., 129n
McCormick, M.S., 115
McInerny, R., 54, 155n, 190n
McKaughan, D., 58
McKim, R., 152
McNabb, T., 32n
Merrigan, T., 26n
Meyer, M., 127
Milbank, J., 50
Mitchell, B., 94–100
Montmarquet, J., 172n
Moon, A., 16n, 17n, 19n
Moser, P., 136, 138n, 152n, 173n
Murphy, C.E., 78n

Newman, J.H., 22–27, 44, 95, 97, 99, 109n, 127n, 133, 188
Nikulin, D., 192n
Noone, T., 62n
Norton, D.F., 30

O'Donovan, O., 130n
Oppy, G., 24n, 73n, 154n

Pace, M., 101n
Pakaluk, M., 38n, 41n
Parekh, B., 195
Pascal, B., 123–124, 201
Pasnau, R., 61n
Paul (St.), 79, 126, 137, 150
Penelhum, T., 19, 83n
Pickstock, C., 50n
Plantinga, A., 16–22, 27, 59, 91, 107n, 108n, 137–138, 156n, 158–159, 161, 172, 186n
Plasger, G., 17n
Plato, 1, 90, 126–127, 188
Pojman, L., 19n, 135n
Price, H., 60
Pritchard, D., 24, 108–111, 171n, 179n, 183–184

Quinn, P., 136n, 152

Rea, M., 19n, 135n
Redpath, P., 55n
Riga, P., 71
Riggs, W., 179n, 186–187
Roberts, R., 172, 174n, 180, 182n, 183
Robinson, J., 157n
Rorty, A.O., 196n
Rorty, R., 7n
Russell, B., 1, 140
Rysiew, P., 30n

Sadler, G.B., 50–53
Samuelson, P., 179–181
Schellenberg, J., 58, 125n, 135–151
Schiller, J.F., 192
Schonecker, D., 17n, 21n
Scott, K., 16n
Smith, W.C., 157
Socrates, 1, 90, 126
Sosa, E., 17, 172, 179n
Spiegel, J., 179n
Spinoza, B., 134–135
Srinivasan, A., 106n
Stacey, G., 86n
Stackhouse, J., 92, 111–112, 125, 131–132
Steenberghen, F. van, 52n
Stump, E., 85n, 89, 112–113, 138n, 141n, 161n, 189–191
Swinburne, R., 21, 58n, 74, 85n

Tanesini, A., 179–181
Taylor, C., 11–12, 92n, 111
Tuggy, D., 35n, 44n

Van Inwagen, P., 103, 107n, 159, 161

Van Woudenberg, R., 35n, 38n, 41n, 42n
Velde te, R., 50
Verbeke, G., 25
Visser, S., 175n
Vos, A., 59

Warner, B., 30–31
Weidner, V., 145
West, R., 183
Whitcomb, D., 180n
Williams, J., 92
Williams, T., 175n
Wippel, J., 51n, 55–56, 60
Witte, J., 191n, 192n
Wittgenstein, L., 109, 128, 133n
Wolterstorff, N., 12–16, 20n, 36n, 41n, 91, 189n, 192n,
Wood, P., 28n, 40, 44
Wood, W.J., 88, 172–174, 180n, 182n
Wynn, M., 25n, 73n

Zagzebski, L., 22n, 107, 171–174, 177n, 178

Index of Subjects

adherence or adhesion to God, 36–37, 68, 77, 82, 84, 89, 113, 119, 150, 206 (*see also* commitment, to God)
arguments in support of faith *see* evidence, of faith
assent:
  and consideration, 78, 114, 118, 195
  degrees of, 1, 13, 155
  and inference, 27, 195
  notional, 24–26
  real, 24, 26
atheism, 135, 142, 145, 198, 213
authority, 13, 32–33, 37, 144

belief:
  basic, 20
  hesitant, 118–119, 206–207
  true, 21, 127
belief-that *see* propositional belief
benefits of ST, 209–210
blindness of mind, 165–166

charity:
  degrees of, 81, 150, 203
  general, 6, 72–73, 75, 78–85, 87, 104, 122, 124–126, 130–131, 150, 162–166, 183, 198, 201
Christian faith:
  as an act of will, 5, 60, 62, 67–68, 70–71, 74, 80, 85, 113, 207
  as an intellectual act, 70, 74, 162
  articles of, 57, 65, 82, 144*n*, 206
  as caused by God, 19, 56, 58–61, 63, 68–70, 81–83, 99–100, 102, 128, 161, 206–207
  certainty or firmness of, 6, 13, 15, 51, 57–58, 62–63, 66, 67–70, 72, 75–77, 79–80, 83–86, 88–90, 99, 103, 110–112, 129–130, 139, 161, 163, 193, 206
  as *criterion* of reason, 84–85, 175–176, 207–208, 210
  definition, 67, 70–71, 73
  degrees or levels of, 13, 57, 79, 81, 110, 150–151, 162, 198
  merit of, 77–78, 115
  as *orientation* of reason, 84–85, 176, 207–208, 210
  paradigmatic, 6, 15, 58, 69, 79, 81, 88, 110, 206
  as *promotion* of reason, 207–210
  specificity of, 27, 44, 56–57, 60, 105
  as trust in God, 14, 36–37, 59, 74–75, 84, 87–88, 100, 103, 107, 132, 198
  as a virtue, 7, 51, 62, 73–74, 78–81, 85, 150, 162
Christian philosophy, 50–56
cognitive deficiency *see* flaw, intellectual
commitment:
  a-rational, 24, 108–111, 114–115, 132, 147, 169–170, 176–178, 189, 191, 196
  to God, 6–7, 14, 19, 27, 110, 147, 162, 182, 191
  to the good, 6–7, 118, 123–124, 141, 143, 146–148, 169, 178, 182, 189, 195, 197, 201, 203
  hinge, 109–110, 128, 185
  nonreligious, 6
  to one's beliefs, 2–4, 6, 16, 22, 82, 94–95, 98, 118–119, 134, 141, 170, 175–177, 183–184, 197
  religious, 5, 172
common sense, 28–45, 127
conciliatory views *see* conformism
conclusiveness, 6, 26, 125, 131–132, 167, 170, 200, 203, 209–210
conformism, 104–105
conscience:
  erroneous, 164–166
  general, 25–26, 164, 166
counterevidence or counterarguments *see* evidence, contrary
credulity, principle of, 33, 194–195

233

devotion, 79–80, 113, 129, 149–150
dialogue among traditions, cultures, and religions, 165–166
disagreement:
  peer, 104, 106–107, 177
  religious, 103
docility, virtue of, 146, 162
doubt:
  regarding faith, 136, 176,
  universal, 28, 109–110, 133, 176, 185, 187
doxastic:
  practice, 115
  voluntarism, 85n (see also will, to believe)

enthusiasm, enthusiasts, 13, 15, 155
epistemic emotions, 169, 177–178
epistemic vices, 177–178
evidence:
  contrary, 15, 21–22, 27, 75, 85, 87, 91, 93, 98, 101–102, 107, 110, 115, 119, 130, 169, 176–177, 188, 191, 193, 195–196, 200
  of faith, 13, 19, 24, 51, 57–62, 64–65, 67–68, 73, 75–78, 82, 84–85, 99, 117, 135–137, 197
  full or conclusive, 2n, 51, 57, 60n, 65–66, 84–85, 110
evidentialism, 18–20, 27
evidentness see evidence, full or conclusive
externalism, 86, 171–172, 189–190

flaw:
  intellectual, 5, 139, 140–141
  moral, 136, 140
formed faith see Christian faith, as a virtue
foundationalism:
  regarding faith, 20
  regarding *scientia*, 20, 189
fraternal correction, 165
free will, 44–45, 68n, 77–78, 161n

God:
  arguments for his authoring revelation, 12, 134–135
  arguments for his existence, 13, 58–60, 135–151, 205
  communion with, 15, 125–126, 129, 131, 141–142, 146–150, 175
  general and confused knowledge of, 18n, 206–207
  as a nondeceiver, 32, 34, 37
  providence of, 30, 192, 194, 204n
  supernatural intervention of, 61, 63, 74, 85, 99, 161
good habits, assumption or adoption of, 6–7, 33, 74, 146–147, 197, 209–210

good, search for, 6, 115–116, 132, 167, 171
grace, operating and cooperating, 68n

habit of faith see Christian faith, as a virtue
happiness, 72, 117n, 126, 136
hiddenness of God, 135–151
honor of God, 78, 110, 114–115
human flourishing, 7, 119, 139, 146–147, 169, 174, 195, 196–197, 200, 203, 210
human freedom, 42–43, 68n, 161n, 175, 191, 193, 196,
humility (intellectual virtue), 178–187

ideology, 195–196
impartiality see neutrality
incompatibility problem, 151–167
inconclusiveness:
  degrees of, 199, 203
  partial see conclusiveness
informal inference, 25–26
intellectual deficiency see flaw, intellectual
intellectual humility see humility
internalism, 86, 171, 189

knowledge:
  probable, 13, 65–66, 68–69
  immediate or intuitive, 20, 64, 127, 188
  demonstrative or scientific, 13, 61–62, 66–67, 69, 77, 81, 114, 161

liberum arbitrium see free will
Locke's epistemological project, 2, 12, 16
Locke's view of faith and reason, 1–27, 57–58, 155
love:
  Augustine's law of, 112–113
  for God see charity
  for the neighbor, 6, 110, 114–115, 130–131, 139, 162–163, 188, 198, 201
Lutheran view of faith, 74

Maritain's distinction between nature and state of philosophy, 55–56
measure of charity (*ratio caritatis*), 78n, 82
measure of faith (*ratio fidei*), 82
miracles, 25, 66, 68–69 (see also evidence, of faith)
moral deficiency see flaw, moral
mutual understanding, 6, 201

naturalism, methodological see naturalistic assumption
naturalistic assumption, 15, 21, 128, 134–135, 151–167, 194
natural theology, 18n, 42, 59, 206
neutrality, 94–100

Index of Subjects

noetic structure, 170, 186–187, 198–200, 205
no-fault unbelief, 135–151
nonconformism, 74–75, 103–105, 159
  (*see also* tenacity)
noncontradiction, principle of, 2*n*, 133*n*, 157, 188

object of faith, 13, 62–65, 79–80, 83
open-mindedness, 178–187 (*see also* humility)
opposing arguments *see* evidence, contrary

parity argument, 19–20, 24, 108*n*
peaceful and respectful coexistence among religions *see* religious tolerance
philosophical forgetting, 12
phronēsis see prudence
practical rationality, 102
preambles of faith, 60*n*, 65–66, 82, 206–207
propositional belief, 14–15, 58, 74, 82
prudence, 25, 69, 173, 178

quasi-fideism, 108–111

racism, unacceptability of, 147, 169, 176, 195
readiness to believe *see* Christian faith, as a virtue
reason:
  autonomy of, 29, 31, 33, 35–37, 51, 57, 82–83, 86, 89, 122, 155*n*
  certainty or firmness of, 57, 69–70, 81*n*, 83–84, 89
  optimism about, 34–35, 38, 165, 189, 208, 210
Reformed epistemology, 16–22, 44
relativism, religious, 75, 87, 160
reliabilism, 29–30, 170, 172, 189–190
religious conflicts, 12, 152, 159
religious diversity, 151–167
religious exclusivism, 103*n*, 158–159
religious pluralism, 151–167
religious tolerance/intolerance, 151–167

scientia see knowledge, demonstrative or scientific
self-interest *see* self-love
self-love, 130*n*, 131, 182
sense:
  dullness of, 165–166
  illative, 25–26

sensus divinitatis, 16–22, 137–138
signs of faith, 14, 63–65, 68, 102*n*
  (*see also* evidence, of faith)
spiritual enhancement or betterment *see* human flourishing
spiritual turn, theory and practice of, 197, 214–215
supernaturalistic assumption, 128, 134, 151–167

tenacity:
  of faith, 27, 87, 92, 93, 98–99, 106, 110, 115
  principle of, 95–96, 98–99, 101, 104–105, 115
theism, by faith and by reason, 190
truth:
  search for, 1, 7, 111, 119, 121–125, 166–167, 183, 201, 207
  realist and anti-realist theories of, 199*n*, 200*n*

unbelief, reasonable or inculpable *see* no-fault unbelief
universal dignity of humans, 144, 147, 169, 175–176, 197
universal fraternity, 175, 193, 196, 201
universal rights, 191–192

virtue ethics, 173
virtue epistemology:
  general, 123, 169–187
  reliabilist, 170, 172, 173*n*
  responsibilist, 170–174, 180
virtues, intellectual:
  character traits, 170–174
  cognitive functions, 170–174
virtues:
  moral, 173, 178
  theological, 62, 72, 74

will:
  to believe, 63, 67, 69–70, 77*n*, 206
    (*see also* Christian faith, as a virtue; doxastic voluntarism)
  quiescent, 161*n*
wishful thinking, 85

For EU product safety concerns, contact us at Calle de José Abascal, 56–1°, 28003 Madrid, Spain or eugpsr@cambridge.org.

www.ingramcontent.com/pod-product-compliance
Ingram Content Group UK Ltd.
Pitfield, Milton Keynes, MK11 3LW, UK
UKHW042042120426
469821UK00013B/254